PARTICIPATION IN LEARNING

Participation in Learning

A PROGRESS REPORT ON SOME EXPERIMENTS IN THE TRAINING OF TEACHERS

BARRINGTON KAYE

What is education if it is not participation and discussion about everything which involves us?

(F.H. in *The Hornsey Affair*)

London
GEORGE ALLEN & UNWIN LTD
RUSKIN HOUSE · MUSEUM STREET

FIRST PUBLISHED IN 1970

© *Barrington Kaye*, 1970

SBN 04 370028 4

PRINTED IN GREAT BRITAIN
in 10 *on* 11 *pt Times Roman*
BY BLACKFRIARS PRESS
LIMITED

TO

Alan, Ann, Anne, Bob, Carole, Chris
David, Don, Elaine, Jan, Janet
Janis, John, Mike, Paul, Peggy
Priscilla, Sue, Wendy and many others

Preface

The word 'experiments' in the sub-title of this book is not used in the sense of rigorously controlled attempts to measure experimental variables. Nor is the book intended to constitute a theoretical validation of undirected methods in higher education. Its purpose is simply that of describing the various ways in which one department of education in a college of education has tried to prepare students to teach in the kind of informal atmosphere which is increasingly to be found in the secondary schools of this country. It is thus in the sense of a 'try-out' that the word experiment is used, and no other.

This is said by way of explanation, not of apology. I have made the point elsewhere[1] that even research proceeds by successive approximations, in which guesses and impressions have just as much place in the early stages as do precisely formulated hypotheses and rigorous observations in the later ones. And whereas research can normally proceed at a pace determined by its own needs, teaching is a here and now situation. Teachers must act, and if there are no guide lines to action provided by academic research, then they must act on such indications as they can find, even – in the last resort – on their own hunches. The results of such actions may legitimately be used to make first approximations to theories, from which more carefully controlled experiments (in the other sense of the term) can be devised.

The present book, then, outlines various attempts to try out the writer's hunch that it is through students' participation in the formulation and implementation of their own courses that they can best be prepared to teach in schools in which, for example, group work[2], inter-disciplinary inquiry[3] and other indirect methods are being used.

It should be added that the use of these methods was not held out to the students concerned as the only, or the best approach to secondary teaching. The need for students to be able to call upon a

[1] In the preface to *Bringing Up Children in Ghana: an impressionistic survey*, Allen & Unwin, 1962.

[2] See Barrington Kaye and Irving Rogers: *Group Work in Secondary Schools and the training of teachers in its methods*, O.U.P., 1968.

[3] See Charity James: *Young Lives at Stake: a reappraisal of secondary schools*, Collins, 1968.

repertoire of teaching methods was continually stressed, and the hope expressed that each would develop a personal style, consonant with his or her own personality and knowledge, which would nevertheless provide sufficient flexibility of approach for the varying needs of the pupils and of the topics to be met.

Part One of the book is devoted to an examination of the revolution in teaching methods which is now taking place in the schools of this country. The changed role of the teacher as a result of this revolution is then discussed, and the students' own attitudes towards their training.

Part Two is concerned with opportunities for participation which were offered to students within a framework organized and directed by the tutorial staff. Details are given of a drama topic in the history of education, and of its subsequent influence on the work of the students with a group of remedial children, and of a topic in the psychology of puberty and adolescence which took the form of a participatory exhibition.

Part Three takes the concept of participation further, and gives an outline of some of the attempts made to give students opportunities for taking part in the planning and organization of their own courses, including their assignments. Some suggested principles of participation in course-planning are then offered.

Finally, in Part Four, some shortcomings of the present system of the training of teachers are identified, and suggestions made for their being overcome.

I should like to emphasize that this book is no more than a progress report of a 'try-out'. It is hoped in due course to set up controls and procedures for the evaluation of the kind of approach described in the following chapters; at this preliminary stage, however, it is more important to try out different ideas and work from impressions, than to secure rigorous evaluation. Those responsible for the training of teachers find progress possible only along a tightrope of the kind familiar from the days of battle-school assault courses: on the one side is the easy drop into the warm mudpond of sentimental romanticism; on the other, the invigorating plunge into the cold bath of academic pedantry. Those balanced precariously on the rope hear both the lazy gossip of their colleagues wallowing in the mud, unable to see for the steam, and the shrill cries of their other colleagues thrashing briskly about in the cold water, unable to see for the splashes. Yet if we are to make any progress at all, we too must venture out along the rope, no doubt toppling from time to time, first into the mudpond and then into the cold bath. Indeed, it may well be that, since most of us can keep only one idea in our heads at any given time – e.g. the formulation of behavioural objectives (a cold bath topic) or creativity (one for the mudpond), such alternation is the only kind of progress possible and – who knows? – it may have the same toning-up effect on our minds as beauticians claim comparable treatment has on the skin.

It should like to record, once again, my thanks to my long-suffering colleagues in the Department of Education, Redland College, and to the students of the College, for their enthusiasm, tact, imagination, forebearance, energy and general good-humour. Special thanks of a somewhat different kind are undoubtedly owing to J. T. Wharton, who was Principal of the College throughout the period described herein, and the nature of whose support and encouragement have made even limited achievement peculiarly worth while. I am particularly obliged to Messrs Allen & Unwin's reader, who made an extremely detailed report on the typescript, with exactly the kind of criticisms and suggestions which every writer likes to receive: detailed, knowledgeable, relevant and precise. I hasten to add that he can in no way be held responsible for the faults that remain.

Bristol and Portishead, 1969

B K

Contents

PART ONE

Teaching and Training

1

A Revolution in Teaching

A fundamental change in the role of the teacher
It is my belief that secondary education in England is on the verge of a breakthrough comparable with that which has already transformed infant teaching, and is in the process of transforming the junior school. To find an infant class today with the children sitting in rows, doing their 'sums' or their 'letters', is the exception rather than the rule. Instead, we expect to find the children busily engaged in a variety of activities, some in groups of three or four, others working by themselves. Not one child, it appears, is doing the same thing as the next. No longer is the teacher to be found in front of the blackboard; indeed, there is often no blackboard at all, and instead of instructing the whole class, the teacher will be moving from group to group, or helping individuals, or hearing children read. There are no longer bells to signal a change of lesson; the children work at their individual or group tasks either until they have finished, or until the need for a change is felt. Some children may persist at their tasks for a whole morning; others move from one activity to another, sometimes working by themselves, at other times joining groups. Yet they all manage to cover a range of activities, and the teacher ensures that basic progress in the tool subjects is made by all.

Nor is the infant class necessarily composed of children of the same age. In some schools children are allocated to classes on the basis of 'family groups', in which five-, six- and seven-year olds may be found in the same classroom. And even the classroom itself is

disappearing in experimental 'open-plan' schools, in which a team
of teachers and ancillaries may be responsible for a hundred or more
children in an open area which includes work bays, play spaces,
quiet corners and reading areas, but is without a single one of the
familiar four-walled rooms that constitute the traditional teaching
spaces we think of as 'classrooms'.

The change in junior schools is progressing more slowly, but it is
already well under way. A class of ten-year-olds may be found
working on a single topic. Such a topic might be 'Water'. One group,
having visited a filtration plant, may be experimenting with home-
made filters. Another group has made a model of a domestic water
supply, complete with valves and taps. A third has made a graph of
the rate of evaporation, using electric lamps of different wattages,
while a large map of local rivers, streams, lakes and pools is in
process of construction by a fourth. What characterizes the children
is their sense of purpose and their understanding of what they are
about.

Of course, not all classes in junior schools will be approaching
learning in this way, nor is it necessarily a good thing that they
should do so. The point I am making is that a revolution is in process
in our schools, a revolution that has already swept through most of
our infant schools, and is at work in our junior schools. The in-
fluences that have contributed to this revolution are many and
varied, and the forms it is manifested in are equally diverse, but one
essential characteristic is shared by all and that is a fundamental
change in what is seen as the role of the teacher.

Traditionally, the teacher's task was to communicate to his pupils
a body of knowledge. The content of that body of knowledge
obviously varied with the age of the pupils and, less obviously, with
the pupils' assumed ability. It also reflected changes in the fashion
of educational philosophies. It included the knowledge of skills,
such as being able to write, as well as the knowledge of facts, such
as the twelve-times table. But as far as the children themselves were
concerned, the syllabus was fixed. Hence teaching method has
traditionally been concerned with the most effective ways of getting
children to master a given syllabus.

But the fact of life is that children vary considerably in their
ability to do this. As a result of inborn differences of intelligence,
aptitude and temperament (though these are now thought to be of
much less importance than before), of environmental differences in
the circumstances of their lives and in the nature of the relationships
with their parents and others, and of differences in their view of

16

themselves and of each other and of the teacher, no two children exposed to the same curriculum will emerge from that exposure retaining the same amount of its content. The whole traditional system of tests, reports, marks, examinations and the rest depends upon that fact. And the skilful teacher in that situation is the one who, given a fixed (that is, predetermined) syllabus, so contrives his presentation of it that each of his pupils retains the maximum part of which he is capable, having regard to these differences.

A fixed or teacher-planned syllabus, then, and children of varying abilities – this is the traditional teaching situation, and the traditional teaching problem is that of adapting the children to the syllabus. The revolution I have spoken of consists of reversing that procedure. Instead of trying to adapt the children to a given syllabus, it is the variety of children's aptitudes and interests that is taken as given, and it is the syllabus that is adapted to them.

This simple reversal of approach is indeed a revolution. For it means that the teacher is obliged to start, not from the straight-forward requirement of certain skills and facts which have to be learnt by all, but from the complex diversity of needs, interests and abilities which exists among his children, no two of whom will be the same. And not only that. He must provide for a vast range of potential interests, as well as for what he finds at first. He must learn to be able to recognise and encourage the first flicker of curiosity until it leads to a genuine search for knowledge and skill. And he must do all this without losing sight of the basic educational necessities, common to his whole class.

For it must not be supposed that, in reversing the traditional relationship between pupil and curriculum, and in making the curriculum fit the pupil rather than the pupil fit the curriculum, we have necessarily thrown overboard all the elements of a traditional education. Clearly, all children must learn to read and write, and to be able to make simple calculations. These are requirements basic, not only to civilized life, but also to any further education. Indeed, the new approach would possibly extend further what might be regarded as basic skills from those accepted as such by the traditionalists. Creative skills are coming to be seen as essential, not only to self-expression but also to the manipulation of those materials upon which our technological society depends. The ability to work with one's hands as well as with one's brain is no longer regarded as a skill suitable only for artificers, nor is the capacity for aesthetic enjoyment thought to be of value only for those who are likely to have the means hitherto needed to employ it. Thus, those who begin

B   17

from the children's needs as opposed to the needs of the syllabus are likely to recognize *more* rather than fewer basic essentials of education.

What *has* been thrown overboard, however, is the requirement that these things are learnt by the whole class together and in a manner determined by the teacher beforehand. The teacher starts, not from a prepared lesson based on the textbook, but from the children's individual or group activities. Certainly preparation is involved; indeed, considerably more preparation is often needed than the traditional teacher might manage with. But in so far as the teacher cannot be altogether sure of the direction, or rather, the directions, which his forty or so children are likely to take in their attempt to understand the world about them, he must therefore prepare for a variety of possibilities. At the same time, he cannot afford *not* to prepare, for he must be ready when the time comes to give the necessary guidance, make the necessary suggestions, give the necessary help to enable each child to carry on with his or her investigations, and what is more, he must be ready to do so there and then. The child who is caught up in the excitement of discovering something new and reaches a point where he needs help or advice, wants it straight away. It is no good for the teacher to say that he will look the matter up this evening, and let the child know to-morrow, for by tomorrow the excitement of today's discovery will have become a distant memory. Thus the teacher, in his preparation, must somehow anticipate the likely direction which each child will take in his or her path of investigation, and make provision against it. And he must do this for every member of his class.

This is not the impossible feat that at first it sounds. The number of avenues that are open to children's curiosity and interests are limited, and teachers come to learn what to expect under certain circumstances. Nevertheless, it is fair to say that the amount of preparation needed with this approach to teaching is generally far more than under traditional teacher-directed methods. On the other hand, the reward to the teacher is infinitely greater. To be a party to a child's discovery of, for example, the balance of nature among the microscopic life of pond water, or the most suitable material for making a speech recording on a gramophone which he has himself made, is at once a privilege and a delight.[1] There is no comparison

---

[1] See the programme 'Finding Out' in the BBC Television series, *Discovery and Experience*, which shows a child in a junior school experimenting with different surfaces in making his own recording. Notice not only the degree of involvement of the child, but also the teacher's attitude towards him: one of encouragement and respect for his achievements.

between this kind of reward and any gratification one might get from the fact that a class of children can recall correctly, say, ten facts about the physical features of Australia, taught to them the previous week. (And, to be fair, it would be a rare class in which all forty children would remember all ten facts!).

Now it must not be supposed from what has been said above that there is no place in modern schools for the traditional class lesson, in which the teacher stands in front of his or her class and explains to them all some new process or piece of information. There are times when such an approach is the right one; that is, it is appropriate to the situation. Moreover, it is important that the children themselves do not mistake for licence the opportunity for self-direction which is being offered to them, and the occasional class lesson demonstrates to them that their teacher has not abrogated responsibility for their learning but has chosen to organize the major part of it along alternative lines. In addition, it is often necessary to explain to the whole class the general procedures which will apply to any given learning situation and this also offers an opportunity for the teacher to demonstrate his or her acceptance of responsibility for the children's learning, as well as to provide a framework within which the greater freedom of the child-directed approach can be grasped without undue anxiety on the part of the pupils.[1]

The argument that education is learning necessary knowledge
This brings us to one of the two major objections that are put forward to this approach to teaching – an approach which we may, for convenience, refer to as *pupil-directed* as opposed to the traditional method which we may call *teacher-directed*. There are, of course, many arguments which are advanced against pupil-directed education and it is not surprising that most of them come from those whose interests are bound up with the traditional system, including a large number of practising teachers and educationists. But in

[1] In my view, not enough attention has been given to children's emotional need for a secure framework from which to venture out in their attempts to understand and control their environment. Very often, the disorder which sometimes attends well-meaning but ill-organized attempts at child-directed learning, and which is regarded as evidence against the approach in general, proceeds in fact from the children's anxieties at being placed in an insufficiently defined situation. These anxieties may well be exacerbated when the children have been accustomed to an unduly authoritarian regime. The freedom to learn for oneself is a freedom, the use of which has to be learned. 'Human kind', said T. S. Eliot, 'Cannot bear very much reality.' That is, not without practice.

substance they can be reduced to two. The first argument is that the aim of education is to equip children with the facts and skills necessary to life in the society in which they are going to live. The children themselves are not in a position to know which these facts and skills are; it is only their parents and teachers who can know this. If we leave children to follow their own interests, it is said, then they may well accumulate a whole lot of useless information and master a number of unnecessary skills, irrelevant to their future lives as adults, instead of acquiring the knowledge and expertise which they are going to need later on. We may call this the *necessary-knowledge* argument. The second major objection to pupil-directed teaching stems from the belief that it is necessary to prepare for the hardships of adult life by experiencing hardship in childhood. 'Life is hard and full of knocks,' the proponents of this point of view assert. 'In order to get on, it is necessary to be able to surmount difficulties and to postpone gratifications. The only way we can do this is by habit.' Education is therefore seen as a disciplining agency and indeed, the word *discipline* occurs frequently in the various formulations of this viewpoint, which we may call, therefore, the *education-as-discipline* argument, and to which we shall return.

Let us first, however, consider the *necessary-knowledge* argument. That children themselves are not able to know what knowledge is likely to be of value to them as adults, and that therefore the teacher must decide what they should learn, appears at first hearing to be irrefutable. And certainly, if we consider such basic necessities as being able to read and write, or to make simple mathematical calculations, then there might be little to argue about were it not for the fact that young children usually require little inducement to learn to read; it is something they see the value and importance of for themselves at an early age. And similarly, the basic mathematical skills of counting, adding and subtracting are ones which young children are normally attracted to for their own sake. And once we go beyond these basic educational tools, the validity of the *necessary-knowledge* argument is questionable. I dare say the majority of the readers of this book underwent a traditional grammar-school or public-school education. How much of what they learnt has *in fact* proved of value to them in their adult lives? They probably all learnt how to solve quadratic equations, how to construct a perpendicular to a straight line with a pair of compasses, which Latin prepositions govern the accusative and which the dative cases, and the dates of Marlborough's battles and a host of similar skills and facts. Yet how many of those readers have ever used those skills and

20

facts in the course of their everyday lives, except as evidence of their own education? And those same readers – how much of the knowledge which *has* proved necessary to their everyday lives have they had to learn since they left school? The fact is that a very large proportion of what constitutes a traditional secondary-school syllabus is totally irrelevant to the needs of normal adult life in the society of today. I would myself estimate that only about 10 per cent of what I learned in secondary school has proved of any use to me since I left full-time education and I dare say the percentage is not very different for most people.

Now if this be admitted, and it is difficult to disagree once generalities are left behind and the actual details of syllabuses are examined, it says very little for the skill of *our* teachers and parents in giving *us* the knowledge and expertise necessary to *our* lives. I cannot help suspecting that I should have made a better job of learning things that would prove to be of relevance to my adult life if I had been left entirely alone, to get on with the business according to my own devices. Nor have we the right to suppose that we should necessarily make a better job of selecting useful information for our children than our parents and teachers did for us. Partly this is because teachers are naturally conservative and partly it is because any skill or information which is made the basis for a traditional teaching subject inevitably becomes ossified and in doing so, is liable to become out of date.

This brings us to the whole question of technological change. There can be no doubt that – provided its progress is not interrupted, or even determined for ever by a nuclear war – the rate of technological change in the world today is going to increase. And increase, moreover, at an increasing rate. The time between the first rough sketching of a good idea and its eventual commercial production is no longer measured in decades, but in years. Within a few years, it may be measured in months. Revolutions in technological processes themselves beget other revolutions, so that within a generation or less, not only have the processes changed but the very principles on which the processes are based have been replaced.

Nor is this accelerating process of change confined to technology; it applies to the whole intellectual infrastructure of our time. Moreover, what is true in any particular area is true of the whole field. With a greater exchange of information between sciences there is a consequent lessening of their boundaries and this very process in turn facilitates further exchanges. New sciences develop on the borderlines of existing disciplines and contribute to them as well as

21

to themselves. The field of communication theory is a prime example of a borderline subject which has had far-reaching effects within the traditional subjects on the borders of which it grew. It is also an example of a subject which has helped to bridge that great divide between the arts and the sciences.

Thus, even if teachers were able to give their pupils the most up-to-date information available today, much of it would in all probability be out-of-date and irrelevant by the time they wanted to use it. And, to be quite honest, the teachers themselves are very rarely in possession of up-to-date information. Far too often they rely upon what *they* were taught when they were at college or university, and while there are those who strive to keep abreast of changes by attending refresher courses and by keeping up with the journals, there are many who are content to teach the same thing year in, year out.

It may be argued that even if a large proportion of what is learnt in school is irrelevant and useless in adult life, nevertheless the learning of it constitutes a valuable basis for further learning and also 'trains the mind'. But in fact, of course, it is rarely a good approach to a subject to learn an out-of-date theory or body of knowledge first, because it may well have to be unlearnt before its successor can be mastered. And the notion that learning anything must be of value, regardless of what use it is, because it 'trains the mind', is a variant of that generalized transfer-of-training fallacy which has now been disproved for over fifty years. Moreover, if the only justification for the inclusion of any item in the curriculum is that it 'trains the mind', for which purpose any subject is as good as the next, one might just as well allow children to study what interests them as to study what interests us.

It may be seen, then, that the argument that a child's teacher can best decide what he should learn is not as irrefragable as might at first appear. It certainly does not constitute an overriding opposition to the kind of pupil-directed education we have been considering. On the contrary, there would appear to be several reasons for not preferring the teacher's selection of items for an ideal syllabus. But before going on to discuss alternatives, it is necessary to examine the second major criticism that is often made against basing education upon children's own interests.

Education as discipline

As I have pointed out elsewhere,[1] the view of education as a kind

[1] See Barrington Kaye and Irving Rogers: *Group Work in Secondary Schools*, Oxford University Press, 1968, pp. 83–8, for a brief discussion of the history and rationalization of this viewpoint.

of necessary suffering is deeply rooted in the British psyche, and shows itself not only in the writings of educationists from Milton and Locke onwards, but also in such folk sayings as 'Spare the rod and spoil the child', which can be traced back at least as far as the fourteenth century.[1] Briefly it stems from the belief that the impulse to immediate gratification of both innate and acquired desires is so strong that, without habituation, the average individual would not be able to resist it. The major aim of education, in this view, is seen as the establishment of a habit of self-denial by the enforced experience of it in childhood. While a reasoned view of life would, in the long term, convince the individual of his ultimate interest in postponing or abjuring short-term pleasures, yet reason is likely to be overcome by our grosser impulses unless we have been conditioned to inhibit them. 'It seems plain to me', said Locke, 'That the Principle of all Virtue and Excellency lies in a Power of denying our selves the satisfaction of our own Desires, where Reason does not authorize them. This Power is to be got and improved by Custom, made easy and familiar by an early Practice'.[2]

I have used the term *conditioned* deliberately, for it is an interesting contradiction in terms that where the disciplinarians speak of the habit of 'self-discipline', they really mean, not the voluntary renunciation of gratification, but the conditioned renunciation of it, consequent upon a programme of training no different in principle from that to which laboratory rats are exposed when they are trained to avoid a given response by associating it with a painful electric shock. We may teach a hungry rat to avoid cheese by the simple expedient of always serving it on an electrified dish. In due course the rat will learn to leave it alone, even in the extremity of hunger. Similarly, we may severely beat a child when we find him masturbating at the age of ten; we may threaten him with insanity, blindness, or the prospect of burning in eternal hellfire if he persists; we may threaten him with what is, to him, far worse than any of these punishments – that is, the loss of our own affection; and as a result of all this and similar experiences it would not be surprising if, when he grew up, he proved diffident in sexual relationships. But to describe his failure to take advantage of such sexual opportunities

[1] See W. G. Smith: *The Oxford Dictionary of English Proverbs*, Oxford, Clarendon Press, 1935, p. 401. It first appears in its present form in 1639 in the writings of J. Clarke but it is to be found in a similar version in Langland's *Piers Plowman* (1377). Samuel Butler repeated it in *Hudibras* (1663) by which time it was clearly a common proverb.

[2] John Locke: *Some Thoughts Concerning Education*, ed. Quick, Cambridge University Press, 1884, p. 25. Quoted by Kaye and Rogers, op. cit., p. 83.

as offer themselves as 'self-discipline' is as precisely improper as to describe the rat's aversion to cheese as 'self-discipline'; both are the result of a successful aversive training programme.

By 'self-discipline' I would understand the ability *voluntarily* to renounce one course of action in favour of another, although the former offers a greater prospect of immediate reward. To 'deny ourselves the satisfaction of our own Desires, where Reason does not authorize them' is to examine rationally the advantages and disadvantages of gratification, and to prefer long-term rewards even though they may be attendant with short-term discomforts. But I think that no one would contend that the hungry rat, confronted with an electrified dish and leaving alone the cheese on it, is *voluntarily* renouncing his enjoyment of it, in any ordinary meaning of the term. Nor would we allow that the young man's abstinence is reasoned, however much we might condone it.

Hence it would seem that one, at least, of the disciplinarian's arguments – that enforced discipline enables the appetites to be governed by reason – is in fact untrue. What enforced discipline does is to submit both the appetites and the faculty of reason itself to the unreasoning government of fear. For it is fear, and not reason, which dictates the young man's continence, just as much as it does the rat's abstinence.

The *education-as-discipline* argument does not rest upon this prop alone, however, so that by knocking it away we have not yet brought it down. Putting aside the question of reason and its part in our lives, one may hear enforced discipline recommended as a kind of hardening agent. 'Deprivation and hardship in some measure are the lot of every man,' it may be said; 'so the sooner one learns to put up with them, the happier one will be.' Which is to say, 'What cannot be cured must be endured'.[1]

Now it is prefectly true that through usage one can come to accept with complacence a measure of discomfort that might otherwise have proved intolerable.[2] But is there any inherent virtue in such

---

[1] Another of those folk sayings which may be traced at least as far back, in one form or another, as *Piers Plowman*. Its first recorded usage in its modern form appears to be in 1763; see Smith, op. cit., p. 566.

[2] As these words are being written, the British Government is apparently attempting to accustom its citizens to accept unforewarned explosions as part of everyday life, by authorizing Lightning fighter aircraft to simulate the effects of the supersonic flight of Concorde air-liners. As with all experiments in building up frustration-tolerance, the initial doses are light and infrequent. No doubt they will slowly increase in severity and frequency until we accept as normal a state of affairs in which our buildings shake, our hearts race, and a proportion of our conversation is lost every few minutes.

acceptance? If we are concerned with technological advance, or indeed with advance in any area susceptible to experimental procedure, it might well be argued that it is in our interests to emphasize rather than to seek to underestimate our discomforts, for it is only through our awareness of them that we shall be led to seek a cure for them. Progress in any sphere will only come when it is recognized that progress is desirable. One man may learn to put up with a squeaking hinge and ultimately will hardly notice it, whereas another will find the squeak so intolerable that he will try any remedy until he hits upon a lubricant. But the latter's door will still be working effectively when the first man's has collapsed from a rusty hinge.

Thus I think it can be demonstrated that an awareness of frustrations, and a refusal to accept them as inevitable, may prove a valuable source of enterprise. A society of hardened unreasoning dogmatists may very well triumph in a world in which mere physical endurance is the criterion of success, but where ingenuity and technical skills are what count, then in the long run it is likely to be that society whose members refuse to accept the apparent limitations of their condition which will come out on top. And it is towards such a world that we are rapidly moving today.

There is, of course, a third prop to the *education-as-discipline* argument, though it is one that is more often held than advanced, and that is a belief in the value of hardship for its own sake. There are those who sincerely hold the view that suffering is good for the individual, and more particularly, for the individual child, not because it leads to a resigned acceptance of hardship as part of the human estate, but because it has merit in itself. This view is sometimes stated fairly baldly in the form 'Suffering enobles', and sometimes it is justified by the reflection that its proponent is a better man as a result of what *he* has endured. To the statement: 'My father beat me regularly and I am all the better for it', there is really no satisfactory rejoinder; for one thing, there is no controlled situation whereby a proper comparison can be made between the speaker, having been beaten as a child, and what the speaker might have become if he had not so suffered; and for another, one might not in any case accept the speaker's estimate of his own worth. It would seem highly likely that important contributory sources of this view, whether or not they might be consciously acknowledged, are the Christian doctrine of original sin, and the unconscious need for punishment which psycho-analysis shows to be the main motive of the masochist. No doubt in many cases the one reinforces the other. Be that as it may, the assertion that hardship of itself is a good thing is not one that I am disposed to attempt to disprove, and those readers who sincerely hold it, and who therefore find a particular recommendation in any system of learning which entails physical or mental suffering for its own sake, need read no further.

So far we have used the term *discipline* to mean rules imposed by others, and we have pointed out that the expression *self-discipline* is often misused: instead of meaning the voluntary acceptance of rules, it has been shown to mean the conditioned acceptance of them. There is, however, a second meaning to the expression, often implied at the same time as the first, and that is a systematic approach to the study of a particular subject, using methods which have proved successful in the past. Thus, when we speak of the 'discipline of history' we mean the patient examination of all available sources with an attempt at their evaluation, in order to arrive at the closest possible approximation to historical truth. Such a process is often pedestrian and always laborious, but in the long run it is likely to lead to a better approximation than inspired guessing, or the intuitive application of some general theory of human behaviour, or the simple-minded recording of whatever information comes to hand without any attempt at assessing its reliability. It is with regard to the employment of system in its study that one speaks of any subject as a discipline.

Now it would seem self-evident that education must entail some experience of discipline in this sense if it is to succeed in an important aim; namely, that of enabling at least some of those who have been educated themselves to contribute to the widening store of knowledge. It may be possible for someone to learn a given set of facts and then subsequently to teach them to others (in the traditional sense of simply imparting information) without necessarily understanding how those facts were come by. But if it is desirable that there should be a continuing revaluation of those facts, and a further adding to them, then it is essential that some of those taught should know how the facts were arrived at, so that they, in turn, can apply the same methods and add to the basic store. Indeed, one might argue that it is more important that someone is taught how a given body of knowledge has been found out than that the body of knowledge itself is handed on, for if the methods are known, then the facts can always be rediscovered, whereas if the methods are lost, the facts themselves can never be modified, and are in constant danger of disappearing for ever. For example, it would be no more than an inconvenience if all existing logarithm tables were to disappear overnight; we could soon set to and reproduce them exactly.

26

But supposing that the understanding of how these tables were arrived at should suddenly be lost – how valuable each single copy would then become! And what if mistakes should arise in the printing of subsequent tables and these incorrect tables circulated for some years so that no one was sure which were the original figures – how could one be sure that any given set was in fact correct?

The 'discipline' of a subject, then, simply means the system of studying it which has led, in the past, to the present store of knowledge that constitutes the subject. Of course, the systems themselves change and are improved, as are the instruments and techniques which are based upon them. Some changes are small, such as an improved stain for the microscopic examination of certain organisms; others are revolutionary, such as Einstein's general theory of relativity. But all methods employ some or other system; that is, they are not whimsical, and it is to the readiness of a student to follow some system in his studies that we refer in 'the discipline of the subject'.

Now some of those who argue that education ought to be a discipline in our first sense – that is, in the sense of its imposing conformity with certain rules on pupils – may do so because they believe that those pupils will not accept discipline in this second sense without some form of constraint. In other words, they believe that children – and it is with children that we are primarily concerned – that children will prefer to work unsystematically and that the only way that they can be got to employ system is by the application of some external force (or by conditioning them to do so, which is simply to say that the force is applied at any earlier date than that under consideration). This is a belief, but it is also a generalisation about human behaviour which is susceptible to proof or disproof. And in fact, of course, it can be and is disproved every minute of the day that children are at play. Can anyone seriously contend that children will not voluntarily employ system who has watched them counting out, or playing 'broken bottles', or engaged in some of the countless skipping games? Go into any children's playground, or listen at any street corner where children gather, and listen to them applying the rules of their games.[1] There is no

[1] See Iona and Peter Opie: *The Lore and Language of Schoolchildren*, Oxford, Clarendon Press, 1959, for a fascinating account of children's rules. Most adults find that reading the Opies' book brings back to their minds all manner of long-forgotten experiences and occasions, and very often the flavour of strong emotional commitment to the rules regarding them may well also be recalled. Details of children's games in Edinburgh are given in James T. Ritchie: *The Singing Street* and *Golden City*, Edinburgh, Oliver & Boyd, 1964 and 1965, the first of which is also the title of a film on the subject.

scholar so pedantic as the nine-year-old in his application of the rules of marbles.[1]

Nor is it only in his games with others that the young child is prepared to submit to system. We have only to think of the immense trouble taken over listing and classifying by train spotters, whose scrupulous method might be the envy of any taxonomist; of the elaborate care in identification shown by young philatelists; of the patient regard for system shown by the child playing with Meccano or any other constructional toy – to recognize that children might be characterized more by a kind of obsessional regard for system than by preference for whimsy. And, indeed, it would be in accord with a good deal of contemporary thought on the subject of mental development to argue that an attempt to attribute order and system to the world about him is an important characteristic of the growing mind.[2]

When we come to examine what children in fact do, instead of allowing ourselves to accept generalizations based on conviction rather than observation, we see that far from being enemies of system, they embrace it at almost every opportunity. Why, then, are they so resistant to it in the classroom, demands the wretched teacher, exhausted after forty minutes spent trying to teach Form IIc the system of Euclid? The simple reason is, that when they are spotting trains, playing marbles, skipping, or memorizing the titles of the Top Twenty, they are following their own inclinations, whereas when they are being required to master Theorem V, they are not. Is this not a universal characteristic of mankind, whether child or adult, that even the most laborious task becomes a pleasure when it furthers an interest? The same teenager who cannot remember a single member of Walpole's first cabinet has no difficulty whatever in memorizing not only the names of all the members of her favourite pop groups, but also the names of their managers, girl-friends, recording companies, together with an inventory of their personal habits, likes and dislikes, and even their hair-styles. And in

[1] See J. Piaget: *The Moral Judgment of the Child*, London, Routledge & Kegan Paul, 1932, for an interesting analysis of children's attitudes towards rules.

[2] See E. A. Peel: *The Pupil's Thinking*, London, Oldbourne, 1960, for a succinct general account of mental development based on Piaget's researches. Those with a taste for historical analogy might compare the child's mental development with that of the Renaissance, when a search for world order was regarded as a legitimate occupation of scholars and one likely to lead to universal solutions; see E. M. W. Tillyard: *The Elizabethan World Picture*, London, Chatto & Windus, 1956.

just the same way, the man who finds the completion of his income tax form an intolerable burden will spend countless happy hours undertaking immensely complicated calculations for his football pools coupon. It is, in fact, true of us all that we take pleasure in doing anything connected with what has gripped our interest, whereas we find precisely the same expenditure of energy over an affair in which we are not interested, if not actually distasteful, at any rate an effort.

It would seem to follow, then, that if we wanted to exploit this capacity of children to learn effortlessly and pleasurably what they are interested in, we must seek somehow to relate their studies to their interests. And it is exactly this that what I have referred to above as pupil-directed education seeks to do. Instead of starting from a prescribed syllabus, the criteria of inclusion of any item in which is that which is thought by a child's teachers and parents to be relevant, or useful, or valuable, or simply 'good for him', the pupil-directed syllabus attempts to start from the child's own interests, and from his capacity for forming other interests.

Now this does not mean that the new teacher is not concerned with the content of his children's studies. He must be so. And, moreover, he has in mind that certain skills and certain information are an essential element in their education. But he is content to allow the children to reach these skills and facts through their own interests, rather than to attempt to impose them without. Indeed, his skill lies in precisely this ability so to respond to his children's enthusiasms that they themselves take the initiative and lead in directions which, the teacher knows, will take them in the general direction he wants them to go. But it must not be thought that what I am describing is simply an alternative way of teaching a prescribed syllabus, only by the use of skills of enticement and encouragement, rather than by skills of instruction and application. The new approach that I am describing, while it may identify certain areas as essential tools of education, nevertheless recognizes that every individual may legitimately end up with a widely different store of knowledge. If we accept – and I think we must accept – that it is not possible for teachers effectively to prescribe the whole syllabus on the basis of what information will be relevant to the child when he is adult and what not, then it follows that we must be prepared to accept that a fair proportion of a child's education may be idiosyncratic – that is, it may be based on that child's particular interests and inclinations.

29

The threefold syllabus

It is this aspect of the whole pupil-directed approach that is mis-understood more than any other, and so at the cost of repetition I must stress that it does *not* mean allowing the child to do what he will, without any regard whatever for the desirability or otherwise of his actual activities. We may say that the teacher has in his mind a threefold syllabus. The first part consists of those basic and essential tools necessary to further learning and to effective living, and as we have seen, the new approach may well include among these not only the traditional skills of reading, writing and simple calculating, but also other skills which traditional educationists might regard as luxuries rather than as necessities – for example, skills of oral communication, artistic expression, aesthetic apprecia-tion, and constructional and other motor skills. The teacher's con-cern is to ensure that this first part is mastered as soon as may be, but he is still content to allow the initiative for learning to come from the child, rather than to impose it according to some pre-determined system.

The second part of this threefold syllabus consists of those skills and areas of knowledge which, while not essential, are nevertheless of major importance and would generally be agreed upon as con-stituting the elements of a sound general education. Here the teacher's concern is that these elements are covered at some time or other in the child's schooling, but again he does not attempt to present them directly because it happens to be Wednesday, or because he has reached a certain page of his textbook; he is content to wait until the child reaches the stage at which one or other of those elements is appropriate to his particular needs.

Now a number of objections to this method of teaching will no doubt immediately present themselves, and they will present them-selves most acutely to teachers who have been accustomed to organi-zing their lessons beforehand methodically and in accordance with some rationale. One such objection is that some skills are dependent upon the possession of prior skills, without which it is pointless to attempt to learn them. Indeed, in certain traditional subjects such as geometry, nearly every fact and technique has a proper place in a sequential hierarchy of knowledge, so that the teacher may argue that no one item can be learnt at any other time than its proper place in the chain of learning. While this may to some extent be true, I think we may be tempted to place too much reliance on the sup-position that children's minds work in a similar fashion to our own. Because syllabus-makers see the logic and symmetry of a subject in a certain way does not necessarily mean that to begin at the beginning and work one's way methodically through to the end is necessarily the most effective way of learning that subject for children. The work of Piaget and his followers has shown us that children's minds work in ways that are wholly different from the mental operations of intelligent adults (and on the whole we may suppose that syllabus-makers are intelligent adults); they may see connections and associations that, to the teacher, are meaningless or even misleading. While, as we have seen, children are no less enamoured of systematic thought than are academics, yet it is the systems of children that they apply, and that may be very different from the systems of adults. What we are concerned with, in the long run, is effective learning – that is, the ability to manipulate as well as merely to recite information, and the ability to adapt, as well as merely to practise skills. In his progress to effective learning, each child may well pursue a path that, to the adult, is inconsequential, illogical, perhaps even perverse. Yet in the end what is important is the effectiveness of what has been learnt. It is a major premiss of this approach that learning from interest, inclination and involvement leads to effective learning, but that learning from fear, habit or a sense of duty may well instead lead to those 'strategies' and substitutes for understanding so effectively portrayed by John Holt in his devastating analysis of how children fail in school.[1]

A second objection to the approach we are discussing here that will spring to the mind of the experienced traditional teacher is that it means that each child must have virtually what is his or her own curriculum. This in turn means that it will become only occasionally possible (or, indeed, necessary) to teach the class as a class. Now this is true, but it need distress us only for so long as we see the teacher-pupil relationship as one in which the former actively instructs while the latter passively learns. I have discussed this view of teaching and its limitations at length elsewhere,[2] and I shall say no more here than that once we accept the desirability of active learning – that is, of children undertaking the responsibility for their own learning and pursuing it, instead of waiting for the teacher to teach them – then we see the need to revise not only our view of the teacher's role, but also the way in which he can best discharge it.

[1] John Holt's *How Children Fail*, London, Pitman, 1964, is, in my view, one of those seminal books which puts into words what one had always subconsciously known to be true. Once the thing is expressed in cold print, however, one can no longer go on acting as if it were not.

[2] See Kaye and Rogers, op. cit., pp. 12–14 and 27–8.

It is with this revision that we shall be concerned in the following chapters of this book.

There remains the question, which I trust has not escaped the reader, of what constitutes the third part of the threefold syllabus. And it is, of course, that particular store of knowledge, and those particular skills, to which the individual child is led as a result of the pursuit of his own interests. Given that the basic tools are mastered, given that what we have referred to above as the elements of a sound general education are, sooner or later, effectively learnt, then the teacher is content to allow that the rest of the child's syllabus shall depend upon his own enthusiasms, shall be, in a word, idiosyncratic.

This is not to say, of course, that it will necessarily differ from the syllabuses of that child's classmates, for there will undoubtedly be a large degree of overlap. And given that the pupils in a particular class spend a good deal of their time working on group activities of some kind or another – and we shall have more to say about this in due course – then there might well be a good deal that is common to all children, apart from those areas which one child may share with, say, one or two others. But what is the essential characteristic of this part of the threefold syllabus is that it does not in detail represent some predetermined scheme devised by the teacher, but reflects the particular topics which have caught and fired the child's own interest.

One might ask, what proportion of a child's education should be idiosyncratic? One can give only a personal answer. During the child's early schooling there will obviously be less room for individuality, not only because of the relative limitations of his physical and intellectual environment, and of his capacity for understanding that environment, but also because in these early years his interests are likely to be caught by everything, so that he is most susceptible to the teacher's suggestions and guidance. For his part, the teacher will be conscious of the need to establish basic skills, so that we may expect that a high proportion of what he does in fact reflects the teacher's rather than his own intentions, though always with the proviso that it is through the skilful exploitation of his interests that the teacher is able to achieve his aims. As the child grows older, so we would expect an increasing proportion of his work to reflect either his own interests, or interests shared with other members of a working group. By the time he reaches secondary school, I would myself hope that a good deal, and certainly more than half, of the child's time would be spent in activities arising directly from the satisfaction of his own curiosity or need for achievement, though no doubt within a framework for which his teachers are responsible. By the time he reaches the fourth form, a child who has received an education on these principles should be perfectly capable of directing, if not the whole, at least 90 per cent of his own education.

I hope no one will have reached this far and still be under the misapprehension that this means that he will have no need of a teacher then. Indeed, we may surmise that his need may actually be greater than it might have been, had he been exposed instead to a traditional teacher-directed education, for as his enthusiasms develop and are fed by his achievement, so the adventure of discovery will lead him to attempt what would have been thought of as far beyond his understanding, both by his instructors and himself, had he remained behind a desk. His attitude towards his teacher now will not be the rather pitying, scornful one of the examination candidate who has got his notes by heart, and feels that he has outgrown his instructor's knowledge; it will instead be the attitude of a fellow-seeker after the truth. And as we know, this is a fellowship which is enhanced rather than diminished by experience. It is to the question of how the teacher may himself become worthy of that fellowship that the rest of this book is directed.

Before examining that question, however, it may be useful to recapitulate what has been said so far. It has been argued that the education system of this country is in the process of a revolution, based on a fundamental change in the teacher's interpretation of his role in the classroom, which is ceasing to be one of directing his pupil's learning in accordance with a predetermined and detailed programme, and is instead becoming one of organizing opportunities and provisions for pupils to direct their own learning. This does not imply a rejection of all traditional knowledge, but a belief that it may be more effectively approached through children's interests. It does not imply a rejection of systematic learning, but a belief that children will themselves see the need for system in their own approaches. It does not imply a repudiation of the teacher's responsibility for his pupils' learning, but a belief that that responsibility can best be discharged by allowing some measure of choice for each pupil, and by recognizing that provision needs to be made for three parts to the syllabus: one part consisting of those basic skills necessary for any further learning; one of those skills and areas of knowledge constituting a common general education; and one of an idiosyncratic area, the content of which will depend upon the individual pupil's interests and inclinations.

2

The Role of the Teacher

In a traditional, teacher-directed lesson, the responsibility for the lesson is wholly the teacher's. He decides what part of the syllabus will be dealt with, how it will be tackled, what examples will be used to demonstrate it, and what work the pupils will do to reinforce their understanding of it. But his habitual authority often extends far beyond the school work itself. Where the children sit, when they shall listen and when write, whether or not they may speak – all these are taken for granted to be within the teacher's right of deciding. He will also say whether the windows should be open or closed, the light on or off, what pictures, if any, should adorn the walls. Indeed, the extent to which teachers are prepared to go in dictating the details of their pupils' activities would be unbelievable, were it not taken for granted. It is a commonplace, for example, that when children are required to copy down notes from the board (a pretty usual activity in such classrooms), not only the wording of the notes (which is in any case often entirely the teacher's), but also the exact disposition of the headings, underlinings and the like are normally prescribed to the children. Not many months ago I was sitting at the back of a third-year class in physics in which the teacher had, characteristically, demonstrated an experiment from the front bench while the children had watched from their places. At the end of the experiment, he wrote a detailed account of what had happened, requiring the class to copy out his words into their notebooks. Underneath the notes he ruled a short line to indicate their termination, and you may be sure he used the blackboard ruler to do so. Then he walked round the classroom examining the books to make sure that everyone was copying out his words correctly. Suddenly there was an angry outburst from the back of the class as he leant over one unfortunate boy, stabbing his finger at the book on the desk. 'How many times have I told you,' he shouted, and from his angry tone one might have supposed that the wretched child had entirely failed to understand the whole point of the demonstration, '*not* to put the line on the *same* line as the last sentence, but on the line *underneath*?' And then turning to the class, he held up the offending notebook, which had in fact been most neatly written out, and repeated his instruction that the line indicating the end of a note should be ruled on the line below the last sentence, and not on the same line, nor yet slightly below it.

No one who has taught for any length of time in a secondary school in England will be surprised by this story (unless it is because I think it worth telling) and I dare say that there are many practising teachers who would be prepared to explain to me that it is necessary to establish exact routines in order to save time, or to inculcate good habits, or even because 'the children themselves will ask if you don't tell them'. Even in such an unimportant detail as the positioning of a final line it is taken for granted that children should not be allowed initiative. Monica Baldwin in her account of life in a closed convent[1] describes the obsessional regulation of the minutiae of everyday life within its walls, but in fact the discipline she endured might be described as liberal in comparison with that in many classrooms, and of course Miss Baldwin had voluntarily chosen the convent whereas few children in our society can escape the sentence of schooling.

Now it is clear that the role of the teacher in charge of children who have some measure of responsibility for their own syllabus must be very different from this. This is not to say that some, at any rate, of the traditional virtues of a good teacher will not be to his advantage; for example, those of patience, a ready sympathy and a sense of humour. But teaching children who are actively engaged in their own learning, and who are to some extent self-directed in that process, involves skills and makes call upon resources quite other than those employed in formal teaching. It is the aim of this chapter to attempt an identification of them.

The role of the formal teacher
We may begin by first considering the role of the formal teacher and

[1] Monica Baldwin: *I Leap Over the Wall*, London, Hamish Hamilton, 1949.

the means by which he fulfils it. Before doing so, however, I should like to emphasize that I am using the word 'formal' strictly in a descriptive sense and without any pejorative implication. Good formal teaching can be enjoyable, stimulating and effective for both teacher and taught, and there are certain circumstances when it may be the most appropriate method to be employed. Our concern here is simply to define the formal situation in order to compare other approaches with it.

By formal teaching, then, I mean a situation in which the teacher directs the lesson according to some prepared scheme in which, while he has taken account of the different abilities and attainments of the pupils, he nevertheless expects the class to learn as a unit. The children sit at their desks in rows, facing the teacher. A typical lesson may begin with the teacher's reminding his pupils of what they already know relevant to the topic of the lesson. He then explains the topic, addressing the whole class with a vocabulary and at a speed intended for all to follow. He may illustrate what he is saying with blackboard diagrams, or with charts, or with a film or filmstrip, or he may conduct an experiment. At the end of his explanation, he may ask questions round the class in order to see whether the children have understood what he has been saying. He may then require them to do some work deriving from his explanation, in which case he may take the opportunity to walk round the class, helping individuals who are having some difficulty.

This is a picture, I suggest, that all of us are familiar with and most of us have spent a good deal of our schooling under such circumstances. What makes the lesson I have described 'formal'? First of all, it is teacher-planned; that is, the teacher decides beforehand on the content and plan of the lesson. Secondly, it is teacher-organized; that is, the teacher decides how his plan shall be carried out. Thirdly, it is teacher-directed; that is, the teacher, having organized the class, ensures that this organization is in fact carried out. And fourthly, it is teacher-oriented; that is, the teacher is himself the source of information, though he may well employ text-books, charts, films, etc. as supporting material.

The physical arrangement of the classroom normally reflects the central importance of the teacher, who sits or stands in front of the children, often behind a bigger desk or demonstration bench. For the formal lesson revolves entirely around him. Without his presence, it simply could not take place. That he is an essential member of the classroom group is demonstrated by the pattern of functional relationships which, if we draw them, look like this:

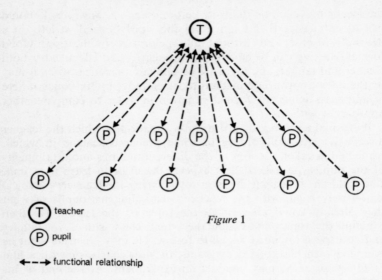

T teacher

P pupil

◄--► functional relationship

Figure 1

In other words, the only relationships that are functional in a formal lesson are those between each individual child and the teacher; there is virtually none between the children themselves. Normally, children address their remarks solely to the teacher, either by answering questions or by asking them. Any communication between children is likely to be illicit.

What are the skills and information necessary to the formal teacher? There is no doubt that the possession of the relevant knowledge comes high on the list. If he is to act as an authoritative source of knowledge, then clearly he must *be* one. As an irreducible minimum he must know the topic he has to explain, and it is obviously desirable that he should also know much more, in order to relate the topic to other topics within the subject, and also to be able to answer questions.

Sequential to the possession of knowledge is the capacity for clear explanation. The formal teacher should not only know his subject, but also be able to explain it simply and clearly, so that the slow children are able to follow as well as the bright ones. In this context, speech is important; his utterances should be precise, carefully articulated, and at the same time sufficiently varied to avoid monotony. And he should know how to emphasize important points in such a way that his pupils pay particular attention to them.

And, of course, he should be able to maintain the order in the classroom necessary to the progress of the lesson. While he is speaking to them, the children should be silent and attentive. When they are working at the exercises he has set, they should be silent and industrious. In so far as the only functional relationships in a formal lesson are those between the teacher and each of the pupils, there is no cause for any interchange between pupils, and in the well-ordered formal classroom there is no such interchange. Nor is there any cause for the pupils to move from their desks. Thus, silence (except for the teacher's voice), immobility and industry are the marks of the well-ordered formal classroom, and it is these marks that are looked for in judging the traditional teacher.

The role of the indirect teacher

We may contrast this picture with what I propose to call 'indirect' teaching, a term I prefer to 'informal' teaching in so far as it is not so much the absence of formality, as the absence of obvious direction by the teacher that characterizes what I have in mind.

The indirect teacher, then, as we have seen, may very well have in mind certain syllabus requirements which it is his intention shall be dealt with during the lesson, and which he has regard to when he prepares his lesson. At the same time, he allows in his preparation for the fact that his pupils will also be given the opportunity to follow particular interests of their own, whether individually or in groups, and he tries to anticipate the direction these might lead. The lesson itself may begin with the teacher's addressing the whole class, as in a formal lesson, and the children may well also be sitting at desks in rows. The teacher outlines the topic, not by presenting it as a field of knowledge which has to be learnt, but by raising questions that might be answered. At this point he may well invite suggestions from the class as to which questions could be attempted, or even whether alternative questions would be more interesting. After some discussion, it is agreed that one or more particular areas would be worth pursuing and at this point he may suggest that the class divide itself into groups, or small working parties, to make recommendations back to the whole class as to how such areas could be defined and investigated. The formation of the groups might be an *ad hoc* procedure, or through some kind of procedure which provides for the declaration of preferences. An important principle followed by the teacher is that children are allowed to choose the areas they wish to work in. The groups then get together and at this stage the desks or tables may be rearranged. The teacher moves round from one group to the next, listening to the discussions, answering queries or, better still, suggesting ways in which queries can be answered, but taking care to encourage initiative among the children themselves. Plans are formed and discussed and after a while the teacher may reconvene the whole class, and suggest that the various plans might be put to the class as a whole, and discussed. This is done and after further discussion, some plans are adopted, others discarded or postponed. New groups might then be formed to begin work on the agreed plans. Some children may undertake to work as individuals, but making specific contributions to the general scheme. The teacher continues as before, circulating, giving advice or suggestions when asked, and stimulating progress by encouragement and approval.[1]

It is clear that in such circumstances, very few of the skills and knowledge necessary to the formal teacher are particularly relevant. It may be argued that knowledge of the appropriate field is just as important as in the traditional class lesson, as the teacher must be able to anticipate where investigations might lead, and what would not be profitable or within the children's abilities. It might be thought that he should also be able to answer the children's questions. While this is true to a certain extent, nevertheless experience suggests that many of the most successful undertakings of this kind have been in areas of the teacher's relative ignorance. Because the teacher may well be learning alongside his pupils he may not therefore lead them, whether through persuasion or example, to approach subjects in the manner approved by the textbooks, and as has been suggested above, textbook approaches are not necessarily the best suited to the children themselves. Moreover, his own knowledge of a subject may tempt the teacher to answer his pupils' questions rather than to suggest that they try to find out the answers for themselves. It may lead him to prevent their embarking on some activity which, while foredoomed to failure as far as finding a required answer is concerned, may nevertheless be a rich source of learning. Moreover, if the teacher does not in fact know the answer to the question the children are pursuing, he may well come to share their own enthusiasm in arriving at an answer. On the other hand, this itself may be a danger in that he may be tempted to suggest methods, which from his general experience, might be more likely to be effective but are less meaningful to the children.

It may appear from all this that knowledge on the part of the

[1] A more detailed account of indirect teaching and some suggestions for its organization will be found in Chapter 4 of Kaye and Rogers, op. cit.

teacher is a positive disadvantage and this is clearly ridiculous. At the same time, it is surprising how, even in primary schools and with subjects in which the teacher thinks himself to be knowledgeable, children who are allowed their heads in following investigations may well raise questions to which the teacher in fact does not know the answer. We may certainly say that exact and detailed knowledge of the whole field of proposed inquiry on the part of the teacher is not a necessary prior condition, as it may rightly be held to be in a traditional teacher-directed lesson.

The capacity for clear explanation is an advantage to any teacher, but again, children may learn more effectively from what they discover for themselves, than from what they are told, however clearly. And children who obtain from their teacher frequent and explicit solutions to their problems may well come to prefer reliance upon him to reliance upon their own efforts. Similarly, clear speech is an undoubted advantage, but it does not hold as critical a place in the teacher's skills in indirect teaching as it does in a formal lesson.

The capacity to maintain order in the classroom has been interpreted, in the traditional setting, as the capacity to obtain silence, immobility and industry. But the first two of these are necessary only because of the requirement in a formal lesson that each child should be able to hear what the teacher says, and because there is no functional need for pupils to communicate with each other. With indirect teaching on the other hand, the relationships between the children forming the various working groups are an essential and continuing part of the lesson, and to seek to obtain silence and immobility therefore would be to seek to prevent the very communications upon which the lesson depends. Moreover, in a formal lesson it is assumed that the work itself will not be sufficiently interesting for the children to apply themselves to it without some kind of external constraint. With indirect teaching, however, it is a basic assumption that the children will become so involved in their work that progress will arise from their own desire to go further. Hence, the ability to maintain order in the traditional sense is no longer of any value to the indirect teacher and any attempt to do so would be to impede the circumstances upon which the success of indirect teaching depends.

If knowledge of the subject is not a prior essential, the capacity for clear explanation and speech of only incidental value, and the ability to maintain classroom order irrelevant, it may properly be asked what in fact *does* the successful indirect teacher need in the way of skills and knowledge? There are, I think, three essentials.

41

The first is the capacity to recognise incipient curiosity and interest. Having recognised it, comes the need to be able to nourish and encourage it. And arising out of this, the ability to see when enthusiasm is flagging, and when therefore, a change of activity or direction is needed. These skills depend upon the experience of contact with children in informal circumstances. They cannot be learnt by rote from a book. By far the best way of developing them is to take part, as an assistant rather than as an observer, in classes in which indirect teaching is already going on. This has the double advantage of not only allowing the student to develop these skills, but also enabling him to see for himself the enthusiasm and impetus which such teaching, under skilled guidance, can generate.

A second area in which the indirect teacher must be competent is the pedestrian but important skill of organization and administration relating to such matters as the ordering and provision of materials and equipment; the organization of visits and expeditions; and the various techniques relating to the mounting of displays, dramatic performances, and the like, including some knowledge of paints, glues, modelling materials, duplicators, craft tools and materials and so forth. And here it is not so important (though it is clearly desirable) that the teacher should himself be able to manipulate these various techniques, as that he should know what is needed and how to obtain it. For once an investigation is under way, and leading towards some tangible result, it is extremely frustrating for the mere lack of materials or tools to be responsible for delay. Among the most important of tools are reference books, and access to a reference library is an essential condition of indirect teaching. This should begin with the class library itself, which should contain as many good reference works as can be afforded. There is no place in this kind of teaching for class sets of textbooks. And it can be fairly confidently stated that teachers nearly always underestimate the level of understanding that children will manifest when they want to find out something about a subject in which they are interested. Books written expressly for the information of children are often written down to their supposed level, giving odd snippets of information instead of systematically presented details. However, publishers are becoming more aware of the need for clearly expressed but technically adequate reference works, and some good series can now be obtained.

One of the characteristics of indirect teaching is that it is often outgoing; that is to say, it involves activities outside the classroom, such as visits to public institutions, libraries, museums, factories and the like. It may also involve inviting experts from many walks of life to visit the school in order to talk to the children about their work. While the arrangement of all this involves no skills that are beyond any literate person, it does require forethought and method, and it is surprising the difficulty that some find in undertaking the simple organization required. It is, of course, a good idea to involve the children as far as possible in these activities, but it is essential that the teacher himself accepts final responsibility for them and checks that they have been done correctly.

An important area of knowledge which the indirect teacher should be acquainted with is that relating to the behaviour of children in groups, the study of which is a branch of social psychology. And a valuable skill relating to this area is that of conducting discussions. Guiding a discussion is a skill that has to be learnt. It involves the ability to lead out those who are shy or inarticulate, and to keep under control the voluble and extrovert, though without discouraging or snubbing them. It includes the difficult skill of formulating conclusions and decisions based on what has been said and intended, not on the teacher's predetermined ideas and preferences. A good discussion leader should be able to give everyone the opportunity to have his say without allowing the discussion to wander off the point, or become boring to the group. He should also be scrupulously fair in his adherence to group decisions, particularly when he does not agree with them. And of course, most important of all, he should be able to resist the temptation to use his own superior knowledge and authority to lead the discussion in the way he wants it to go. This does not mean that he should not allow, or even encourage, decisions or conclusions which fit in with his own plans, provided they have been reached through the children's own initiative. But it is very easy for a teacher, who has half-formed some some particular plan of action, so to influence a discussion group that they are led, despite themselves, to agree to do what the teacher has previously decided they should do. There is nothing more infuriating than a pseudo-democracy in which the trappings of free choice are used to conceal an authoritarian regime. Under such conditions neither adults nor children give of their best.

So far we have been considering the situation in which one teacher is solely responsible for a class of children. Team teaching and

43

co-operative teaching[1] entail a further skill and one, moreover, at which teachers are not notoriously adept; I mean the skill of co-operation. Accustomed to having complete responsibility for what goes on in a classroom, the formal teacher gets into the habit of making a large number of decisions on the spot. Indeed, as I have pointed out above, he normally takes it upon himself to make decisions in so many areas as virtually to deprive the children of any initiative whatever. It may therefore be understood that experienced teachers often find extremely irksome the need for continual and detailed consultation which good co-operative or team teaching entails.

It may be seen, then, that the skills and knowledge demanded of the indirect teacher are considerably different from those traditionally associated with successful classroom lessons, and the fostering of them understandably requires an alternative training programme. It is the purpose of this book to outline some experiments which the author has been connected with, aimed at providing such an alternative. Before doing so, however, it is intended to examine the students' own attitudes towards the training situation, and it is to this subject that the following chapter is devoted.

[1] The distinction between team teaching and co-operative teaching is one that has come, in this country, to be associated with teaching different age-ranges. The term *team teaching* is generally applied to secondary schools, and it tends to imply a group of teachers, often under a team leader, having joint responsibility for some part of the curriculum, which is usually divided out among the various experts in the team, each of whom may give one or more 'lead lessons' in his approach to the topic or part of the curriculum with which they are concerned. These lead lessons will be attended by all the children for whom the team are responsible (who may number two hundred or more in the case of a year group in a large school), while follow-up work may be done in classes or smaller groups, under the direction or guidance of the members of the team. *Co-operative teaching* is normally applied to a primary-school situation in which a group of class teachers take joint responsibility for all or a part of the curriculum of their classes. This enables them to specialize in different areas, often by using their rooms as subject- or area-centres. Lead lessons to the whole group of children are not usual in primary schools; the children may move from one subject centre to the next, either according to some programme or in relation to their individual work. There is a good deal of variation and try-out currently in progress in both team teaching and co-operative teaching.

3

Students' Attitudes

Those responsible for the training of teachers are often the worst
offenders in failing to practise what they preach. As educationists
we often stress the importance of understanding the motivation of
the learner before planning any educational programme. Before
going on to discuss how best we can prepare our students to fulfil
the kind of role that has been outlined in the previous chapter, it is
therefore proper that we should give some time to an examination
of the students' own views, and it is to this examination that the
present chapter is devoted.

University departments of education
Most universities in England and Wales have a department of
education in which students who have already obtained their degrees
and who wish to train for the teaching profession may follow a
course for one academic session leading to a professional qualification.[1] This qualification used to be called the Teacher's Diploma,
but the designation Postgraduate Certificate in Education is generally
now preferred.

University departments normally train secondary teachers, though
there are one or two offering courses preparatory to primary teaching.
Traditionally, they have prepared students with school-subject

[1] For full details see the current *Handbook of Colleges and Departments of
Education* published by the Association of Teachers in Colleges and Departments
of Education.

degrees to teach those subjects in secondary schools, particularly in the grammar schools and in such of the independent schools as welcome trained teachers. Until very recently, many public schools avowedly preferred to recruit their teaching staff purely on the basis of the class of degree achieved and on the personal qualities of the applicant, regarding the training qualification as of little significance. Some appointing bodies are even said to have taken the view that a candidate with a training qualification was to be avoided, perhaps because it indicated an attempt to bolster up a poor degree, perhaps because it was genuinely felt that training unfitted students for teaching. Certainly it can safely be said that the majority of independent-school heads would prefer an untrained first-class honours graduate to a trained second-class man. This bias against professional training has been reinforced by Government policy, which has recognized untrained graduates as qualified teachers, no matter how irrelevant the subject of their degrees to the needs of their pupils.[1] This irresponsible policy has at last been reversed as far as primary teaching is concerned, but it is applicable to secondary teachers at least until 1974, and these are the main concern of university departments of education. The fact that those graduates who feel sufficient concern to prepare themselves for teaching by undertaking a postgraduate training course thereby put themselves in jeopardy – since they disqualify themselves if they fail – has obviously made it difficult to maintain high academic standards on the postgraduate course and, indeed, failure on the theoretical papers is generally much lower than one might expect.

The course leading to the postgraduate certificate consists of two parts: theoretical and practical. The theoretical course normally includes courses of lectures on educational principles, educational psychology and child development, history of education and health education. Courses on sociology, philosophy and comparative education may or may not be included. There will also be classes on the methods of teaching various subjects – students taking those classes in the subjects which they intend to teach; normally, of

[1] The list of qualifications which entitles their holders to recognition as qualified teachers includes not only all degree subjects, but also such qualifications as a First Class Colliery Managers' Certificate or the Associateship of the National College of Rubber Technology. Nor is there any requirement that the subject of the qualification should be relevant to the qualified teacher's appointment. The possessor of a degree in Sanskrit, for example, is thereby qualified to teach in an infant school, if he be appointed. See *Scales for Salaries for Teachers in Primary and Secondary Schools: England & Wales*, London, H.M.S.O., 1965, Appendix V.

course, their own degree subjects. Finally, university departments sometimes supplement the postgraduate course with a number of ancillary courses. In so far as the majority of students will not have done any psychology, philosophy, sociology or human biology before, it can be seen that the courses in these subjects must necessarily be extremely sketchy. To attempt even an introduction to four or more new academic fields of study in the two terms available (since one of the three terms is normally given over to teaching practice) is hardly the way to rigorous scholarship, and it is not surprising that departments of education often have very low academic prestige among the other university departments. From the students' own point of view this would, perhaps, matter less if the course were properly integrated, so that at least a coherent intellectual structure could be studied. In fact, however, many university education departments are content to offer a number of discrete lecture courses, leaving the students to attempt their own synthesis, and it is not unusual for the lecturers offering those courses to draw them up without bothering to consult their colleagues to see if any cross-reference might be done.

As I have said above, the component parts of the theoretical course have not been experimentally justified for inclusion in it. Educational psychology is included because 'the students ought to know how children's minds work', though it is not unknown for this course to be chiefly concerned with the learning behaviour of rats; the history of education is included because 'teachers ought to have some knowledge of the historical development of the educational system', though the course may well include a detailed consideration of the provision for religious instruction in state schools in the nineteenth century while ignoring the influence of socialist thought in the twentieth. The work of Freud and the psychoanalytical school, which has probably been more responsible than any other coherent psychological theory for our present view of child behaviour, may well be ignored altogether, or simply referred to in an aside. Moreover, there is no time to treat anything systematically and comprehensively. It is hardly surprising that students who have just spent three years in the intensive study of a branch of one subject for an honours degree should view the education course, considered as an academic exercise, as little more than a joke.

There are other factors contributing to the students' low estimation of the postgraduate year. University education department courses are often deserving of criticism, not only because their theoretical components are superficial and fragmented, but also because their practical components are unrelated to the student's needs. A common pattern for the three-term year is for the middle term to be wholly devoted to teaching practice. Method classes in the first term may occupy no more than one or two hours a week, during which the lecturer may content himself with a number of generalizations which are seen by the students, apprehensive of the coming practice and mindful of the lack of order which they remember their own teachers suffering from, as being totally inadequate to equip them with the capacity to control ill-disciplined classes. Arguments for and against the teaching of formal grammar may seem of little moment to the prospective teacher of languages who is wondering what he should do if he cannot keep order. Moreover, the qualifications of the methods lecturers themselves as effective teachers in school may well be in question in the minds of the students, particularly as the giving of demonstration lessons is no longer regarded as *de rigueur*.[1]

Then, when the teaching practice itself arrives, students may expect to be visited by their supervisors at most twice a week and more commonly far less often. Supposing that they have a teaching timetable of twenty lessons (and many have more) – that means that at best only a tenth of their actual teaching is seen by the supervisor to form the basis of his advice and of his assessment. Moreover, in some departments the members of staff regard the teaching-practice term as an opportunity to catch up with their reading and research, with the result that they may look upon any time spent supervising students on teaching practice as a tiresome interruption of their own studies. Under such circumstances it is not to be wondered at that students sometimes complain of rare visits and an apparent reluctance on the part of visiting lecturers to spend time discussing their teaching problems.

[1] The fashionable argument against the giving of demonstration lessons is that to do so would be to perpetrate the notion that there is a single ideal way to teach, shown by the demonstration. I agree with those who regard this as a heretical viewpoint, but I nevertheless wonder whether the effect of successful demonstration lessons on the relationship between lecturers and students might not justify the facing of this danger, which in any case could be guarded against by a good variety of lessons from a number of different lecturers. Certainly it has been my own experience that students are very much more ready to listen to advice after having seen the lecturer deal with problems himself; while to invite and be prepared to discuss criticism of his own lessons is to establish the kind of *rapport* that enables him to make effective criticism in turn. Moreover, the fact that his lessons inevitably justify criticism need not – unless he is entirely hopeless – lower the students' estimation of his advice. Students recognize that no one is without fault and make allowances for it.

The feeling that insufficient practical help is given to the student teacher is not the only other factor contributing to his low estimation of the postgraduate year. It is sadly true that a fair proportion of students in university departments of education are there, not because they have ambitions to enter teaching, but because their ambitions to enter some other profession or occupation have been disappointed. To become a teacher is a recognized alternative open to the student who fails to get the class of degree or personal recommendation necessary to land a better job. Moreover, for many, and particularly for those whose indolence or irresolution make the conditions of a student's life pleasant, the prospect of a further year at university is itself attractive, particularly if it is known that the demands as far as the work is concerned are not particularly exacting. Indeed, it is not very long ago that a professor of education at one of the older-established universities used to begin the course by telling his students that they now had the chance to do all those things in the university which their degree studies had not left them time for. On the whole it is fair to say that the postgraduate year is looked upon by many students as a chance to relax after three years' hard work, a pleasant holiday to compensate for failing to land an exciting job, and possibly a second opportunity to look around for an alternative.[1]

The colleges of education

The training colleges, renamed colleges of education at the suggestion of the Robbins Report,[2] are traditionally responsible for training primary teachers, secondary modern teachers, and specialist teachers of non-academic subjects such as domestic science, physical education and handicraft. They can be divided into various groupings in a number of ways: into general colleges offering both primary and secondary training in a large variety of subjects, and specialist colleges dealing with one age-range or one subject; or into local authority colleges, run by county or borough councils, and voluntary colleges, run by voluntary bodies (normally, of course, religious bodies); or into day and resident colleges, the former often dealing

[1] The limitations of the teaching staff of university departments of education are discussed by W. Taylor in *Society and the Education of Teachers*, Faber, 1969, pp. 219 et. seq.

[2] See Committee on Higher Education: *Higher Education*, London, H.M.S.O., 1963, vol. I, para. 351, p. 119.

49

largely with mature students; and so forth.[1] For present purposes it is proposed to confine discussion to the local-authority general college; differences between that category and the other colleges are of little relevance to the topics we shall be concerned with.

The minimum qualifications for entry to a college of education are normally five O-level passes. However, with the increasing demand for higher education, many colleges have been able to insist on a higher standard for a large proportion of their intake, so that a fair number of students may well possess the minimum university entrance requirements of two A-levels plus three O-levels. Normally, and since 1962, the students undertake a three-year course of study in which the professional study of the theory and practice of education is pursued concurrently with the study of one or more subjects: art and craft, biology, commerce, domestic science, English, geography, religious education, or science, for example. It is a firmly-held principle of colleges that the study of a subject is not pursued only in order to amass the knowledge necessary to teach it. Students preparing to teach infants may well study science to an advanced level, although they will not expect to teach it as such. Students preparing to teach in secondary schools, however, will normally be teaching their subjects and the study of them is therefore part of their professional training as well as furtherance of their own personal education.

In addition to the study of one or more main subjects, students take short curriculum courses, specifically designed to give teachers content as well as methods of teaching general subjects. These may include English, mathematics, art, physical education and so forth. It must be remembered that primary school teachers are expected to cover most aspects of the primary school syllabus, and if they are members of a small school staff, they will be expected to cover the whole syllabus.

Thus, the college course includes the theory and practice of education, one or two main subjects which may be studied for the relevance of their content to the student's teaching, and/or as part of their personal education, and a group of subjects taken with a view to teaching them.

The teaching-practice pattern varies considerably from one college to another. Some colleges arrange a block practice of several weeks

[1] Details of the various courses offered by the colleges of education in England and Wales are to be found in the *Handbook of Colleges and Department of Education*, op. cit.

at the end of each year, others vary the times of the practices; some colleges are content with two, longer practices; others provide a day-a-week practice in place of one of the block practices. However, all students in colleges of education have the advantage, as compared with those on the postgraduate course, of a number of practices extended over a period of years, and the kind of apprehensive anxiety common among the graduates with regard to their classroom performance is somewhat less apparent among college students. Moreover, college students are often introduced to the classroom by degrees; they may at first be responsible for a small group of children, instead of having to take a whole class.

Colleges of education have traditionally concentrated on classroom skills and while there may well be cause for complaint among students as regards the actual quality of the advice and guidance offered, nevertheless most colleges seek to keep in touch with the best teaching methods employed in schools, and give their students an opportunity of absorbing them. Because of the importance, particularly to a primary school teacher, of understanding children's behaviour, the study of child development normally plays an important part in the theoretical course in education and this may be related to practical work with children in and out of school. The subjects that together make up the course in the theory of education are more or less the same as those to be found in the university departments: the principles of education, educational psychology and child development, health education and history of education. A few colleges are beginning to offer courses in the philosophy of education, and one or two in the sociology of education. The general academic level of college work is below that in university departments, though rather more attempt is made to integrate the course and to relate it to the students' practical work.

I have suggested above some of the factors which affect the attitude of postgraduate students towards the one-year course in professional training offered in a university department. It is clear that a number of the conditions governing those attitudes will not be present for college students. At the same time, it cannot be pretended that there are no grounds for concern. The colleges have the advantage that their students have chosen at the outset to enter the teaching profession, and the prospect of their doing so to some extent informs their attitude throughout the three years of their course. Moreover, the fact that in most colleges there is some purposeful contact with schools tends to keep in mind the relevance of their studies to their ultimate careers. And of course, the fact that the colleges are organised solely for training teachers gives them an undeniably professional ethos.

At the same time, there are two important undercurrents among college students which militate against a full commitment to their studies. One is that, particularly with the increasing demand for higher education, many of the students are university rejects, who must necessarily look upon a college course as second best. The other is that the vast majority of college students are young women, most of whom can expect to get married at the end of their course, or within a year or so of their becoming teachers. Their attitude towards the course is inevitably somewhat dilettante, and as the three years progress, neither the relaxed complacence of those who have become engaged, nor the frenetic social activity of those who have not, encourages a serious attitude to study.

There is, moreover, a generally relaxed air with regard to work among college students. Failure rates are low, course requirements outside the teaching practices are not high, and students may comfortably cruise through their courses without overworking themselves. While the certificate awarded on the successful completion of the course is normally divided into two or three grades, the attainment of a distinction grade does not give to a teaching career the demonstrable impetus that a first-class honours degree does in many walks of life. The grade of certificate obtained, in both theory and practice, is looked upon as a temporary assessment, and teachers know that promotion and successful advancement depend far more upon enthusiastic reports from heads of schools in which they have taught, than from the standard of their certificates.

There is a different source of malaise commonly to be found among college students, which derives not so much from their own attitudes towards authority, as from the attitude of the college staff towards them. Traditionally, training colleges have been establishments to which it was safe to send older girls; safe in the sense that their parents could expect with a reasonable degree of confidence that their daughters would not be impregnated, either by wild young men or by wild young ideas. And the colleges have only very recently begun to drag themselves out of the nineteenth century as far as their attitude towards student behaviour is concerned. Most colleges have elaborate rules regarding times of coming in at night, even times of going to bed and the wearing of dress and cosmetics. In many colleges, to dress fashionably is to attract unfavourable comment from members of staff, which may lead to reproof or even reprisals. College principals sometimes argue that it is school heads who set the pace with regard to dress and cosmetics, but they rarely carry this argument to its logical conclusion by allowing students to wear whatever they please while not actually on teaching practice. Similarly, there is normally little interest among college students in politics or, indeed, in any controversial issues. The intellectual atmosphere is muted, conservative and above all, one in which conformity is well regarded. A newly qualified teacher, writing of her experience in a college of education, says: 'We were required to listen and accept: there was little opportunity to question. The course seemed less concerned with thought and independent judgment than with amassing facts, receiving opinion and studying mechanically.' The generally repressive atmosphere and lack of intellectual stimulation led to apathy: 'Nothing much was in fact required of us so eventually we did nothing much.' She concludes that: 'It has always seemed to me very possible that perhaps the three-year college course was purpose designed to produce a semi-profession of docile, institution-respecting teachers.'[1]

To be fair to college tutors, this state of affairs is often supported by the students themselves. Perhaps as a result of the well-known policy of recruiting applicants who have been Sunday-school teachers, college students are themselves conservative in attitude, conformist in outlook. One may listen to a group of students discussing current events with the sinking of the heart that comes from knowing that their views will be precisely the same in forty years' time. College tutors[2] do not suffer from the same sense of academic inferiority that may be found among their university counterparts. They are normally appointed from among practising teachers, and such an appointment is regarded as a promotion; while they do not usually expect to compete for university appointments. But what marks them out particularly from university lecturers is their relative lack of academic freedom. Colleges of education, whether maintained by a local education authority or by a voluntary society, are hierarchical in structure, and the principal of a college is comparable with the head of a school in the extent of his authority. Thus, college tutors can at best fulfil only an advisory capacity with regard to student acceptance, college discipline, curriculum determination, and the allocation of staff and resources, and in some colleges they may

[1] L. Tinkham: 'Learning one's lesson,' in A. Cockburn, & R. Blackburn eds.: *Student Power: Problems, Diagnosis, Action*, Penguin, 1969, pp. 86, 88, 94.
[2] Usage tends to prefer college tutors and university lecturers, though the distinction is not a technical one. Both normally give lectures and conduct tutorials as part of their duties.

well not even be asked for their advice. The tradition of the auto-
cratic headmaster, personally responsible to his board of governors
for every aspect of the life of the school, may no doubt make
occasionally for great schools, but it may also develop a cringing
subservience in his staff – a quality that is not compatible with high
levels of academic attainment.

It is true that the Government has declared its intention of securing
the adoption of the recommendations of the Weaver Report,[1] which
urges that all colleges should establish academic boards, but old
habits die hard, and many years must elapse before college tutors
feel able to express views highly critical of college policy without
apprehension.[2] A case comes to mind in a college with an academic
board of some years' standing: a senior member of staff felt strongly
that his academic freedom had been arbitrarily curtailed in a number
of ways which prevented the proper discharge of his teaching duties.
He tabled documentary evidence at a meeting of the academic
board, urging that the board was responsible for academic freedom.
It was suspected that the documents implied criticism of the principal
and the board preferred not to read them. It is difficult to imagine
a similar situation arising in a university senate.

As I have said above, the course provided in a college of education
tends to be much better integrated than that offered in a university
department (which is not to say that there is no room for improvement in it), and there is a tradition of pastoral care for the student
which, while it no doubt enables college students to make the
transition from school work to organised private study more readily
than in universities, at the same time is coupled with a degree of
surveillance over their private lives that more spirited students find
objectionable. College staff usually have a fuller teaching timetable
than do university lecturers; whether for this reason or another, the
volume of research issuing from colleges of education is meagre.
Indeed, the criticism made above of university syllabuses – that there
appears to be little or no need felt for the experimental justification
of its validity – is equally true of the colleges of education, in which
generally matters of policy are decided, not by demonstration and
controlled experiment, but by recourse to intuition, unsubstantiated

[1] *Report of the Study Group on the Government of Colleges of Education.*
London, H.M.S.O., 1966.

[2] Cp. Taylor, op. cit., p. 244. This is not to assert, however, that all university
lecturers are necessarily free from apprehension on this score.

assertion and the widespread belief that 'what was good enough for me is good enough for them.'[1]

Attitudes common to university and college students

So far I have concerned myself with the differences between students in university departments and colleges of education in their attitudes towards the professional courses of training they have embarked upon. There are a number of further considerations, common to both, which are of relevance to our subject. The vast majority of students have themselves come either from grammar schools or from independent schools in which both the method and content of their education was of the grammar school type. A large proportion attended primary schools in which lessons were taught formally, though this proportion is beginning to diminish. Hence, very few of them have had any classroom experience other than that of being taught in a traditional, formal manner, with the teacher directing the lesson along lines which he or she has (or perhaps has not!) prepared beforehand. While those who are preparing to be primary teachers may recognize that methods in schools for the under-elevens have changed, nevertheless their own experience is almost wholly that of being taught formally.

Their own *successful* experience, be it noted. This is a most important factor in their attitude towards all methods of teaching. University and college entrants represent the top 20 per cent of school leavers in academic attainment; all but a negligible minority have a minimum of five O-level passes in G.C.E. and many, of course, have a much greater record of examination successes. Whether as a result of a retentive memory, or a high general intelligence (whatever that is), or a liking for the teachers, these students have successfully benefited from the kind of teaching they have themselves received. No doubt they have all had some experience of its limitations, but the fact remains that it has been responsible for their present success and it is not surprising, therefore, that their attitudes towards traditional methods are on the whole favourable. Indeed, while those who are intending to teach in primary schools may be prepared to examine alternative ways of arranging a classroom to having the children sit in rows of desks, those who are aiming at becoming secondary teachers usually fully anticipate teaching in precisely the same way that they themselves were taught, except that they hope to model themselves on the better teachers they have themselves learnt under. Admiration of a particular teacher is often

[1] Further limitations of college staff are discussed in Taylor, op. cit., p. 203 et seq.

55

a reason adduced for the choice of teaching as a profession and while it is personal qualities which stand out in the students' accounts of the best teachers they have known, their mastery of traditional teaching techniques is always mentioned with approval.

The majority of students, then, have no cause to be critical of traditional methods; they have achieved their own success under them, and they anticipate using the same approach themselves.[1] Moreover, they conceive this approach as consisting of a number of rules which it is their purpose in attending a teacher training institution to learn, and which it is the duty of the tutors and lecturers to teach them. Students are often suspicious of the reluctance of education lecturers to provide explicit and detailed instruction in method. They are prepared to cite the proposition that there is no one best way to teach when defending apparent disaster in their classrooms or teaching practice, but they disallow the same proposition as a general principle governing the college or university course in education. Moreover, even when told that what lies behind good teaching are such commonplaces as an understanding of children's problems, thorough and relevant preparation, a readiness to explain patiently and carefully when explanation is called for, the desirability of getting children to do things for themselves instead of watching the teacher do them – principles which are as appropriate to indirect methods as they are to formal class teaching – students persist in thinking that their mentors are for some reason deliberately withholding from them the 'tricks of the trade', which they see as certain techniques which can be learnt and applied in all relevant situations.

This attitude is doubly distressing, not only because it is ill-founded, but also because it introduces an element of mistrust in the students' view of their tutors. Indeed, it is not unknown for students to say to their tutors: 'You are yourselves all experienced teachers on the staff; why do you conceal from us the secrets of successful teaching?'

[1] It will be remembered that we are speaking of student teachers here. Evidence that not all students are uncritical of traditional teaching methods has been brought sharply to the attention of university and college authorities by the various strikes and sit-ins that have become a familiar feature of the scene in higher education. Student politicians and revolutionaries are well aware of the crucial role that control of the curriculum and the methods of teaching it plays in the 'manipulation of the manipulators', to use a favourite phrase; see, for example, Stedman Jones's chapter on 'The meaning of the student revolt' in Cockburn and Blackburn, op. cit., p. 49, et seq. Rebel student teachers, if any exist, have been noticeably inactive so far.

There are, of course, those students who believe that certain subjects 'teach themselves'. This is a common view of handicraft students, for example, who will often claim that their subject is so intrinsically attractive to boys that there is no need for them to learn how to teach it at all. And those who expect to spend most of their time teaching subjects in the sixth form may, perhaps with rather more justification, claim that problems of securing order in the classroom, and the fostering of effective learning among their pupils, need not concern them.

But most students are all too aware of the need for a plan of action in the classroom, and a plan, moreover, which is demonstrably successful. So far, their own experience of such a plan has been largely limited to formal lessons. It can readily be seen, then, that there is a double problem in teaching 'new' methods: the students must not only learn how to apply them, they must also be convinced of the need to do so. Hence, any programme aimed at providing students with an opportunity to acquire the techniques and experience necessary to successful indirect teaching must also have built into it some means by which the students may discover for themselves and at their own level, the value of an indirect approach to learning.

In the following chapters are outlined some attempts to provide such a programme. It must be emphasized, however, that if these attempts do not merit the description 'experiments' in the sense of carefully controlled procedures governed by experimental controls, they fully justify it in the more everyday meaning of the word – i.e. that of something tried out. They were launched in the belief that the need for a new approach to teacher training was sufficiently urgent to justify their trial adoption. In the absence of a rigorous demonstration either of the inadequacies of traditional methods, or of the efficiency of alternatives, one is obliged to fall back upon personal impressions. My own impression, heightened by a return to England after a decade overseas, was that there was urgent need for a new approach to the training of teachers if the institutions concerned were not to be left behind in the wake of educational progress. I report these attempts, not because I see them as models to be followed, but so that others similarly engaged may benefit from my mistakes.

PART TWO

Some Experimental Approaches

4

Students and Responsibility

Students' resistance to new teaching methods
From what has been said in the preceding three chapters it may be
seen that in attempting to introduce new methods into a training
programme for student teachers, one faces a formidable array of
difficulties over and above those problems attendant upon the
introduction of any change into the running of a conservative
institution. Moreover, despite the widespread adoption of those
approaches to teaching which I have described as tantamount to a
revolution, there nevertheless remains a large body of teachers, often
occupying important positions in school hierarchies, who are themselves opposed to such changes. Very often these teachers are the
most vocal of their opinions in the staff room. Their declarations
of faith in the old, well-tried methods are usually accompanied by
the advice, to student teachers, to disregard everything they are told
at college. The students, flattered by the inclusion of themselves into
the category of those who are 'getting on with the job' as opposed
to those college and university lecturers who are full of newfangled,
highfalutin' ideas but have themselves forgotten what it is to deal
with a classroom of unruly children (if, indeed, they ever knew!),
are also impressed by the older teachers' ability to achieve instant
silence in their classrooms – an achievement which seems especially
enviable in the face of their own apprehension.

As I have already pointed out, the students often begin with a
predisposition in favour of traditional, formal teaching, the vast
majority having themselves achieved entrance to college or university

by their successful achievements under such methods. They come expecting to learn how to employ the traditional methods they are familiar with, and expecting to learn them in a traditional way.

There is thus considerable initial opposition to be overcome by the university or college lecturer seeking to introduce indirect approaches to learning, particularly for students preparing to teach in secondary schools. For while students are generally prepared to concede that indirect methods are sufficiently widespread in primary schools to justify their having at least some experience of them, they will normally make no such concession when it comes to teaching children of secondary age. Coupled with their own reasonably successful experience of formal teaching is their own apprehension of what might happen in a classroom of young adolescents if the familiar restraints of teacher-directed lessons were removed.

It is thus essential to show students not only that indirect methods are desirable in secondary schools on theoretical grounds but also that their adoption does not in practice lead to immediate uncontrollable chaos. And in addition, something has to be done to overcome the intellectual inertia characteristic of many student teachers, some of the sources of which I have suggested in the previous chapter.

Experience suggests that the most fruitful area on which to begin an offensive on complacence is that of the students' own experience of learning. If we can demonstrate to the student in terms of his own experience that an alternative approach to academic study can be made that, perhaps even despite himself, engages his interest and leads him to work hard out of sheer enthusiasm, he may then be prepared to consider the application of a similar approach to teaching children, particularly if he can be shown the method in action. Hence, it is in my view a necessary precondition of introducing indirect methods to student teachers that they are given an opportunity to experience such methods themselves at their own intellectual level.

The limitations of formal lectures

The need to start from the student's own experience was brought home to me most vividly during a year's sabbatical study leave spent at one of our older universities. In order to supplement my reading, I attended a number of lecture courses, many of them given by distinguished scholars. And as a form of relaxation from my studies, I joined a students' dramatic society, well known for its theatrical experiments. Both these experiences proved significant, though neither in the way I had anticipated.

The lectures were in subjects in which I was particularly interested, and they were given, as I have said, by authorities in their field, some of them of international repute. I looked forward keenly to widening the boundaries of my knowledge and to resolving a number of problems that had presented themselves in the course of my reading.

Attendance at a variety of lecture courses soon revealed to me, however, that I had forgotten how badly delivered the great majority of lectures were. Lecturers forgot their references, mislaid their quotations, repeated themselves, interspersed their sentences with 'er's' and 'ah's' and coughs and throat–clearings and a hundred other irritating habits. They either delivered their lectures in an unvarying monotone, without any attempt to emphasise the impor- tant points, or they gave every utterance such over-emphasis that after underlining the first three or four notes, one gave up. But most of all, the lecturers had clearly given no thought whatever to the problem of trying to make their matter memorable. They saw their responsibility as simply that of disgorging themselves of the facts which they had learned, and they left their audiences to deal with this regurgitation as best as they could.

I soon found that my fellow students were as bored as I was, the difference being that they saw this boredom as an inescapable part of a university education and for the most part endured it without complaint. The remedy open to all university students – that of absence – was always available in the last resort, and as the term progressed so did the audiences diminish: at first fitfully, with one or two even returning after a single absence, and then more dras- tically until, by the time the term was half over, many of the audiences were reduced to a third or less of their initial size.

Two successful lecturers

It would not be true to say that I found all the lectures equally wearisome. Of the dozen courses I attended, rather more than half were undoubtedly tedious; two or three were relieved by occasional bright periods; and two were entertaining, one because the lecturer engaged his audience in dialogue and managed to keep them thinking, the other because his material was intrinsically fascinating and was, moreover, presented in a thoughtful and stimulating way. The success of this second lecturer (who, incidentally, was not a regular member of the university staff, but an outside expert, brought in to describe his experimental work) intrigued me, and I set about trying to pin down the elements of his approach. They appeared to rest on two

63

general principles, both contrary to customary university lecturing practice. Most lecturers evidently saw their task as the presentation of the principles of their subjects. They illustrated these principles with examples if they had time or if they had remembered to prepare some, but these examples were clearly regarded as inessential to the main task of setting out the principles. The outside lecturer, on the other hand, gave most of his time and attention to the detailing of examples, which he presented vividly and accurately. He then left his audience to arrive at the principles for themselves, with perhaps a few hints at how they might do so.

Again, from discussion with my fellow students it was clear that my own enjoyment of these lectures was shared. Their interest was aroused by the examples given. Sufficient details were always provided to satisfy initial curiosity and to stimulate further speculation. The fact that they were then invited to make their own inductions was not only a challenge, it was also a direct appeal to their intellectual maturity. The lecturer was, in fact, treating his audience as intellectual equals: here are the facts, he was saying – you and I can see what they mean.

The other lecturer whose performance I enjoyed did in fact give precisely that: a performance. He relied for its effect upon the response he obtained from those members of the audience who rose in answer to his invitation to point out the fallacies of the seemingly absurd propositions he put forward so provocatively. And for all its apparent spontaneity, his performance was as carefully prepared as that of the variety gag-man's turn, to which it bore a marked resemblance. In making this comparison, I am not seeking to denigrate the lecture as an intellectual demonstration. Quite the reverse. It was, in fact, a highly sophisticated and successful descendant of those Socratic discourses which the Western world regards as among the highest products of civilised thought.

Of the twelve or so lecture courses I attended during my sabbatical year, these two were the only ones I enjoyed and looked forward to. I bore with several of the others to the bitter end out of a sense of duty, but some I simply could not endure, and I quit (along with many others) well before they were halfway through. Sitting in the hall during these wearisome, interminable perorations, I wondered how many of my students had found my own lectures as unendurable as this. And having spent most of my academic life teaching in universities overseas, where the tradition of absence from lectures had not developed, either from a greater courtesy on the part of students, or from an exaggerated respect for the wisdom of lecturers,

I had not had even the rough and ready guide to excessive tediousness which a diminishing audience would have revealed.

A student drama group

That attending lectures was a singularly inefficient educational medium was not, however, the main lesson I learned during my year's study leave. Important though this (for me) discovery was, it was a negative finding. If formal lectures were to be demoted from their central position in the apparatus of higher education, what was to take their place? And appropriately enough, from the symbolic point of view, just as I had learnt my negative lesson from my formal activities, I gained a clue to my positive discovery from my informal ones.

As I have said above, as a form of relaxation from reading and lectures, I joined a students' drama group. This not only gave me an opportunity to indulge a childhood ambition to act, but also enabled me to get to know students under conditions of informal equality. The fact that all the members of the group shared a common purpose meant there was no need for me to explain my presence, and the inevitable *longueurs* during rehearsals and planning meetings gave me a chance to hear the students' views and observations about their work without the unnatural forced atmosphere that often characterizes an interview, however apparently informal. What struck me very forcibly was the contrast between their studies and the drama production in terms of their feelings of obligation and commitment towards these two activities. If there was any conflict between times of lectures and times of rehearsals, the latter were always given priority. And even where tutorials had been arranged with their tutors, and a rehearsal was called which clashed, they would normally attend the rehearsal, saying that they could always find some excuse to satisfy the tutor. Time devoted to studies, essay-writing or class discussions was usually begrudged as time wasted, whereas there was apparently no limit to the amount of time they were prepared to devote to rehearsing, planning or simply discussing the play in general terms. The same student who complained that he had been asked to read an article in preparation for a seminar discussion the following week, did not bat an eyelid when the director of the play suddenly produced a copy of Stanislavsky's textbook on method and required him to read it before the following evening. (And what is more, he stayed up until two o'clock in order to do so.) In short, the students generally found their academic studies for the most part heavy going and tedious, and they begrudged the time

E 65

spent on them, whereas they regarded the demands put upon them by the dramatic production as enjoyable in their own right, and they never seemed too tired or bored to continue.

Yet it was not the case that all these students were particularly interested in drama. While one or two had a special interest in the theatre, and hoped to continue professionally, the majority of the students regarded the drama group as simply a pleasant diversion, much as I did myself. Nor were they particularly talented, either at acting, or directing, or at any of the various other activities connected with the theatre. What was it, then, that accounted for the enthusiasm with which they applied themselves to these productions, in comparison with the apathy with which they commonly regarded their studies? After all, they had chosen to come to university to study, not to act, and they had presumably registered for courses in subjects which they found interesting. Nor was it the case that excessive demands were made upon them in their studies. They had, for the most part, a light programme of lectures to attend, with perhaps a weekly discussion group or practical class, and at most a fortnightly meeting with their tutors. The major part of their study time was their own, and they were free to arrange it to their best advantage. Nevertheless, they behaved as if their studies constituted a terrible regimen, while the very real demands of the dramatic production seemed to them delightful and easy to meet.

From watching them at rehearsals and planning meetings, and particularly from the way in which those with particular responsibilities (for directing, for stage managing, etc.) discharged them, it became increasingly clear to me that it was not the dramatic activity itself that the students found so engrossing but the fact that they were wholly responsible for it. While it was true that they had some responsibility for arranging their studies, at least in comparison with their recent experiences in school, nevertheless this was only the relatively minor responsibility of organising their study time. The academic courses they were following were fixed, the lectures and classes were arranged by the university, the books prescribed, the topics decided. The students' role was simply the passive one of attending the required courses, reading the prescribed books, writing essays on set topics. Although they were of an age when their coevals at work were regarded as adult and were given adult responsibilities, yet in everything that concerned their relations with the university, the students were treated as children. Nor was this attitude limited to their academic studies. They were required to be in their colleges by a certain time, there were limitations in their visitors; areas of the town were out of bounds to them. Treated as if they were irresponsible children, it was small wonder that from time to time they behaved like irresponsible children. Yet, whenever they had a chance to exercise responsibility – in relation to their societies, student newspapers and magazines, exhibitions, charity organizations, expeditions, etc. – they acted sensibly and responsibly.

Giving students responsibility

The problem as I saw it was essentially that of so organizing a course of study that it tapped at least some of the enthusiasm I had seen displayed at the meetings of the drama group. And the key to this seemed to me to lie in somehow giving students greater responsibility for their own courses; not merely in choosing them and then attending them, but in actually planning them and in carrying them out.

The notion that students should have some responsibility for course-planning at first seemed absurd. Having myself been processed through the academic machine, I had emerged with a collection of degrees and diplomas which entitled me to wear the gown of a 'master' of my subject; i.e. I was licensed to teach it. And I had hitherto subscribed to the view (inasmuch as it had never occurred to me to question it) what I was somehow better fitted to decide what the students should be taught than they were themselves. I saw 'academic freedom' (that rallying-cry of the pedant) as consisting largely in the right of a number of degree-holders to control the circumstances under which others might be admitted to their sacred number. Yet the same arguments that I have used above to justify a large measure of freedom among schoolchildren in choosing and planning their own studies apply, with even greater force, to further education. And it is worth remembering that even the universities themselves originally consisted of groups of students (of different 'nations' or countries, hence the term 'universe') who invited learned scholars to teach them and, in several medieval universities, could sack those who they felt were not teaching them well.[1]

I was fortunate, on my return from study leave, in being in a position in which I could try out some of the ideas which had occurred to me. As head of the education department of an expanding college of education, I was able to initiate experiments without the restrictions either of administration or of tradition which I had

[1] See Hastings Rashdall: *The Universities of Europe in the Middle Ages*, Powicke and Emden, eds., O.U.P., 1936, for details.

met in a university department. I was in addition responsible for the development of a small postgraduate course, and for this I had complete freedom to plan and organize the course as I wished. The syllabuses were extremely vague and hence very flexible; the fact that assessment of the students' achievement was based wholly upon course work meant that I could experiment without the fear that they might not be able to answer questions in a final examination paper.

During the past few years, I have tried out a variety of approaches to the training of student teachers, both in the three-year certificate course and in the one-year postgraduate course. I would not wish to claim that all these experiments have been successful. Nor has the pressure under which I and my colleagues in the education department have worked allowed us to set up the kind of experimental situation from which we could have based our conclusions on comparative data of some pretensions to academic rigour. Our findings are therefore all necessarily impressionistic. The one characteristic common to all our experiments has been that we have tried to give our students a greater measure of responsibility for their course in education than is normally the case. It is this *participation* in planning their own courses of learning that gives the present book its title. And it is an underlying assumption throughout the book that students will always respond to such participation with integrity and an increased sense of their professional role. The teachers of today carry a responsibility to society that is greater than at any time in our previous history, not only because there is a subtle but continual increase in the shift of those responsibilities for social education which hitherto have been regarded as largely or wholly belonging to the parents, but also because the teachers must prepare children for a world which must inevitably be very different from their own. They must, in other words, accept a large measure of responsibility for the society of tomorrow. There is only one way of developing a sense of responsibility, and that is by having experience of responsibility. If we want our teachers to act responsibly, then we must give them responsibility. This is what we have tried, in various ways to do in the experiments outlined in the following pages.

Training students to apply indirect methods in schools, and using indirect methods in that training, necessarily means that we are continually working at two levels: the first level being the children's work, and the suitability of various approaches to it; the second level being that of work with the students themselves. Tutors attempting this are confronted with a dilemma. The students, in attempting some piece of work at their own level, will often find themselves in situations, and undergo emotions (for example of frustration or elation), which experience tells us that children will in turn be faced with. Should one bring the students' work to a halt, while one draws their attention to their own circumstances (and possibly thereby increases their sense of frustration, or dissipates their elation) so that they can recognize and sympathize with similar events when they come to deal with children? The faculty of self-analysis is a difficult one to develop. Yet it may be that without such a pause, the parallel will not be apparent to the student. We have not solved this dilemma, though of one thing we are convinced: the value of the students themselves first undertaking work at their level in the same kind of way that they will subsequently try out with their pupils. Thus, before sending our students into schools to organize group work in their classes, we first require them to do group work among themselves in college. In the following chapter, an example of this is given.

5

A Drama Topic

Group work with children

As an approach to learning based upon the exploitation of children's initiative and co-operative inquiry, group work has for long commended itself to primary teachers. More recently it has come to be seen as a method equally appropriate for secondary classes, especially when associated with inter-disciplinary inquiry. It is also a natural concomitant of team teaching.

Group work takes a variety of forms. Two elements are essential to its success: firstly, that it must make provision for children to choose freely the topics which they are to pursue; and secondly, that, having so chosen, they must have a further measure of freedom to direct their own pursuit of them. Neither of these provisions necessarily implies that the children are under no restraint whatever. Freedom to choose a topic is perfectly compatible with a limitation of topics from which to choose; such a limitation might be that provided by the teacher with due regard to the syllabus he has in mind. Similarly, self-direction in their investigation does not mean complete licence to do whatever they wish, and again it is perfectly compatible with a large measure of guidance and advice from the teacher. Indeed, experience suggests that one of the problems the teacher faces in group work – at least with a class inexperienced in this approach – is that the children tend to lean too heavily on the teacher's guidance, and his main difficulty is not one of restricting their freedom, but one of encouraging them to use such freedom as they are offered.

70

In group work, then, children work together in small groups of four, five or six children each, on a variety of topics. These groups are formed either through the children's choosing which of a number of topics to work on, or through their choice of each other as group-mates, or through a combination of both factors. Normally, the topics are different aspects of some central overall topic which the whole class is concerned with, and provision will normally be made for the groups to report back to each other; perhaps by displays, or performances of some kind, or through reports, lecturettes and folders.

I have given elsewhere the rationale of group work as a method suitable for adoption in secondary schools.[1] In the same place is also outlined a programme of training secondary teachers in this approach as a normal part of their teaching repertoire[2]. I do not propose to repeat the justifications given there for the inclusion of this method in the training programme, but instead to discuss some of the problems involved in its adoption, and to suggest some solutions.

Topic work with students

An important difficulty facing those who wish to include group work in a training programme for students preparing to teach in secondary school is the students' unfamiliarity with this approach in their own schooling. Moreover, as has already been pointed out, they are pre-disposed in favour of the kind of traditional class-teaching through which they have achieved their own academic success.

Even in their primary schools the majority of student teachers have experienced, for the most part, formal lessons. Those that come from areas in which selection is still practised at 11 plus almost certainly attended streamed primary schools and were themselves probably in the A streams. Thus, by the time they reach higher education they have already had experience of ten or more years of formal class teaching, and as far as they are themselves concerned, of relatively successful class teaching. It is not surprising, therefore, that they look upon alternative methods with considerable suspicion, and adopt them – even experimentally – only with some reluctance.

[1] Kaye and Rogers, op. cit., chapter 6.

[2] ibid., Chapters 2 and 7. See also Barrington Kaye: 'Training Secondary Teachers in Group Work Methods', *Times Educational Supplement*, July 15, 1966, p. 149, and 'Problems in Training Secondary Staff in Group Work Methods', ibid., March 15, 1968, p. 861.

Not having had experience of self-directed learning, the students find it difficult to believe that children will in fact become engrossed in their work, whatever assurances their lecturers may give them. For this reason, if for no other, experience of group work among themselves is an essential preliminary for students who are to use group-work methods on a teaching practice. In order to distinguish it from the group work with children that follows, this preliminary experience has been called *topic work*.[1]

Topic work with students, then, is a means of giving them prior experience of group work, and the two terms are used in this way to avoid confusion in discussion and administrative arrangements.

Topic work can be approached in two ways: either by giving students the opportunity of investigating the same kind of topics that they can then use, subsequently, with children; or by suggesting topics within their own syllabuses. Each approach has its advantages and disadvantages. If students undertake topics which are also suitable for children in schools, they will be able to discover sources and materials to which they can refer when they take the same topics with the children afterwards. On the other hand, this very convenience may be a disadvantage in that they may be tempted to suggest short cuts to knowledge as a result of their own preliminary researches, such short cuts perhaps bypassing important learning experiences. Moreover, having once made what was (let us hope) a successful investigation themselves, they will find it difficult to be flexible in allowing children to approach the subject in a different way. It is extraordinarily easy to become committed and inflexible in one's approach, especially if that approach has itself been success-

---

[1] Topic work is also a term used to refer to a way of working in primary schools in which a topic is studied by a group or by the whole class. The terms *group work*, *topic work* and *project work* are often used synonomously, though properly the following distinctions ought to be drawn: *group work* is a means of organising children by dividing them into small groups on the basis of their own choices, and allowing them some measure of self-direction; *topic work* designates not a means of organization but the kind of work they are embarked upon, which is a study of some topic out of which the skills and areas of knowledge included in the traditional curriculum flow naturally; *project work* is a kind of topic work in which some activity other than the simple recording of data is involved. It is thus quite possible for all three approaches to be simultaneously employed. For example, the mounting of an exhibition showing the work of Oxfam would be a project suitable for a whole class at almost any age level. Group work might be the approach by which children are organized for this class project, and some of the groups might well concern themselves with such topics as the nutritional values of staple foods, subsistence farming, the population explosion, etc.

ful. A further disadvantage might be that through familiarity, they would become bored with the children's discoveries and unable to share with them the excitement of the investigation itself.

On the other hand, the approach to topic work with students in which a topic is chosen which relates to the students' syllabus, rather than to a school syllabus, has the disadvantage that the students themselves, while admitting the value of the method as far as they were concerned, may yet argue that it does not follow that it is suitable for work with children. Nevertheless, this approach has the merit of demonstrating that a particular aspect of their theoretical studies which might otherwise be thought to be dull and uninteresting, can become fascinating and rewarding, and it requires no great stretch of imagination to realise that the same mechanism might well be as true for children as it is for students.

It is thus proposed to describe an example of topic work with students in which the topic was one within their own curriculum.

A drama topic on the history of education: preliminary discussions

The drama topic described below was one of four topics offered to a group of second-year students in a college of education as a preliminary to experimental group work in secondary schools, and the procedures adopted were deliberately made as nearly as possible comparable with what might be found in a secondary-school situation.

About one hundred and sixty students who were preparing to teach in secondary schools were invited to choose from four alternative topics:

 (i) an investigation into the use of sociometry in schools;

 (ii) a series of environmental studies of the city in which the college was located;

(iii) a social survey of local community services;

(iv) a dramatic representation of some aspect of the history of education.

These four topics were presented by four tutors to the whole group, each tutor spending not more than five minutes outlining the kind of development it was hoped that the topic would follow, though it was emphasized that these initial ideas were simply starting points, and that the students would be free to develop them in accordance with their own views.

73

I myself chose to suggest a drama topic for a variety of reasons, the main one being the experience I have already described, during a sabbatical year spent at one of the older universities, of the tremendous enthusiasm and drive which students put into their amateur dramatic productions, contrasting forcibly with their general lack of enthusiasm for their academic studies. As I have said, it had occurred to me to wonder whether it might not be possible to tap the springs of this enthusiasm in relation to some aspect of the students' own course of studies. What characterised these dramatic activities, it seemed to me, was not so much their form and content (students, after all, studied drama in the various literature courses without displaying comparable energy) as the fact that they were largely self-directed; that is to say that the students themselves had (and accepted) full responsibility for the final productions. I felt that if I could contrive a learning situation in which students were accorded at least a major responsibility for the direction of their studies, it might be possible to arrive at a similar result.

It was clear that such a responsibility must begin with the exercise of free choice, for it is through choice that commitment begins. Hence the fact that the students chose the drama topic rather than any other was, in my view, an important contributory factor to its success. (And, of course, the same argument holds of the alternative topics, all of which began with the inestimable advantage that they had been chosen by the students who undertook them.) Moreover, in presenting the various topics, the lecturers were careful to emphasize that the initial choice need not be final. After the introductory outlines of the four topics had been given (which took only a few minutes), the students were invited to gather round the four lecturers, who positioned themselves at the four corners of a hall, and put questions to them. Several students took this opportunity of visiting all the lecturers during this stage, which lasted for about three-quarters of an hour. They were then asked to complete a card, giving their name, and arranging three of the four topics in their order of preference. Again the point was made that they would not be bound by this choice, and an opportunity would be given for them to change topics, if they so desired.

It may be objected that in allowing such flexibility, students were being presented with an unreal situation, irrelevant to the harsher circumstances of the 'real world' in which there is often little or no choice, and in which, even when an opportunity for choice is found, there is rarely the chance to revise one's preferences once they have been stated. This objection is, of course, a variant of the familiar argument that the best preparation for the hardships of the adult world is the enduring of hardships in childhood and youth. If this were true, then the best adjusted of our citizens would be those unfortunate enough to have been born into circumstances of squalor and poverty, neglected or even rejected by the adults around them, victims of deprivation and cruelty, who have grown up without ever having known comfort, affection or contentment. Yet it is easily demonstrable that it is precisely from these circumstances that most of the psychopaths and delinquents of our society come. I cannot agree that the enduring of hardship of any kind, whether physical, emotional or intellectual, can be justified as a good in itself. This does not mean that I am automatically in favour of licence and indulgence. The key, in my view, to this pseudo-controversy lies in responsibility. Given real and meaningful responsibility, it is my experience that the majority of children (and students) – unless their spirits have already been broken by a regimen prescribed by one of our disciplinarians (who, I have noted, are often not averse to indulgence where their own creature comforts are concerned) – respond by voluntarily accepting whatever hardships have to be endured in order to fulfil that responsibility. And it is the engendering of this kind of freely-accepted self-discipline that is, surely, one of the true ends of educational endeavour.

Let us return to our students, who have been left having exercised their free choice by arranging three of the four topics in order of preference, and who had then been released to have coffee. An examination of the cards showed that there was some considerable imbalance between the groups in terms of their first choices. Indeed, it would have been very surprising if the 160 had conveniently arranged themselves into four groups of forty! At the same time, it was felt that an approximation to equal-sized groups would have the advantage of being more directly comparable with a normal class, as far as organization was concerned, and of course, it seemed more equitable in terms of the number of students to each lecturer.

From second and third choices on the cards it was clear that it would be possible to arrive at equal-sized groups while leaving the majority of students in topics of their first choice. However, it was agreed that this would have done violence to the principle of freedom of choice; moreover, this same problem would, in all likelihood, be met subsequently by the students themselves on their group work with children, and it seemed a good opportunity to discuss it.[1]

[1] This is an example of that possibility of feedback from one level to another, which I mentioned earlier.

When the whole group reconvened after coffee, the fact that first choices led to unequal groups was announced, and the students were asked how they would react to a reallocation of some of them on the basis of second and third choices, in order to arrive at a more equitable distribution. As had been expected, they greeted this proposal with strong disapproval, several saying that there was no point in being asked to make a choice if that choice was then going to be ignored. This point was taken up in general discussion, the lecturers agreeing with the point of view, but asking for a practical solution. The students pressed for groups to be formed on the basis of first choices, regardless of inequalities of size, and to this the lecturers ultimately agreed.

This discussion was of value in several ways. First of all, it demonstrated that students' opinions were respected – an important principle to establish when their previous experience had been, on the whole, that they were not. Secondly, the process of arguing in favour of the principle of first choice of itself made those choices more meaningful. To use psycho-analytic jargon, the students libidinized the choices they had already made. And thirdly, the discussion itself, to which both students and lecturers contributed freely, dramatised the whole matter and made it memorable, so that the lecturers were able to refer to it when the students themselves were facing similar inequalities in the sizes of the groups they were trying to form in their work with children. And to be fair, a number of students spontaneously recalled their own experience and feelings, and used them to justify unequal groups of children on their own group work.

After the discussion, the lecturers met the groups of first-choice students in separate rooms to discuss the topics they had chosen.[1] As this was the last meeting of term, and the topic work was scheduled to begin in earnest next term, it had been agreed that this initial meeting in topic groups would be used to discuss in general terms what might be done, and to decide upon an outline course of action, so that at the first meeting in the following term, the four outlines could be presented to the whole group, thus enabling the

[1] It will be appreciated that, in what follows, I am using the drama topic group as an illustration simply because in doing so, I am able to draw upon my own experience. The other three topic groups, which met at the same time, followed a very similar course, though there were naturally some differences of procedure dictated by the different topics. What characterized them all, however, was the degree of interest and involvement in the work itself.

students the opportunity to revise their choices which had already been promised to them.

About forty-eight students had opted for the drama topic as their first choice. In presenting it I had said very little about the content of the topic, but had used the five minutes to emphasize that every opportunity would be given for the development of imaginative ideas, and I suggested that we could use the services of 'writers, actors, producers, handymen, electricians, painters, designers, historians, poets, eccentrics, sculptors, printers, musicians, dressmakers, creators and originals of every kind'. This was said in the hope that, whatever talent the topic might attract, the students who opted to join it would not do so on the supposition that no greater demands would be made upon them other than they should be passive, unimaginative and simply *nice*, or that by never creating a disturbance of any kind, whether intellectual, moral or social, they would somehow be contributing the utmost that might reasonably be asked of them. Subsequent events justified this hope. The drama topic group included a large number of lively students, always ready to suggest new ideas themselves and to examine those offered by others with a critical but favourably disposed intelligence – a combination that led to some excellent discussions. It also included a fair number of such noncomformists as had somehow slipped through the various recruiting procedures by which the teaching profession appears to try to ensure that no one with any claim to be an original thinker should become qualified – procedures which, fortunately, are not a hundred per cent effective.

I had determined beforehand that the topic should be based, as far as possible, on the students' own ideas. However, consistent with my own advice that the group-work teacher must be prepared to provide his class with a framework within which a choice could become meaningful, I had worked out a rough idea which I was prepared to outline. This was that we might take the history of the training of teachers in England as a subject near to the students' hearts and present it as a series of short scenes showing the historical development of training during the nineteenth and twentieth centuries. It has also occurred to me that this might be done by a series of *tableaux vivants* accompanied by a narrator, and that these might be related to a worksheet to be distributed to members of the audience.[1]

In the event I need not have worried about a lack of students' ideas. I had hardly got out the teacher-training suggestion before

[1] The idea of the *tableaux vivants* had been suggested by Anthony Powell's novel, *The Kindly Ones*, which I had been reading at the time.

alternatives were forthcoming: the public schools; church and state; the Education Acts; the classroom through the ages; the development of the universities – all of them topics which were eminently suitable for dramatic performance, all of them strongly supported by different members of the group. Even the Education Acts, which at first appeared to have little dramatic potential, were shown to be full of material by an enthusiast, who offered to write a short script within the next few days to demonstrate the suitability of this topic.

This suggestion gave me the idea of having a second meeting before the end of term at which the alternatives suggested could be voted upon, after a couple of days had been allowed to their supporters to prepare a documented and illustrated case for their adoption. Small working parties were at once appointed and their remits agreed, which was to undertake some preliminary research into the kind of material which might be available, to outline very briefly the way in which it was envisaged that the performance might be developed, and to make some suggestions for its presentation. At this stage I mentioned my own idea of a series of *tableaux vivants*, linked by a commentator, and while this suggestion was received in a kindly fashion, it was immediately followed by a host of alternative proposals, and I once again discovered that unpalatable truth, forever withheld from the authoritarian teacher, however benign, that his own ideas are not merely not the only ideas, they are also not necessarily the best ones.

The time for reporting back had been fixed at two o'clock on the day before term ended. Half an hour before the meeting was due to commence I received word that a crisis had developed in a school at which another of my students, in a different year of training, was doing teaching practice – a crisis which demanded my immediate attendance. I left word with my topic group that I had been unavoidably called away, but that they should elect a chairman and carry on without me; I would try to get back before the end of the discussion.

The crisis proved to be one of those unfortunate misunderstandings between school and college which sometimes arise on teaching practice – mainly through insufficiently explicit information having been provided by the college in the first place. By the time I got back to my topic group, the discussion had been going for over an hour. I sat at the back of the room, not wishing to interrupt the proceedings. It rapidly became apparent to me that something had gone wrong. The group was no longer bubbling over with new ideas and enthusiasm as it had been on the previous occasions.

Instead, there was a good deal of unnecessary disagreement with the chairman (who proved to be the enthusiastic advocate of the Education Acts for a topic, who had offered to write out the whole script two days before), and there was also a continual undercurrent of bickering among various members of the group, even while one of the working parties was presenting what proved to be the last case – that for the universities. It was clear that the working party in question – a small one of five students – had gone to a lot of trouble already. They listed various sources they had tracked down in the library in which could be found contemporary accounts of life at the universities at different stages of their history, and they were ready with a number of suggestions by which certain highlights of university development could be effectively presented through a dramatic performance. But they were uneasy and they seemed to me to be speaking more defensively than their material justified. When they had finished, the reason for their defensiveness and for the undercurrent of bickering, immediately became apparent. Instead of performing his role objectively, and allowing questions to be asked of the university working party, the chairman exploited his position by comparing the university proposal unfavourably with his own preference, that for the Education Acts. It soon transpired that he had done this all along, and hence the majority of those present, who had undertaken a good deal of preliminary work in the expectation that their own preference would at least be given a fair hearing, were now justifiably resentful of the manner in which the meeting was being conducted.

It was an extremely interesting situation, especially as the chairman had, I presumed, been elected by the rest of the topic group. It was also one of those situations in which I had to decide – as the one ultimately responsible for the group – whether there was more to be learnt from allowing things to develop without my interference, than from taking over. Somewhat regretfully, I decided that the group was too newly-formed and inexperienced to be able to cope with the kind of frustrations that were developing, especially as there would be no opportunity in the near future to meet again, and work through the dilemma. At the same time I had no desire to undermine the chairman's confidence, either in himself, or in the scheme he was proposing. I therefore took advantage of the end of the university working party's hearing to ask him for a brief recapitulation of what had transpired so far, using my late arrival – for which I apologised – as my excuse for doing so, but without making any attempt to take over his function as chairman.

He reported the proceedings faithfully enough, as I gathered, but from his manner of doing so, it was clear that he had assumed already that his own working party's suggestion – the Education Acts – was the topic to be adopted, on the grounds that the working party which was supporting it was the largest, though they were by no means a majority of the whole topic group.

I then asked what procedure he proposed adopting for voting on the topic to be adopted – was it to be by show of hands, or would a secret ballot be more satisfactory? He was clearly surprised at this question, and there was a noticeable stir of interest among the other members of the group.

'It hardly seems necessary to vote at all,' he said, 'since our group is obviously the largest.'

'But it is far short of an overall majority,' I pointed out, 'And it is possible that members of the various working parties may vote for topics other than their own.'

A lively discussion followed, during which it became apparent that we should have to give some thought to the procedure of voting – nearly everyone having agreed that a vote was essential. Did we agree to adopt the topic which received the most votes, or did we want an overall majority of votes (i.e. more than half the number of members of the topic group) before we would adopt a topic? If the latter was agreed upon, then we should probably have to employ some form of redistribution of votes. There was the alternative possibility that we might try to present all the ideas that had been worked out – either separately, or by combining them into some kind of general history of education. This latter proposal was soon dismissed as likely to lead to a confused production, but it was pointed out that the Education Acts could be combined with any one of the other proposals without much difficulty.

Time was running out. While the acceptance of the democratic procedure of voting had restored much of the confidence that the chairman's arbitrary approach had lost, it was necessary to come to some decision before the end of term if the initial impetus was not to peter out. Through the chairman I asked whether the members of the group would prefer to postpone the selection of the topic until the following term, which would give further opportunity for the working parties to prepare their cases, or to choose before the vacation, so that they would know what they would be doing.

All but a few were for choosing before the end of term. The chairman then pointed out the problem of deciding upon a voting procedure, and reminded the group of the arguments they had just had on the subject. At this point I offered to work out a voting procedure which would ensure an overall majority for the topic chosen, and suggested that we meet again very briefly the following day to put it into action. My offer was accepted. I thanked the working parties for the evident hard work they had already put into their proposals, apologized again for my lateness, thanked the chairman for his part in the proceedings, and the meeting closed.

The following day we met again briefly as arranged. The voting scheme I proposed was a simple redistribution of the votes cast for the least popular topic, to proceed stage by stage until an overall majority was reached. For this purpose, all members were asked to place three topics in order of preference. But before voting began, I suggested that we should remind ourselves that the Education Acts – which had evidently attracted a good deal of support already – could well be combined with any one of the other topics, so that while we could include it as a topic in its own right, we should also feel that we were not necessarily cutting it out altogether by choosing one of the alternatives.

The members of the group then voted on slips of paper. Interestingly enough, the Education Acts as a separate topic received only the third largest number of votes. The most popular topic was that of the classroom through the ages, and it required only a single redistribution of the votes cast for the least popular topic for the classroom to receive an outright majority of votes. I declared the result (having thought it wise to reassume the role of chairman on this occasion) but reminded members of the group that it might be necessary to confirm the decision next term if the membership of the topic group changed significantly as a result of the opportunity to revise their choices that had been promised to students. In the meantime it was agreed that all present members of the group would undertake some preliminary reading during the vacation.

I have discussed these preliminary meetings in some detail because they illustrate several important points in group work, whether with students or with children. The first is the importance of convincing the members of the class that free choice really means free choice. It is to be expected that, when children or students are accustomed to the teacher's direction in all things, they are understandably suspicious of any declaration of intent of freedom of choice, and are ready to retreat into apathy or resentment at the first signs that their suspicions are not without cause. This had already been demonstrated in the reactions of the whole group of second-year students to our question of whether the topic groups should be made equal by the transfer of some members to their second-choice groups. It came out again in the undercurrent of hostility which the chairman of the topic group had aroused by his biased conduct of the meeting.

A second important point which these meetings brought out was the need for the teacher (or tutor in this case) to keep a continual watch on the group procedure to ensure that the wishes of all members are considered – not just of those members who are articulate or forceful in the expression of their views. This underlies the importance of devising and keeping to procedures for the conduct of meetings, the taking and implementing of decisions, the allocation of tasks, etc. The teacher will often be tempted to shorten or even to dispense with such procedures on the grounds that they take up too much time; it may well be that in this he will receive the encouragement of one or two of the most vocal members of the class. But he will be wise to insist on adherence to whatever procedures have been agreed upon. It may be noticed that here, as in all democratic procedures, those most impatient with them are often those who most despise the concept of democracy itself.

The drama topic: development of work in groups
When we reassembled after the vacation, we had before us and available for topic work eight successive weekly afternoon sessions of one and a half hours each. Provision was made for further changes in the topic groups, but in fact there was very little such movement. This bears out my view that the sense of commitment to a choice is often more important than the choice itself, since it seems unlikely that all the members of the different topic groups could have known exactly what was going to be done in the topics when they first had to choose. On the other hand, since all groups made provision for self-direction, it might well be argued that a valid choice could in fact be made at the outset.

After this provision, it could be said that the drama topic group was now properly formed, and could begin work in earnest. During the first few discussions I took the chair myself, to ensure that there was no repetition of the difficulty last time, and to keep the project moving. Our first task was to agree on various principles: how the production should be mounted, what form it should take, how many separate acts we should present, whether it should be a costume-and-props performance or not, etc. It was not difficult to get ideas from the members of the group on these various points; what was difficult was to persuade the proponents of the ideas to accede to the democratic process in adopting them. Here again I was struck with the fact that, with this approach to learning, the main problem was that of dealing with enthusiasm instead of apathy – a pleasant change from the more customary teacher-directed approach. It was important to give everyone who had a suggestion full opportunity to explain it, even though this necessarily was time consuming. I was determined that no one should feel disgruntled because his or her viewpoint had been ignored, or not taken seriously. It was important that the group should become accustomed to the implications of self-direction.

By the end of the first session we had agreed on a number of important principles. The performance was to be a series of short scenes, each one representing a classroom of a different period, with incidents designed to bring out the characteristic problems of the time. They were to be linked by a narrator, whose character was still the centre of controversy: while some were for making him a well known historical personage, perhaps reading out a relevant passage from one of his works, others thought that continuity might be given to the whole performance by having a single, neutral narrator. It was also agreed that costumes might be used, but that they should be confined to the principal actors, while the extras should have a universal black garb. Props were to be few and symbolic rather than representative.

I suggested that at this stage we might form a number of working parties whose task it would be to undertake the initial research for each scene, outline a script and make suggestions for its production. I emphasized that at this stage these suggestions might be provisional only, and that working parties must be prepared to accept considerable modifications of their schemes, if necessary. For this reason I suggested that, although the groups that actually took part in the scenes might well be the working parties, yet we should leave open the question of membership of those groups until next time. We should also have to think about the appointment of a co-ordinating group, with overall responsibility for the production, but that again could be left to our next meeting.

This procedure was agreed to, and it then became necessary to select a number of working parties. We did this by first of all agreeing as a whole group on the number of scenes, and their historical setting. These were to be the medieval scene, a Tudor classroom, a Victorian classroom, a classroom at the turn of the nineteenth century, and a classroom of the future. Members of the topic group then chose which of these scenes they wished to join working parties for. Again, there was a certain amount of inequality in numbers, but we agreed that this did not matter so long as there was a minimum of four in any one.

A most interesting incident occurred during this first allocation to sub-groups. As I have said elsewhere,[1] it is my belief that the choice of whom one is to work with is as important as the choice of what one is to work at, and for this reason I allowed the working parties to form themselves as they wished, without any formality of procedure. One of the main disadvantages of such an approach is that it is difficult to ensure that isolates and rejectees (to use the language of sociometry) are incorporated into groups easily.[2] I had not anticipated any particular difficulty in this respect. What became apparent during the process of forming the working parties, however, was that the student who had been chosen as chairman for the discussion when I was away, and who had conducted that discussion with a marked bias in favour of his own views, was now finding it difficult to fit into any of the working parties. At one stage of the proceedings, he looked across to me and said, half comically, half tragically, 'It doesn't look as though I'm wanted!' At this, one of the groups which had already formed and contained, as I noticed, several members with strong personalities who would be more than a match for him, said: 'Why not join with us?' and he gratefully accepted their offer.

I was strongly tempted to use this incident, which had gone unremarked by most of the students, to illustrate the problem of the isolate in group formation, but I decided that to do so would be to exploit the ex-chairman's vulnerability unfairly. This leads me again to this problem of using and reinforcing the experience of topic work with students. Naturally, they are continually finding themselves in situations which are analogous to the situations they will later be placing their children in. On many occasions they react to such situations in much the same ways as their children will react. How, then, is the tutor to emphasize this comparison and draw from it the relevant teaching pointers?

One way is to try to make dramatic the incidents which they will then subsequently remember, as indeed we did over the question of the original distribution into topic groups and the proposal that we should equalize them. Often, however, there is neither time nor opportunity to delay the progress of the topic work, especially as

[1] See Kaye and Rogers, op. cit., pp. 28–9 and 48 et seq.

[2] Ibid., p. 50.

the work itself quickly involves the students and they become understandably frustrated if they are continually being held up in order for some analogy to be made, the more so as the problems they will themselves face when they come to use group work with children are still remote and unreal. At one stage I experimented by setting aside occasional ten-minute intervals, during which the students were required to describe, at the back of their files, their own reactions to this or that set of circumstances. My intention was that these notes would then form suitable references when it came to talking about the problems of group work with children, but I must confess that I was unable to persevere with this scheme, largely because I myself resented the time devoted to it nearly as much as did the students themselves.

At our second proper meeting the following week, the five groups took it in turn to outline the progress they had made. In fact, they had all made considerable progress. A large number of sources had been located, and the reading of them accomplished by a division of labour within the working parties. Several had already roughed out scripts and begun plans for the productions. The meeting was lively and exciting; as usual, the main problem was that of restraining the over-enthusiastic.

During the explanations of each group's proposals, the members of other groups made suggestions and criticisms. All of these were thoughtful and sensible; not one was frivolous. It was clear that the topic had got away to an excellent start despite the set-back of the first meeting, and the sense of commitment and enthusiasm which I had hoped for was already apparent.

At the end of the readings, I proposed that we now formed the groups who were to be responsible for each of the separate scenes. I also pointed out the need for continuity and co-ordination and proposed that, in addition, a separate co-ordination group be formed, with overall responsibility for production and direction. This gave an opportunity for members of the topic group with special interests to declare them. We were fortunate in having students among us with interests in lighting, music, costumes, stage management and production. These formed the nucleus of the co-ordinating group. We then formed the sub-groups, which were mainly, but not exactly, composed of members of the relevant working parties. It was then agreed that each sub-group should have a representative on the co-ordinating group, whose job it would be to ensure that sub-groups were kept informed of central decisions, and in turn that sub-group decisions were declared to the co-ordinators.

The co-ordinating group immediately went into session and began to lay down general points of procedure for continuity; for instance, those regarding props and furniture. It was agreed that each group should draw upon its own members for its principal actors, but that it would call upon others for extras. Suggestions were made for symbolic scenery, which could be hung upon a black backcloth, and one member undertook to rough out some costume designs. Another member agreed to prepare a lighting plan. And the co-ordinating group announced to all sub-groups a programme for the remaining seven weeks, which included the provision for a draft script a week hence, a completed script the week after, with rehearsals to begin the week after that.

Before the group broke up, all sub-groups had made arrangements for further meetings during the week, despite the fact that the time allocated for the topic on the timetable was no more than one afternoon session every Thursday. In other words, we had already reached the position where the topic was no longer seen as a passive learning activity of the kind in which the students simply turned up with their notebooks ready. Instead, they had themselves accepted responsibility for the progress of the work and were prepared to devote their free time to it.

As part of the topic work, the students were required to keep logbooks. I asked each sub-group, including the co-ordinating group, to keep a file, recording all meetings and decisions, and from these I was able to keep a check on their progress. The allocation of tasks within each group was also recorded, and notes were contributed by the individuals concerned on what they had done. This enabled me to see what contribution each individual was making.

Now it might be objected that individual students were likely to do only the kind of work that they found interesting, and that therefore this approach did nothing to teach them the 'discipline' of study. To begin with, I can see nothing wrong in allowing students (still less, children) to study what interests them. It can easily be demonstrated that any syllabus is an arbitrary selection of topics from the whole range of what might be done; it seems more satisfactory that the student should do this selection on the basis of his own interests, rather than that it should be done by his teacher, on the basis of his own prejudices. It may be objected to this, that the student will then omit whole areas of knowledge which are vital to a full understanding of the subject. Yet my own experience has been that almost any topic selected at random from within what might be called a traditional subject area, leads to a concern with other topics, and that – given the opportunity and encouragement to do so – the student will be led to cover the field from the impetus arising from his initial studies. Moreover, the pursuit of knowledge, if it is allowed to work its magic on the student, will lead him to accept a self-imposed discipline under which he would soon rebel if it were dictated by his teachers. The meetings of the sub-groups were a case in point. Normally, any proposal to hold an extra meeting of a seminar or lecture course in order to deal with some matter not covered in the course itself, would be greeted with a marked lack of enthusiasm; for it to be held in the students' own free time would be regarded as outrageous. Yet the students themselves were prepared to arrange a large number of meetings in order to carry forward the work they were engaged upon, simply because they had accepted responsibility for its progress, and therefore felt the demands of the work itself. Nor was it the absence of a tutor that made these extra meetings palatable. I was often asked if I could attend the meetings, and they would be arranged at a time when I could attend, even if that were inconvenient to the students themselves. Of course, when I did attend, I took care to restrict my participation to that of an equal member of the group: answering questions when they were directed to me, making suggestions when I felt they might be welcomed, but never assuming more responsibility than the group accorded me.

The second meeting of the whole topic group, the following Thursday, was a brief one. The co-ordinating group announced some further decisions regarding the continuity of the scenes, and the question of the narrator was discussed. However, no decision was reached on this matter, and the meeting broke up to enable the sub-groups to continue with their preparations. Going round the different groups I found that a great deal of research had already been done and most of the groups had a clear idea of what they were going to attempt. The Victorian group, for instance, had decided to divide their scene into two sections to represent the two nations of rich and poor, to be presented on stage simultaneously, each alternately 'freezing' and acting. The following excerpts from this group's file record their decisions.

September 29th (Week 1)

Decision to divide stage into two halves, having two *tableaux* – one frozen and other in dialogue with a co-ordinating line having two separate contexts.

(a) Typical female institution for orphans and deprived children, etc. Emphasizing situation in which teacher is repressive figure.

(b) Private tuition in a wealthy home emphasizing provocation exercised on governess by children and schooling in the fine arts as opposed to the three Rs.

It was decided that no further conclusions could be reached until detailed results of the research work were reported and therefore everyone was allocated this task for the meeting next week. Two members of the group volunteered to write a skeleton-type version of the script and then produce it for discussion at a general meeting.

October 6th (*Week* 2)

The results of individual research work were produced and assimilated. A further suggestion arose: whether to substitute the presentation of a typical Froebel-type lesson, therefore representing the 'new' thought of the period, in place of the presentation of a private tuition lesson? The possibilities of this suggestion were considered, but it was thought to overlap the work of the next group and was therefore refuted.

On the grounds of basic historical fact the following situations were agreed upon as a foundation:

1. *Repression – corruption*

Inspector visiting school (system of 'payment by results') – lecture given to class before his arrival, emphasis on discipline and prompting of more intelligent children to be forthcoming – entrance of inspector, silence, standing, etc. – sets class a problem and leaves to visit other classrooms – teacher immediately goes to children telling them answer, children become noisy, are suppressed and one child in particular ordered into the corner and intimidated – teacher back to desk – entrance of inspector who then commends teacher on 'high results' of class.

2. *Privilege – influence*

Drawing room in wealthy household – one young girl embroidering, one having a conversation in French with her governess – one typical 'little Lord Fauntleroy' enters and disrupts scene (by means of throwing a frog, etc., at the governess?) – governess attempts to chastise him and is precociously reminded by the child of his parents and her inferior position.

Details of the costumes were briefly considered and the necessity for contrast recognized. It was decided that one *tableau* would be essentially 'grey' in colour with no ornamentation whatsoever, whilst the other would be very colourful with rich furnishings suggested by textured fabric drapes and covers on chairs, etc.

Pictures of the costumes of the period were consulted in *English Costume of the 19th Century* by I. Brooke and J. Laver. A meeting was decided on for Sunday October 9th to begin work on compiling the script.

Important tasks were assigned to individual members: design, script, co-ordinating representative, secretary.

The co-ordinating group decided on the following timetable, which was duly announced to all the other groups:

Oct. 13th Groups should have a rough script ready and some idea of timing and casting worked out.

Oct. 20th Materials and costumes should be organized by this date, and there should be a first rough run-through.

Oct. 27th Half-term. During this time groups should be accumulating costumes, props, etc.

Nov. 3rd Costumes should be almost ready by this date. There will be a second run-through.

Nov. 10th Complete run-through with lighting.

? Dress rehearsal.

Nov. 17th Production.

A number of other production points were discussed, and the suggestion was made and agreed upon that the audience should be required to give some kind of evidence that they had learnt something from the production – perhaps by means of a programme-cum-questionnaire. The audience would be the members of the other topic groups.

During the following week, each group met a number of times to pool their ideas, and to construct a draft script. I attended one or two of these meetings, though – as I have said above – my presence was entirely superfluous as far as the progress of the work was concerned; the impetus of the idea, and the commitment to it on the part of the members of the topic group, carried them forward without any encouragement from me.

By the third Thursday (October 13th), most groups had a rough script ready. Further progress was held up, however, until the important question of the character of the narrator was decided, and I therefore began the meeting by inviting general discussion on this question. Feelings ran high on this matter for some reason[1], and it seemed important to devote sufficient time to enable everyone to have his or her say. Ultimately it was possible to reduce the various suggestions to two: (a) that there should be a single narrator to give a commentary throughout the production, and ensure continuity; (b) that each group should provide its own narrator. These two proposals were put to the vote; (b) was passed by a substantial majority.

After this decision, each group read out their rough script and explained how they proposed to produce it. Comments, criticisms and suggestions were made by the other groups. There was a feeling of satisfaction and a certain amount of mutual congratulation that so much had been achieved. At the same time, it was recognized that there was very little time left and certainly no excuse for complacency. A number of decisions were taken: that there should be a clock and a window in each scene to establish continuity; that the 'pupils' for each scene could be dressed in a neutral black uniform, which could be varied for the different scenes by the addition of token extras – for example, a paper ruff for the Tudor period, etc. The co-ordinating group agreed to finalise the design of the windows and clocks, and to draft a questionnaire for the audience. One of the members was designated in charge of music and undertook to find pieces suitable to the different periods.

The co-ordinating group met again the following Monday, and composed a notice, calling the co-ordinating representatives from the various sub-groups to a meeting that Wednesday, with draft designs for costumes, set layout, list of props and suggestions for window and clock designs. The notice prudently listed the names of the representatives, with the instructions that they should tick their names when they had read it. It also provided for substitutes if they could not attend in person.

The meeting on Wednesday was a successful one, and all the required details were ready. The co-ordinating group assembled them, made a number of minor alterations in order to ensure continuity, and then cut stencils and duplicated a five-page leaflet giving all these details, including the designs of furniture, costumes,

---

[1] I never discovered why feelings were so strong on this point, though I suspected that it was because one of the group very much fancied himself in the role of a narrator who would take on a series of character studies of famous writers of the times.

90

and the individuals responsible for the various items, in time for the full meeting of the topic group next day, Thursday, October 20th (Week 4).

By this time I had decided that I should hand over responsibility for the whole production to the co-ordinating group, and suggested that they elect a chairman to take the meeting. They chose the group's secretary – a girl who had already shown her efficiency in drawing up a detailed programme for meetings, casting, lighting, etc.

As laid down in the programme, the meeting of October 20th was given over to a first full-length rehearsal. This brought about the realization that it would be necessary to have more than one copy of each script! It also high-lighted the fact that most groups still had to make decisions about innumerable small aspects of their scenes. At the same time, it helped all members of the topic group to see the performance as a dramatic whole. Despite its patchy presentation, it was possible to see that it did have a certain coherence and integrity. The Victorian group recorded in their file:

October 20*th*
First full-length rehearsal. Many inadequacies, e.g. absence of scripts, props and continuity with music, etc. However, session was beneficial inasmuch as each group was made aware of the activities of the individuals and of the whole.

From the point of view of our own particular group this meeting was very unsatisfactory as we only had one copy of the script and had not had a previous rehearsal or adequate discussion; however, it did serve to emphasize certain problems, e.g. 'freezing' must be more exaggerated and resolute; positioning on stage; numbers in classroom; timing and recognition of cues, etc.

Details of scenery and costumes were confirmed with the continuity group and tentative decisions for future rehearsals made.

The following week was half-term, during which all members of the sub-groups who were acting as pupils were asked to obtain a black uniform of tights and rollneck jersey. The co-ordinating group had made notes of all the criticisms made during the first rehearsal, and these were passed out to the groups in question. They agreed to work out a day-by-day timetable of all rehearsals (which involved the booking of various rooms and halls), and to provide a representative to take note of any continuity problems. They also agreed to duplicate the entire script. Meanwhile the lighting member had prepared a draft layout of the lighting requirements of each group, and meetings were arranged with the college drama tutor to discuss the use of the stage.

On their return from the half-term holiday, the various sub-groups began to arrange individual rehearsals, recording their arrangements on the timetable sheet the co-ordinating group had posted on the noticeboard. A sense of urgency had begun to communicate itself to all the topic group members. The members of the co-ordinating group spent the morning of Thursday, November 3rd, duplicating the overall script. At two o'clock the fifth general meeting was due to begin, but sub-groups asked for, and were allowed, half an hour to go over various points before the planned rehearsal.

In fact this rehearsal proved a setback. After two groups had performed, it seemed that little if any progress had been made since the previous general rehearsal a fortnight before. This was, in fact, not because the members of the groups had not been working hard, but because each group was trying to rely upon its own membership for direction. The need for an overall, independent director became evident to me during the afternoon, but I was reluctant to make the suggestion myself, hoping that the topic group as a whole had by this time sufficient resolution to meet its own problems. The feeling of the meeting became edgy and unhappy; criticisms started to become personal. At this point, the student whose biased chairmanship of the preliminary meeting had endangered the topic at the outset, suddenly spoke up, pointing out that the present meeting was a waste of time, and that what was needed was an overall director. After some discussion, the force of his arguments were recognized. It was clear to many that he would himself make a good director, but before his own name was put forward he nominated another student, whose comments so far suggested that he had a clear idea of what was needed. All members of the sub-groups agreed to act under his direction, and to accept his decisions. A revised timetable of rehearsals was then drawn up.

The change is reflected in the diary of the Victorian group.

November 3rd
(1.00 – 2.30 p.m.) Unofficial rehearsal, major points from previous meeting discussed and finalized. Each half watched the others run through their scene without any freezes and then criticized them; this was done twice. The whole scene (plus freezes) was rehearsed four times and the necessity for word-fluency made most apparent – otherwise no major technical difficulties.

The general meeting proved interesting – the medieval and Tudor scenes were rehearsed and then a motion was put forward for a director and finally one was nominated. Future individual rehearsals were decided upon with the stipulation that the director must be present.

November 7th

The first rehearsal under direction of appointed director. Five run-throughs with many points arising:

1. Change of script: a few minor changes, e.g. the opening speeches of Miss Penton (the schoolteacher) being altered to stress the theme and similarly the French speech of the governess; more emphasis given to insolence of young boy; punch-line changed.
2. Decision to write problem on board facing audience so that teacher can be seen writing in answers – teacher hurriedly rubbing away answers on inspector's return emphasizes dishonesty.
3. A few positions on stage, e.g. young boy turning back on governess to exaggerate insubordination.
4. Decision to give Miss Penton a limp and walking stick because of her injury – this proved to be in character![1]
5. Governess to faint at sight of spider, therefore emphasizing her fragility.

Necessity to learn new lines now hindered further developments.

The effect of a 'professional' director is immediately apparent, and similar improvements were made in all the scenes. The members of the sub-groups accepted the authority of the director without question. I was particularly interested in their choice. While he was obviously well qualified to direct from the point of view of the relevance of the comments and suggestions he had made, yet I was nonetheless surprised that he had been chosen, as he was not particularly popular, and had a nervous, hypercritical manner in normal conversation that I would have thought would have disqualified him from the position. However, it would seem that the topic group as a whole recognised his suitability, whatever they might have felt as individuals, and indeed he proved an excellent director, displaying reserves of patience, perseverance and tact that surprised me.

By this time I had myself been invited to join in two of the scenes;

[1] The student playing Miss Penton, the schoolteacher, had been involved in an accident the previous week.

in the medieval scene I took the part of a naughty pupil, and was roundly beaten, to everyone's delight; in the turn-of-the-century scene I played the part of a severe and pedantic teacher. By now the drama topic had achieved a priority in everyone's everyday affairs to the extent that nothing was allowed to stand in the way of rehearsals. The drama topic group as a whole was carried forward with that sense of community of purpose which is one of the chief springs to action and rewards of co-operation.

The meeting of November 10th was devoted to a complete run-through with scenery and lighting effects, and such costumes as were ready. Elaborate lighting scripts, scene-shifting layouts and music scripts were produced and co-ordinated. Meanwhile a member of the co-ordinating group had drafted a programme and questionnaire, and this was approved and duplicated. Last minute changes to the productions were made, and the various props were assembled.

During the last week, no day went by without a meeting of at least one of the sub-groups. The director gave all his spare time to the topic, as did the co-ordinating group's secretary, who was now doubling as stage manager, as well as accepting responsibility for the conduct of meetings. A full dress rehearsal was called for the afternoon of the Wednesday before the scheduled performance. By now a very creditable standard of production had been reached, and the director wisely decided to rest content with a single run-through.

The drama topic: the performance

The performance itself, in front of an audience composed of the three other topic groups, plus several other invited groups, went off extremely well. There were no real hitches and no one forgot his lines, though there was a good deal of apprehension in the wings.

The medieval scene was preceded by an extract from Chaucer, setting the scene 'whan Richard II is king; troubable years whan Wycliffe is preching agains the Church'. The curtain then rose on a monastic schoolroom in which the teaching monk drearily rehearsed Latin grammar, which the boys were required to get by heart. The scene emphasised the emphasis on rote learning; no attempt was made to teach the understanding of the passages that had to be translated. Quotations from common texts were used, and a contemporary poem, complaining of the poor scholar's lot was recited.

In the Tudor scene, the main part of the syllabus was still Latin, but a little English had by now crept in. The meagreness of the schoolmaster's pay was augmented by tips from the pupils' relatives, and profits from any school cockfights. In this scene the narrator commented on various aspects of the performance, drawing attention to the limitations of the education of the time by quotations from contemporary writers and documents. After a dismal day's work, interrupted only by the horseplay of the dinner break, lessons ended with a disputation which itself broke up in a free fight.

The Victorian scene, as we have found, was presented in two separate sections; one, the drab interior of a Board school during the visit of an inspector; the other, the home of a wealthy family in which the children were taught the gentle arts by an intimidated governess. This was an extremely well-presented scene, into which a lot of thought had been put by the group responsible, and it received much applause.

The Turn-of-the-Century scene was the responsibility of the sub-group which contained most of those students who had supported the Education Acts as an alternative topic. The scene was presented as an empty elementary schoolroom; as each pupil entered, he recited a passage from one or other of the Acts and Reports of the time. The first excerpt was spoken with lively enthusiasm, but as the years passed and the quotations grew increasingly idealistic, so the manner of presenting them grew less hopeful until the final passage, taken from the first edition of the *Handbook of Suggestions for the consideration of Teachers*, published in 1905, recommended that:

> The essential condition of good Education is to be found in the right attitude of the teacher to his work . . .
> The teacher must know the children, and must sympathize with them, for it is the essence of teaching that the mind of the teacher should touch the mind of the pupil.

This was presented in an apathetic, almost funereal tone, and the class, which had grown progressively less lively with each quotation, was by now dull and resigned to the entrance of the pedantic teacher, who proceeded to conduct a lesson no less rigid and authoritarian than those that had preceded it.

An interesting feature of this group was that the student who had originally been its leader and most enthusiastic supporter, and who had taken the chair at the first discussion, had left it at the request of several other groups who wanted him as their narrator.

Finally, the Future group showed a child in a room designed for automated teaching, subjected to a variety of electronic teaching devices, including a hypnopaedic, sleep-learning machine. The narrator to this scene assumed the breezy manner of a modern salesman, confident of the superiority of his own goods, and he answered the objections raised by the members of the group who had been planted among the audience, with splendidly glib evasions. The curtain rang down on their final cries: 'Is this progress?'

The drama topic was over. I invited the groups to add their comments at the end of their files, assessing the value of the topic.

The co-ordinating group commented:

The Production: Thursday, November 17th
The play had a quite professional finish with no prompting needed and no major hitches. When the first laugh came we all breathed a sigh of relief. Lighting and music and the sets were all effective and quite smooth.

Everyone did a certain amount of ad libbing which made the acting more spontaneous. Members of the audience seemed to feel that the flashing lights between the scenes were a little distressing and also that the scene changes were too long. This lengthy pause had been essential during rehearsal but was not required to the same extent today.

The future scene was successful and the audience plants[1] caused a diversion and added interest. The statement – Is this progress? – left a question in the minds of the audience and was dramatically effective.

In its own way the play was educational and thus served its original purpose.

The Victorian group recorded their comment on the final production in the following way:

The Performance: 9.15 a.m., Thursday, November 17th
Firstly, I must say, on behalf of the group, how much we all enjoyed the performance. Of course we all suffered grave apprehensions whilst waiting behind stage, but once started we felt at ease, and entered into the feeling of the sketch. Although the second entrance of the inspector was slightly delayed, we felt that this did not mar the performance as a whole, and all other hitches which we experienced during rehearsals, did not occur today.

The audience was very receptive and laughed at appropriate times, and the level of their involvement was maintained through-

[1] The sub-group who acted the classroom of the future had planted a number of their members among the audience to ask awkward questions.

A DRAMA TOPIC

out, thus giving us confidence and encouragement. Indeed, we
feel that the whole performance was an enlightening success and
fulfilled its aim of presenting to the audience a light but informative
history of English Education.

When all was over, we felt rather deflated, yet satisfied that all
our work was worthwhile, and we would like to thank the director
for all his help, given with infinite patience, throughout rehearsals.

After the performance, I called the files in and marked them.
The drama topic was over and I posted a notice congratulating its
members.

Drama Topic Group

Now that I have had time to read the files, I want to say how
impressed I have been with the work of this group – not only
with the production itself, which I thought was very good, but
also with the quality of thought, effort and enthusiasm that went
into the preparation – research, organization, administration,
rehearsals, etc.

In assessing the work I have had to concentrate on the internal
evidence of the files themselves, and I have tried to take account
of the different sizes of the groups, and also of the effects of changes
of personnel.[1] You will understand that this is a difficult task
when the subject of the files – i.e. the production itself – has a
quality of its own which obviously cannot be captured fully on
paper, and also when a lot of the work which went into the production does not show in the files. For this reason I decided to
award an overall assessment for the whole topic work, and to vary
this only by the addition of plus or minus according to my judgment of the file. One group,[2] however, has produced a file of such
outstanding quality that I could not keep to this plan, as far as
this group was concerned.

Files are returned, with comments, on the trolley. Will all
members of each group please initial my comments to signify they
have read them, and then return the files by next week.

My sincerest congratulations to the whole group. I should for
my part welcome suggestions and criticisms regarding my own
organization (or lack of it!) of the topic. Do not be polite –

[1] Resulting from the fact that at different stages in the production various
members left the scene sub-groups to join the co-ordinating group.
[2] The Victorians. I assessed their file as A; all other files were marked between
B+ and B−.

G   97

remember that next year's groups may benefit from your suggestions. If you wish to remain anonymous, by all means do so.
Comments can be returned with the files.[1]

Finally, I presume that everyone has learnt the moral from this
activity: that, given sufficient freedom and encouragement, it is
possible to tap the springs of enthusiasm and creativity in learning,
and transform even the dullest subjects (Education Acts?) into
an exciting and rewarding learning situation. But this will not
happen without a good deal of preparation and thought *beforehand*
on the part of the teacher – it is your task in the next few weeks
to think how you can tap these springs for the children you will
be teaching next term (not to mention those you will be teaching
for the next forty years!).

December 23rd   b.k.

---

[1] In fact no further comments were made, but the various final summings-up
of the topic in the files had already included some good critical observations,
most of them valid, and it may be that no one had anything further to add.

6

Group Work in Schools

Follow-up of the drama topic
There was no doubt that the drama topic had succeeded in at least
one of its aims: that of demonstrating that the pursuit of knowledge,
given the circumstances of choice and self-direction, could be
exciting and rewarding. The sub-groups' files showed that, during
the 'research' stage of the work, not only had a great deal more
reading been undertaken by the members of the groups than they
would normally have done, but also that their reading had been
both adventurous and selective. Instead of keeping narrowly to the
recommended textbooks, they had investigated the resources of the
library. They had also related their reading in literature to the topic,
and at one time, when the suggestion was made that the narrators
should be well-known historical characters, a selection of suitable
excerpts from the writers of the different periods had been made.

The actual knowledge of educational history acquired by the
members of the drama topic group was, of course, incidental to the
main purpose of the exercise – that of experiencing the organizational problems of the group-work approach. As I have said above,
my attempt to make these problems memorable by taking time off
the topic work, as it were, and persuading the students to record
their feelings at different stages of the work did not prove very
successful – partly because of the impatience caused by the interruption in their work, partly because of the sheer artificiality of this
device. However, that their experience would be relevant to the time
when they came to apply group work in schools was not overlooked

99

by the students, as the following comments, from the Turn-of-the-Century file show:

Comments on the work as a whole
The session on this Drama Topic has proved most interesting and beneficial. The subject matter involved, i.e. 'History of Education', was chosen because we are to go into this in detail next term. We must all have learnt something about it already, by putting together and taking part in this production.

If we can learn knowledge in this lively, enjoyable manner why can't children?

All projects have a beginning, and ours, as most beginnings, seemed at first to be confusing, with an idealistic end in view, and no one really knowing where to turn for help. But, together, as a large group, a pattern emerged, and this pattern was a pattern of progress, not only in knowledge, but in working with a group of people, dividing labour equally, and striving towards a thoroughly presentable production. We have all met the snags which might occur when doing this with children, and we have all had the experience of taking part in such a project and should therefore be able to understand a child's feelings towards it. If a child can get as much out of such a topic as we have from this, it is most certainly a method which must be tried in school.

Naturally, some members may stand out more than others, but the quiet ones will learn about responsibility to their group, by helping with the smaller administrative jobs, which need to be done just as well as the larger, more important tasks.

In fact, I should definitely like to fit in a topic of this kind with children and see how they get on with it, and what they gain from it. It would also help a great deal in getting to know the children as individuals.

As has been said above, the topic work with students was arranged as a preliminary to their own group work in school. During the following Spring term, these students were attached to classes in selected comprehensive and secondary modern schools for a morning a week, in groups of three and four students to a class. They were prepared for this, not only by the experience of their own topic work, but also through lectures, classes and demonstrations on informal methods, the organization of group work, the formation of groups, the use of materials, the organization of visits, display, the creative use of such teaching aids as tape recorders, film cameras, overhead projectors, and the psychology of small groups. As the approach to this group work has been outlined elsewhere,[1] I propose to confine my remarks here to the use made by the students of their own topic-work experience when they came to do group work in schools.

In their group work, the students were asked to form themselves into small teams and to offer possible schemes of work in relation to a list of offers of classes from various schools which was posted on the notice board. Several of these offers were of a very generalized kind, leaving the students a good deal of freedom in their schemes. Some of the students who had been members of the drama topic group took this opportunity to submit schemes of work based on a dramatic approach.

Art and drama in a scheme for group work

One of these was a scheme for an art class with third-year children (i.e. thirteen-year-olds) of below-average academic ability. Four students, including Anne,[2] the secretary and stage manager from the drama topic, and Bill,[1] the lighting expert, proposed a scheme in which creative work with paper (collages for scenery, paper sculpture for costumes, and papier mâché for masks) should be used with spontaneous dramatisation. From their preliminary visits to the school – a large, country comprehensive school – the students learned that the children were extremely backward, and used to working under the teacher's close supervision.

The students had a long discussion before the group work began on whether or not they should take samples of the kind of masks, collages, etc., that could be produced with scrap paper (and which they had themselves been learning about in their basic art classes). The following notes from their group-work file report this discussion.

Meeting: Thursday, December 1st

(a) There was discussion at great length as to whether or not we should take in examples of work that had been done using the materials the children would use during this topic work.

    (i) It was decided that if the children saw these examples they would not want to carry out the preliminary work leading up to this.

[1] See Kaye and Rogers, op. cit., Chapters 2 and 7.
[2] Here and elsewhere in this book the names of the students concerned have been changed.

101

   (ii) There would not be the opportunity to build up the interest in the project if such a jump was taken.

   (iii) There would be no individual thought during the preliminary work as we would wish there to be.

(b) It was thought that the best method was, by way of introduction, to teach techniques that might be useful to the children during their later work in costume, etc. This would be done by dividing them into four groups of about four to five children. Each of us would then take a group and demonstrate a few simple techniques in our own particular field of paper work. They would then try a few experiments using these techniques. We would also give a brief outline of our scheme and an explanation of why they were having the preliminary work.

(c) We were also to ask the class teacher what previous work with similar material the children had done.

In fact, it turned out that the children had not done any similar work previously. It was also pointed out by the art teacher that 'paper was quite a treasured commodity in the school'! The students, not to be outdone, asked the children to bring newspapers, magazines, scrap card and boxes, and chicken-wire (as a basis for the masks).

During the first two lessons, the students gave the children some instruction in various techniques of papercraft, allowing them either to remain in one group and practise that technique, or to move between groups. They also began the slow process of encouraging them to think for themselves, and to make their own decisions, which these children, used to being told what to do in the smallest of matters, found it difficult to bring themselves to, not only on account of lack of practice, but also because such previous experience of initiative as they had shown had generally led to failure or punishment or both.

It is clear from the tone of the students' reported discussion and from the care which they showed in leading the children into accepting responsibility for their own work, that they had developed a high degree of sensitivity to the children's problems. Here is a report of a meeting held after the first lesson.

Group Meeting: 5.30 p.m., Monday, January 16th
It had been originally intended that each group should move on to another student in order to gain experience in another technique

in paper work. However those children working with Bill and Terry had progressed so little that it was useless to stop the children working in a particular technique without their having achieved much, in order to justify a move. We decided that it would be best to give the children free choice of the techniques they would like to practise during the lesson. This we thought would allow them to move on if they were wanting to, or to stay if they wished to complete a piece of work, or progress to greater skill in the field of papercraft in which they were working. By doing this we thought we would avoid the children becoming bored or disheartened at the outset if any were on the brink of so doing. On the other hand it was decided that a little specialization would not be detrimental to the later project but rather an advantage, providing, of course, they weren't all specialists. This was hardly likely to happen with the amount of concentration this group appeared to have.

The children began to respond to the students and – what was more important – to show some signs of self-confidence. By the third lesson, the students felt that they were ready to discuss and choose the topic to which the papercraft techniques were a preliminary. Their discussion notes before this lesson show how far they had learnt the group-work approach.

Meeting of Group to discuss Lesson 3: January 20th
It was agreed that at this lesson we should start working on our main project – work on a central theme which would lend itself to creative work with paper, and to eventual dramatic expression. It was felt that the children should themselves decide on this theme, and that ample opportunity should be given for discussion on this. At the same time we thought that we would be advised to go prepared with some ideas of our own, so that we can prompt the children should they be unwilling to offer ideas of their own. At an earlier discussion the children themselves suggested a saloon scene.[1] We feel that there are other more adaptable themes, such as a native tribal dance (Zulus), or knights of old, and would like to make the children aware of possibilities in other fields, such as these.

For this lesson, then, we plan a general introduction of the topic, leading to general discussion of the subject matter of the central theme, which we hope will be monopolised by them, with

[1] It transpired that they were acting Western scenes in their drama classes, so even this suggestion was not original.

SOME EXPERIMENTAL APPROACHES

suitable prompting from us where necessary. We will allow time
for the children to discuss this amongst themselves, before finally
deciding on the theme – by a vote.

Once the theme has been decided, we will try to get them to
see for themselves how paper work could be involved, and
indeed what will be required. We will again allow time for informal discussion, in which we hope they may decide for themselves which particular aspect of the work each is interested in.
It is then hoped that some division of the class into groups
according to this interest can be made : a group concerned with
costume, with hand props, with scenery, etc., depending on what
is required.

The discussion of possible themes proved quite lively. The
students divided the children into small groups to discuss ideas,
and then brought them all together as a class to hear the various
ideas (which were written on the board) and to vote on them. At
the children's request, each was allowed two votes. The results,
as recorded in the students' logbook, were as follows:

	Votes
A Viking scene – an attack and battle	9
A Zulu scene – war dance and fight	0
Drunken saloon – drunks fight over cards	7
Robin Hood – robbing the rich	0
Egyptian scene – a temple, pyramids	0
Stone age – early man, monster fights	13
King Arthur – knights, jousting, fair	2
William Tell – crossbows, shooting the apple	1
Ali Baba – thieves thieving	0
Total votes cast:	32

The students observed in their file: 'It is interesting that some
had not used their vote (eighteen were present) for a second topic,
and the three girls had all voted for the drunken scene.' The pre-
dominance of the male sex in this class no doubt was the reason
for the emphasis on fights and battles in the suggested themes,
though it might well be argued that these children's experience of
rejection and failure would have led to a good deal of stored-up
aggression.

The production of stone-age masks, a large backcloth of a primal landscape made from paper collage, animal 'skins' made of paper with coloured strips pasted on, and two elaborate monster costumes, all proceeded at a good pace, with the children showing increasing enthusiasm and initiative. Some even offered to come into school during half-term to work on the masks, much to the amazement of the art teacher. Even the three girls, who were notoriously uninterested in any kind of work, began to show interest and specialized in the production of stone-age wigs, which they made from carpenters' shavings fixed in chicken-wire caps. By the fifth lesson the students were commenting :

The children seemed to take over from us this lesson, they were much more keen and had many new ideas. In fact, we found ourselves with little to do.

Two lessons later, most of the masks and skins had been done, and the large backcloth was nearing completion. New groups were formed to work on the monsters, whose great heads were a riot of colours. Another group had formed to consider the production of the actual performance, and met separately to discuss their ideas.

By the eighth lesson, Anne is writing :

We had managed to acquire a fairly long length of hessian, which we thought could form the two monster bodies. These became my responsibility, so together with the girls, and three boys who were not needed elsewhere, we set to work. The boys acted as dummies for us, while the girls set to work pinning the lengths of hessian around them. I was very pleased with the way the girls involved themselves this lesson, and by the end of it we had one completed costume for three boys, and one almost completed for two. The boys who were going to be the monsters decided that they should get some practice at moving around together, and their 'rehearsal' caused a little commotion in the classroom so I had to stop them before they had disrupted everyone else. Otherwise everyone worked very well in this group, and I was very pleased with the work they had produced by the end of the lesson – as usual we could have done with a great deal more time !

The following week the performance took place. One of the children who had been a member of the production group assumed responsibility for the performance. There was only time for two run-throughs, both under his sole direction.

The students recorded their final lesson with the children.

Lesson 9. March 16th

Some of the children were waiting for us when we went up to the art room during the coffee break – we thought this showed a certain amount of enthusiasm for the work we have been doing ! . . . When the rest of the class had arrived . . . we asked the Production Group if they would meet and discuss the form of the play, who should do what, and also who should wear what. Willie (one of the boys) assumed the leadership of this group and the rest of the children accepted him quite happily. We left the organization of this entirely up to him, and we feel that he did a very good job of it.

They took quite a long time getting into their costumes, and some adjustment was necessary, but soon they were ready for a first run-through. This was a little chaotic – the form was a little obscure, the action not quite clear. The action was to be two tribes fighting each other; monsters appear and there is a fight in which the weaker one is killed, and the victor turns against the primitive men; the two tribes unite against their common foe, the monster.

Willie did not take part, but directed the action. He had instructed the boys that they were only to mime the fight, and that as far as possible they were to avoid actually hitting anyone with their clubs and spears, because the paper costumes would not stand up to very rough treatment – this factor did restrict the possible action to a certain extent. In the first run-through, they did not really keep to this rule, and many running repairs were necessary – Larry assumed the main responsibility for carrying out repairs.

We called everyone together and discussed how the play could be improved – clearer division between the various events was suggested, and also less hard hitting with spears, etc. There was time for one more performance, and this was much more effective, and we felt that dramatic work had been quite successful.

The students included in their logbooks a profile of each child. That on Willie, the boy who directed the dramatic performance, makes interesting reading.

It was surprising to hear that Willie had been a serious trouble-maker in that class, and Mr L. (the art teacher) had had to take strong disciplinary action with him. This term he has seemed quiet, but authoritative – very ready to shoulder organizational responsibilities and readily accepted in that role by the other boys. He now seems to be a very responsible boy and has done an excellent job of organizing the Production Group and in *directing* the final dramatic work.

The students' comments on Willie illustrate a common experience in group work : that given the opportunity to take responsibility for their own work, children who have previously appeared to be trouble-makers can become helpful and responsible members of a working team. In a traditional, formal teacher-directed lesson, the only outlet the natural leaders have among their peers is to lead them in rebellion. Under group work, however, the teacher can canalize their energies in organizing their less out-going fellows, often with surprisingly successful results.[1]

It should of course be remembered that the aim of this scheme of work was the art work produced, and the dramatic performance was incidental to that aim. Nevertheless, the performance fulfilled a vital function as far as the children were concerned, for it gave them a specific purpose to relate their work to, as well as providing a set of criteria against which to judge the effectiveness of their productions.

The students ended their logbook by giving their own assessments of the value of the group work. Anne wrote :

Assessment of group work

I found this term a very valuable and enjoyable experience. I feel sure that we were lucky in that by choosing an art and drama topic we were more able to participate in and enjoy the work with the children, than those who chose a more 'academic' project.[2] The very nature of the work made it easier to work *with* the children, than to direct operations from 'above'.

Personally, I welcomed the chance of forming a more informal relationship with the children, and in this case I feel that it was

[1] See Kaye and Rogers, op. cit., p. 51.

[2] In fact, of course, it is the attitude of and procedure adopted by the teacher, rather than the actual topic, that determines the success of group work. That these students had, from the start, an admirable approach to their scheme is well demonstrated by the excerpts quoted from their logbook.

very successful. These were nineteen third-year children in the remedial form. They were not, under normal circumstances, either inclined to, or able to turn out any very successful work. The informal nature of these lessons greatly helped to draw these children into the general activity of the class. By half-term even the least interested amongst the class were showing some interest, which gradually grew into genuine enthusiasm as the project gathered momentum. Many of the children in this class hadn't worked so hard or so long in an art lesson before ! Mr L. (the art teacher) was genuinely surprised at the involvement which they showed.

Undoubtedly, the informal atmosphere and the ratio of student/child was responsible for the work these children were prepared to put in. Obviously the student/child ratio of 1 : 5 was a very unrealistic one as far as present-day teaching is concerned. I feel, however, after this experience, that something approaching this atmosphere could be obtained in normal teaching circumstances. It would require very careful organization on the part of the teacher, and a certain amount of confidence, so that the groups of children could be allowed enough freedom, but I feel sure it would work.

The opportunity to work as a team with other students, was also a valuable experience. It gave the opportunity to see other techniques being put into practice and to evaluate the different approaches to group work.

I feel that this was an invaluable experience from which both we and the children benefited.

Of course, as Anne says, the student/pupil ratio is an extremely artificial one which – except for a few sixth-form classes – the teacher would not normally expect to come across. But among the aims of the group work was that of giving the students an opportunity to work together as a small team, and from this point of view, the number of children they were dealing with did not much affect the situation. A second aim was to demonstrate the fact that, given the chance of self-direction in work that they had themselves chosen, even remedial children can develop a degree of responsibility for their own work that teachers who are used only to formal methods would not believe possible. As the students themselves reported, there were times when 'we found ourselves with little to do'. And a third aim was to give the students a chance to get to know a few children well, freed from the constraints normally to be found when dealing with a large group of children. Their sensitive profiles demonstrated that they had made good use of this opportunity.

A dramatic approach to English with a remedial class

Among the offers from schools of classes in which teams of students could do group work was one of a small class of twelve children, who were described as 'lowest ability, first-year remedial children'. As the school was a moderately large country secondary modern school, it was sure that the class would be very backward indeed, and would certainly include emotionally-disturbed as well as educationally retarded children. The scheme of work was to be 'any topic involving written or oral English'.

Three students from the drama topic group, including Tim, the director, chose this class, and offered a topic based on the sea and ships, using spontaneous dramatization as a stimulus. Their file tells the story of their first visits to the school.

Preliminary visits

We entered the school for the first preliminary visit with very open minds. We knew that we wanted to do dramatic work and because of the town's locality[1] we thought that marine drama would be appropriate. We left our scheme as general as this until we had met the children and their teacher to discover from them what work had previously been done in drama, and what were their general abilities. We had many different ideas and rudimentary schemes but we wanted to keep them in the embryonic stage until we had assessed the situation in which we were to teach.

The first visit answered the majority of our questions. We met the children and saw some of their work. We also saw them at work. From the class teacher we learnt their capabilities and failings. None of us had worked with remedial children before and we learnt much from the class teacher and from talking with and watching the children. Now that we had a clearer conception of the classroom situation we were able to plan a rough outline of the scheme we wished to pursue. Our problem now lay in the fact that we had too much material which we could use, and only ten weeks to accomplish the project.

[1] It was situated on the coast.

The second visit, with further discussion with the class teacher and the children helped to clarify our ideas. We began to discard material. For example, one of our original ideas had been to portray cabin boys through the ages. Although we had thought that this would be interesting for the children we now saw that it would be too advanced for them. They would not be capable of making their own detailed research and the project would become too teacher-directed. Similarly, we ousted a scheme concerning the Flying Dutchman. Through discussions, mainly with the class teacher although often involving the children, the scheme of work suddenly fell into place. One moment it was a mass of muddled ideas and then we began to plan it, lesson by lesson, and the project to our relief became clearly defined. We were able, at this stage, to allocate certain areas of the topic to the members of the group. Each of us was to concentrate on an era of history and develop it in some way for the purposes of the project. The three eras chosen were those containing the different methods of sea transport : rowing boats, as portrayed in the Vikings, sailing ships, and modern liners.

We decided that we needed to begin the project with an activity that would make an impact on the children. A good way to do this, we concluded after lengthy discussion, was to begin with a play of our own making. After further discussion we decided that a good subject for this play would be the story of Christopher Columbus. This would be known to the children. We wanted to bring the children into this play. We did not know how they would respond and so we looked on this as an experiment. Their reaction to this would greatly affect our viewing of the lesson outlines for the following weeks. We also decided to have a film the first week, because we thought this too would be exciting for the children and would help their understanding. The film chosen, *Sailing to the Cape,* was excellent for our purposes since it showed clearly many of the details we wanted the children to grasp, for example, pulling up an anchor and hauling down sails.

Since we had our first lesson planned, the third preliminary visit was used to check on arrangements and organization. We had to make sure of a film projector and similar articles. We had to make sure that we had accounted for everything, since our next visit would be actually to teach.

This excerpt reveals that the three students had already learnt a great deal about group work. I was particularly impressed by their willingness to abandon ideas that they had worked out, and by their general readiness to adapt the scheme to the children's reactions. This is one of the most difficult aspects of group work for students to master, particularly when they are unsure of themselves in the classroom in any case. From their previous teaching practice they have learnt at least one lesson : that, as far as traditional class-teaching is concerned, it is always better to over-prepare than to under-prepare. They have no doubt all had the chilling experiencing of reaching the end of their material halfway through a lesson and realizing that there remain twenty or so minutes in which the children have to be occupied. When the children are dependent upon the teacher's direction for their activities, such an experience can leave its mark on student teachers. Hence, the willingness to rely upon the children's initiative, and to be ready to modify their approach in relation to its reception, augured very well for the success of this group. I was pleased, too, with their thoroughness. It is important to approach the selection of a film for group work imaginatively, but it is also important to have in mind such pedestrian but vital matters as whether or not there is a film projector.

The students set to and roughed out a short playlet, set on board Columbus's ship, full of details of action involving the hoisting of the sails, changing course, dropping the anchors, etc. Here is their account of its presentation.

Lesson 1. Thursday, January 12, 1966

The lesson period was broken into two main parts: the play and the film, each with its own discussion time. We arrived at the school at 9.15 a.m.[1] As the hall in which we commenced our lesson was still occupied by the senior school assembly, we went to Room 25 to introduce ourselves to the children and prepare them for the work. We did not give them any indication of the nature of the work that was to follow, but asked them to put on their plimsolls and have a pencil and paper ready just in case they needed them. Then we took them to the hall and asked them to sit on the floor at the front, while we put the sextant and box of ship's biscuits on the top of the piano. Tim put on his seaman's jacket and cap; then we began the play.

We began by keeping word for word to the lines we had

---

[1] As the school was a considerable distance from college, they had been excused assembly by the Head.

written but after a few sentences we began to ad-lib. This did not seem to bother the children in the least,[1] in fact, it added to the excitement as we could play it according to audience reaction. We did, however, stick to the sequence of events which we had planned. The children joined in willingly. Some were lookouts, peering through the fog for land, others manned the wheel or hoisted sails, while others let down the anchors. In this improvization it was important to make sure that they could comprehend the size and shape of articles and materials which they were supposed to be handling. For example, if just left to man the wheel, we found that they envisaged only a small wheel. It was important to show them just how big the wheel would actually be. Similarly, the lowering of the anchors was done by chopping a rope, so here they had to pick up a heavy axe and swing it on to an imaginary rope. This was directed by pointing out in the dialogue exactly where the rope lay, in which direction it would run and where the blow had to be landed. The play was brought to an end by the successful landing of the ship and the crew ate ship's biscuits.

Next, the children split into natural groups and we discussed life at sea and the play.

One of the boys, Graham, who is particularly nervous, had been upset earlier that morning. The class teacher told us that the boy could not co-operate and would not even speak, so she advised us not to press him into taking part in the lesson. Although we made several attempts to talk to him he just stared blankly and made no attempt to communicate. The first time he made any effort to participate was when he accepted a ship's biscuit.

Each of us led our own individual discussions, very informally, just getting to know the children. They spoke freely without inhibitions and were very eager to talk and ask questions. They all enjoyed the play and many of them said that it was very exciting. The discussions (commented on below) lasted for about ten minutes and then we all went to the film room for *Sailing to the Cape*.

This was an excellent film and linked up very well with the play as it was about a sailing ship which travelled from Sweden to South Africa and on its journey experienced the calms of the Doldrums and the storms of the Roaring Forties. Many of the

---

[1] I am not very clear why the students should have thought that it would.

scenes were very dramatic and also very factual. In some scenes a sextant was used, exactly the same as we had used in the play.

From the discussions which followed the 18-minute film, it was obvious that it had greatly aroused the children. We did not split them into discussion groups but just held an informal discussion, everyone with everyone. Many of the points in the film lent themselves to further discussion, such as the reason for the name Roaring Forties, measuring the actual wingspan of a 14′ albatross, and the fact that there were no lifeboats on the ship. It was especially interesting that towards the end of the discussion the whole group seemed to split up into smaller natural groups of three or four. This brought the lesson to a close.

Comment

We were all very pleased with the first lesson of the series as the children were really excited. We were successful in arousing their interest which was our prime aim. This was undoubtedly due to the novel methods—at least, methods novel to the children – that we used. The play which we acted was an appropriate opening gambit. The discussions allowed us to get to know the children, allowed them to give back their ideas and gave a high degree of personal contact within the groups.

Because the children were excited they wanted to participate and were well behaved and co-operative. They spoke freely and quite fluently which was quite surprising.

The class had only ever been shown one film before, so this pleased them, too. They were very observant and asked questions after.

Personally, I did not find the team teaching at all dismaying but quite the reverse. It was a very enjoyable experience.

Here again we see the students' flexibility of approach, ad-libbing as the play develops, particularly in order to meet the special problem (which they had not anticipated) of the extremely limited knowledge of the children they were dealing with. Their sensitivity is again shown by the fact that they appreciated that Graham's accepting a biscuit was in fact a sign of participation, and by their interest in the natural groupings the children formed. Their choice of props for the play also showed a high degree of imagination.

The students had by now roughed out a programme for the ten weeks of group work, based on their original idea of sea transport

H

through the ages, and after the initial presentation of Columbus's voyage, they returned, in their next two lessons, to the Vikings. Suggesting to the children that they should together work out a small playlet similar to the one they had presented, they began by discussing the physical aspects of life on board a Viking ship : the feel of the heavy oars, the weight of the brass helmets, the sound of the drum used to keep time in rowing. Assembled in the hall, and sitting aboard an imaginary longship in the middle of the floor, they rowed across the narrow seas towards England.

After each episode the children were encouraged to argue about what they had done, and to make suggestions as to how the acting could become more realistic. This comes out in the students' comments after the lesson :

> When the children began to consider what they would be wearing, e.g. heavy helmets, sandals instead of plimsolls, they started to build up a mental picture of themselves rowing a Viking ship. They began to have discussions among themselves as to what they could and could not do on board such a ship. The value of this type of reasoning on their own parts was demonstrated later when they were trying to decide upon a rhythm to adopt for rowing the boat. They tried out one rhythm, which was obviously too fast, and from this mistake were able to adopt a rhythm of satisfactory speed. Through this trial-and-error method the children learnt more of the basic essentials of rowing than they would have done from a teacher-imposed rhythm. The children obviously empathized more deeply in the second attempt at rowing, most of them being physically exhausted at the end of the exercise.

From this activity, the children were then given a further chance to discuss the scenes they had enacted, which included (at their own suggestion) the reactions of a group of Anglo-Saxons to the Viking raid, and were then taken to the library to use the books for a piece of imaginative writing.

The following week the students took in pictures of Viking ships and armour, and the children were allowed to make helmets and shields from cardboard. Armed with these, they re-enacted the scenes, with even greater enthusiasm and involvement, and again wrote an imaginative piece. This was followed, the next week, by a visit to a museum, to study models of old-time sailing ships, leading to a dramatization of the age of exploration. One of the incidents dramatised was that of Cortez's meeting with Montezuma, and this led Graham, the deeply-disturbed boy, to write an imaginative piece describing the scene. The class teacher said that this was only the second time he had written anything since he had been in school.

Most admirable of all, however, was the students' critical attitude towards their own efforts. Tim observes:

> The discussion would have been greatly improved if I had got more of the faults and improvements (regarding the spontaneous dramatic production) from the children. I tried to get some from them, but not all.

Earlier, in their report on the Viking scheme, another member of the group commented:

> It would have been much more valuable for the children if we had incorporated their ideas into the activity. They were obviously going to adhere to our pattern fairly closely,[1] and even if they were not, this would not have mattered, and so from this point the activity should have become largely pupil-directed. When they said, 'Let's be ancient Britons,' instead of saying, 'Yes, that's what we are going to do,' it would have been better to say, 'Yes, that's a good idea. What do the rest of you think of that?' etc., and then let them lead into the activity.

After the age of explorations, they came up to modern times with a study of present-day liners. Again, they led the children into improvised drama—this time with the scene of a shipwreck—and using this as a stimulus, followed it with oral work with a tape-recorder, and written passages. A visit to the docks was included in these lessons, during which the various devices for ensuring safety at sea and in the event of shipwreck, were examined.

For the last two visits, the students asked the children to make their own suggestions. After some discussion, a number of ideas were mooted, and ultimately three schemes were suggested. One was chosen by vote and immediately acted out.

The play was about a ship's captain. He and his mate went to a prison to obtain a crew for their ship. It was fascinating to see

[1] In other words, the children's suggestions were in line with the outline plan the students had drawn up.

the prisoners discuss among themselves whether or not they should go with the captain. They decided to go with the captain. John Welling became a prison warder although we do not know how he obtained his office, whether it was by self- or class-election. The second scene of the play took place on board ship. The prison crew discovered dynamite in the hold. They held a meeting and decided to force the captain to stop the ship. Unfortunately, the play had to finish with the argument between the prisoners and the captain.

Before the students handed their group-work files in, they were asked to give their views on the value of the work they had done. Here they are:

Impressions and opinions on the group work
I found this practice very useful and very enjoyable and I thought that at our stage of teaching experience, it was a good idea to have us go out and teach with other students, because one feels more confident than if one was on one's own, and one also gains more confidence as a result of doing something well in front of people whom one knows.

The main problem about such a group practice is surely picking a topic which will interest each student, and also hold the children's attention for the whole period. Fortunately we were able to do this. Our topic was a very broad one, and left much scope for individual variation. This is, I think, essential, especially if the children are allowed as much self-guidance as possible.

I found it very interesting to watch the other two teach, and to learn from their ideas and ways of putting things over. It is a good idea, I think, when someone else is teaching, almost to act as one of the class, trying to experience how the children feel, and such a practice as this is really the only chance one gets of doing anything like this. It was a good, broadening experience. Another advantage of such a practice is one which we really missed out on. We should have criticized one another more. Perhaps, being close friends, the other two did, but as a group we didn't pull one another about very much. It is difficult to criticize constructively of course. Perhaps we didn't feel confident enough.

But I would say that working in a group does help to give one confidence, not only because of the reason mentioned in the first paragraph, but also because one is able to get better results, mainly, I suppose, because one doesn't have to worry about discipline – trying to keep one's eye on the whole class at once. And then again, when splitting the class into groups, one has two other people to work these groups up into something substantial, whereas if one was on one's own, the children might tend just to while away the time until one could get round to them.[1]

The last real benefit from the student's point of view is the experience itself, of working with other people and making something worthwhile and substantial as a result of combined effort. It's very nice to pull one's weight, there is a feeling of responsibility and trust in it, something like the satisfaction one gets from playing in an orchestra. I think it was all a very good idea.

I would say also that the children benefited in two very real ways from this practice. Firstly, they had a lot more individual attention than they would otherwise have had, and secondly, they had the experience of being spoken to by three completely different people, whom they would otherwise not have known at all. I think we broadened their experience in the same way as they broadened ours.

The second member of the group, also a woman student, had this to say :

The group-work experience as a means of teaching
For the Children.
On our group work the pupil/student relationship was in the ratio of 4 : 1. We were therefore able to spend a greater length of time with individual children. This was, I feel, advantageous to the children especially since they were a remedial group. A few of the children had speech difficulties and the small natural discussion groups which we were able to form because of the low

[1] This, of course, was this student's guess. If it were true, normal group work in which one teacher has responsibility for up to six groups, would not be possible. However, as this student was to discover on her subsequent practice (when she carried out a successful group-work project with a class of children for which she was solely responsible) in fact children – given the opportunity to work by themselves – are capable of a high degree of involvement and self-direction. On the other hand, it must be admitted that the present class consisted of very disturbed and backward children, whose capacity for sustained work was in any case extremely limited.

pupil/student ratio were helpful in overcoming these difficulties. We had time just to talk to the children which the class teacher with an average of thirty or more children is unable to do to such an extent. This I feel was helpful for the social and personal development of the children.

The low pupil/student ratio also helped the children with their writing. We had not the experience of the class teacher but we had time to help the children sort out their own problems. Instead of just giving the children a spelling that they might know themselves, we had time to stay with them while they worked it out.

The group work was helpful for the children because it probably presented them with a different type of work and approach.

For Ourselves.
The group-work experience was an excellent opportunity to try out new ideas in a controlled situation. The situation was more controlled than a teaching-practice situation for there were fewer children and more students to cope with them. We were working with friends and so had support and guidance from them. For us the group work was our first experience of team teach-in. This was something which we could probably never try so easily again. The fact was that we enjoyed team teaching, and recognized its advantages. If in the future we have the opportunity to carry out some team teaching we should probably take it.

The ideal classroom conditions provided a good opportunity for trying informal work. Drama with a full class is difficult to control and organise. In this situation we were able to try more ambitious things. We gained confidence in handling this type of work. We also learnt a lot about teaching drama. Sometimes the actual drama would not be very good but the work arising from it was excellent. On other occasions the drama was carried out with great enthusiasm and feeling but the written work was sadly lacking in this. We therefore learnt that drama should not be judged merely by the practical work. The work arising from the drama may compensate for and even follow poorer practical work.

Finally, the comments of Tim :

The group-work experience as a means of teaching
This was a thoroughly enjoyable experience which in every way

was a great chance to experiment and learn from both a sub-jective and an objective situation.

Subjectively, I found it very useful working closely with two friends on a common plan which, from the beginning, remained very flexible. It was good to argue and reason our own ideas with each other in order to get a common plan and aim. This meant that with two others criticizing a basic idea, your own had to be almost foolproof. In fact, we changed our minds many times before we arrived at a final plan of attack. Even when the lessons were under way, we still let ourselves be channelled into other ideas as the children were taking over from us. We were aware of the pitfalls of not being flexible.

Having to co-operate and look at each other's teaching had many advantages. The pool of ideas was widened. Because we were friends, however, we did not really criticise each other's actual teaching enough. Perhaps we would have gained more had we done so, but watching others teaching did help in one's thinking of one's own teaching.

I found the freedom of the experience the most exhilarating part. A free hand to change plan and ideas was good. It allowed us to make mistakes and correct them as we went. It also allowed us to avoid the pitfalls which came in practice but which in theory we could not see.

Objectively we could see the effect of team-teaching upon the children. We wondered if three teachers in the classroom at the same time would prove dismaying for the children but they seemed to take quite naturally to the situation and it did allow us to get to know them well.

Group work has given me, personally, an extra insight into the teaching situation. It has given an extra dimension to the mechanics of the job because it was a freedom, controlled by having to consult a 'group' of people in the same situation as myself. In discussion it was refreshing to hear the different opinions and ideas of the other two members of our group and look at the same situation through their eyes.

Our scheme of work was particularly interesting to me because of the way we applied ourselves to the job. We did not take one group of children each but shared the responsibility of all the children. Neither did we all teach separately and simul-taneously but took charge individually of all twelve children whilst the other two watched and helped as needed. In this situation the emphasis of teaching was changed from person to person and the children had to respond by continually changing groups and subgroups. In this way the structure of the class became a sort of amorphous mass moving in a united direction, yet ever changing within itself.

I thought that this might be rather unsettling for the children, but I think I underestimated the tremendous versatility of children and the way they can adapt to change. I think that this was as refreshing for them as it was for us.

Looking back on the experience, I find it very difficult to think of any real changes that I would have made if I had the same time again. One change which I would make would be a change of emphasis from oral English to written English. At the beginning of the scheme we wanted to develop only oral work, but as two weeks passed we began to realize the possibilities of written work which were at our disposal.

In assessing the value of this piece of work, it is important to bear in mind that this was a class of extremely backward and disturbed children, normally taught throughout the day by one teacher (a teacher skilled in dealing with handicapped children). The boy who eventually accepted the ship's biscuit, Graham, was described by the teacher as 'being obsessed by death'. He was under psychiatric treatment, and the students observed in their profile of him, that 'whenever he spoke to a teacher, even if in the corridor or under any circumstances, he always held his hand up halfway, near his face.' Graham's reaction to the students' first entry into the classroom was to begin crying. He preferred to be left alone by himself, and had no wish to join the first visit to the museum. Yet as the students persevered, he began to respond to them and by the fourth lesson he was asking for a part in one of the dramatic improvizations. When the class visited the docks, late in the scheme, Graham wanted to come, and asked a great many questions.

The value of group work to students

Of course, as the students themselves commented in their files, the group work they were given was an entirely artificial teaching situation. But this does not mean that it was not a valuable one for them. In arranging it for them, I was acting on a number of assumptions. Firstly, that they had to discover for themselves the potential springs of action that can be tapped when a small group of children are allowed to pursue together some topic or inquiry or project which they themselves have chosen, and in the pursuit of which they have been allowed a good deal of self-direction. The students had already discovered the strength of such motivation as far as they were themselves concerned in their own topic work. But it was necessary to demonstrate that a similar motive could be drawn upon with secondary schoolchildren. By allocating students to classes in the ratio of one to every four or five children, I was able to provide a situation in which each student could observe this magic working at close hand, without at the same time having the responsibility, and the anxiety of looking after the whole class.

A second assumption I was making was that, without this stepping stone as it were, students preparing to teach in secondary schools would not attempt to apply group-work methods. It was not enough that they knew that they were being used in primary schools successfully, nor even that they had themselves had successful experience of the approach in their own topic work. They had to discover for themselves, and at close quarters, the impetus to work, the sense of excitement and application, that group work can bring, and again the student/pupil ratio of 1 : 4 or 5 enabled them to do precisely this. Given this demonstration, and given their experience of the method in the somewhat rarified atmosphere we had created, it then seemed possible that the students would be encouraged to try and develop group work with their own classes when the opportunity arose. And indeed, this was what happened on their next practice, in the following term, when they were given a block teaching practice without college supervision, and encouraged to use group work in at least one of their schemes of work. This the majority of the students did. I do not myself think they would have had the confidence necessary to do so, without the prior experience which we gave them.[1]

[1] Though it is proper to record that since the events described above, I have myself moved away from the view that working with a single small group of children is a *necessary* precursor to accepting overall responsibility for the organization of group work in a classroom. One reason for my change of opinion is that there is the danger in a student/pupil ratio of one to five or six that the student tends to act as the leader of the group and a 'mini' teaching situation develops, whereas if the student is responsible for two or more groups, he is obliged to leave each one while dealing with the other, and hence the need for the autonomy of the groups cannot be evaded. Moreover, what seemed experimental two years ago has come to be accepted as a normal state of affairs; both tutors and students have come to accept group work as a normal part of training, and the need to prove that it works is no longer of paramount importance.

There was, however, a third purpose in arranging the group work in the way that we did. This was to give them the experience of working as a team. Team teaching as an approach to secondary teaching that is particularly suitable for mixed ability grouping is being tried out in an increasing number of schools, and it seemed to me that it was our responsibility, in training teachers, to give our students at least some experience of working in a team. Here again, the fact that the teams were small, and that the number of pupils for which they were responsible was rarely more than one class, proved an advantage rather than the reverse, for it enabled the students to meet all the problems of team teaching proper, but in a limited context and with limited responsibility. That some of the students themselves realized the value of this experience, and availed themselves fully of the opportunities it offered, is shown by the records of the three students who presented the scheme of work on ships and the sea.

Finally, the group work gave the students the chance to get to know as individuals a few children of secondary-school age in a way that the limitations of normal class teaching altogether prevent. Having once built up close relationships with them, it was my hope that they would never again be able to view a secondary class, however large, and however formal the approach which they might be adopting, as no more than a multiple of that faceless, and wholly hypothetical invention of pedagogic writers : the secondary schoolchild.

There is one point I must make here. Both the students' schemes described above are of group work with remedial groups of children—in the latter case, with a severely remedial group. I must emphasize that I chose these examples because of the relevance of the students' own notes to the topic under discussion, and not because of the suitability of the schemes chosen. In particular, I do not wish to be taken as thereby implying that group work—or, indeed, any of the informal approaches referred to in this book—is suitable only for work with remedial classes. Students have used this approach successfully with mixed-ability classes and—when given the opportunity—with examination classes. The view that traditional, teacher-directed lessons are not always the most suited to the needs of less able children is slowly coming to be accepted as valid (if grudgingly, in some quarters); the corollary that teacher-directed lessons are not always most suited to the needs of able children is one that is strongly (sometimes almost hysterically) resisted. It is my own view that informal methods and traditional teacher-directed lessons both have their place in the repertoire of the secondary teacher of today, whatever range of ability he or she is dealing with.

7

A Psychedelic Exhibition

The drama topic in the history of education had proved a rewarding enterprise, which had fully justified its adoption. Remembering the dramatic productions I had taken part in while on study leave, and the time and effort my student friends had been prepared to devote to them in contrast with the scant attention they had given to their studies, I felt that we had achieved some measure of success with our topic work in drawing upon that reservoir of enthusiasm normally untapped by the demands of the curriculum. However, it did occur to me to wonder whether the success of the drama topic was not in part due to the traditional hold of any dramatic activity. Dramatic productions, after all, are well known as being tremendously demanding of time and enterprise, and it may well be that those students who chose to take part in the topic, did so with the anticipation of becoming involved beyond the normal expectations of a study group in education. I therefore decided to try an alternative topic the following year – one for which there was no particular tradition, and one in which, therefore, the students would be obliged to draw upon their own resources in a way that was not immediately apparent at the outset.

I had no special preference as to content except that it had previously occurred to me that, with the general pressure of the first-year course, insufficient time had been allowed for the study of the psychology of puberty and adolescence, and I had this possibility at the back of my mind.

124

A psychedelerious happening

It so happened that during the Christmas holidays following the end of the group work I have described in the previous chapter, I was in Chalk Farm in North London, and I noticed on the wall of the old Round House, recently taken over as a workshop for modern arts, a poster advertising 'a psychedelerious happening' on New Year's Eve, with the pop group, the Pink Floyd. The Pink Floyd had become exponents of music to the accompaniment of moving coloured lights and I had read somewhere or other that the effect was similar to the hallucinations induced by lysergic acid, the drug LSD. I had myself taken this drug some years before as part of a series of psychological experiments in electro-encephalography, and I was curious to see whether it was in fact possible to contrive the vivid hallucinatory patterns which lysergic acid characteristically induces, without the aid of the drug itself.[1]

The admission ticket was suitably printed in different coloured inks, and nine o'clock on the evening of the last day of the year found me standing in a slowly moving queue, entering the old railway repair shed by way of a somewhat dilapidated flight of wooden steps.

Inside the building was a smallish crowd of perhaps eighty or so people standing in the cold, dim, round hall, watching the projection of a coloured light pattern on a huge cinema-type screen, in front of which the pop group were playing energetically. The colours moved pleasantly, not unlike those films of the movements of primitive single-celled organisms, magnified many times. Colours slid across the screen in great blobs, which changed shape, bulging and fragmenting and then slid off to be replaced by others. Other lights, placed below the level of the players, threw their shadows across the coloured background, and these, too, pitched and swelled. From time to time, stroboscopic lights, attached to

[1] At the time I sampled lysergic acid and mescaline sulphate, the possibilities of their having serious after-effects was not widely discussed. However, both drugs were accompanied by a number of extremely unpleasant side-effects such as nausea, and a painful sense of an overfull bladder together with an inability to urinate, which made the experience less rewarding than Aldous Huxley's romantic accounts had led me to expect. My own theory of the effects of these hallucinogenic drugs, for what it is worth, is that they impair the nervous control over ocular focusing, with the result that when an attempt is made to concentrate one's vision, one perceives a number of alternative focusings, often rapidly oscillating between one and another. This undoubtedly gives a sense of depth to the object one is viewing, as well as an alternation between clarity and fuzziness. Huxley tells us that he saw to the heart of a flower. My own view is that the vagaries of his vision obliged him to look closely at a flower for the first time.

the gallery above our heads, began to flicker in the faces of the audience.

Not more than half a dozen people were making any attempt to dance. The majority simply stood in front of the group and watched the changing pattern of lights. It was not unpleasant and the variety of the colours and shapes prevented it from being monotonous, but as a perpetual experience it was totally different in quality from that of a drug-induced hallucination.

Wandering round the dim and draughty hall, watching the fit-fully-lit faces of the audience, it occurred to me that what was missing in the entertainment – if entertainment it was meant to be – was any provision for their participation. It was true that they could dance, if they wished, but then they could have done that well enough to simple music, without the added advantages of moving coloured lights. At the same time, I could not dismiss the occasion as entirely pointless and without profit. It struck me that there was something in this that could be exploited educationally, though it was not until several days later that the idea of a psychedelic exhi-bition occurred to me. This was to be essentially a participatory exhibition; one in which the viewers were required somehow to take an active role. With so many exhibitions – whether of works of art or of goods for sale – the role of the viewer is a passive one. I was reminded of an excellent exhibition of kinetic art I had visited in Stockholm some years before. Each exhibit somehow involved the viewer in participation. One of Tinguely's mobiles, I remem-ber, had to be mounted like a bicycle, and pedalled; with another, the onlooker – if that is the right word – had to manipulate various levers and buttons, insert brushes with coloured inks, and then an abstract painting was produced which could then be taken away. The painting was signed by the artist who designed the machine and a space was left for the addition of the viewer's name. There were also do-it-yourself modern sculpture kits : a number of wire strings through which were threaded variously-shaped blocks of carved stone. The viewer's job was to arrange these blocks in an aesthetically-satisfying relationship to each other.

It was at this point that I realised that the participatory exhibi-tion, which might be psychedelic in construction, could be based upon that study of the psychology of puberty which I had felt was not given sufficient emphasis in the first-year course, and in this way I arrived at the idea of a 'puberty psychedelic participatory exhibition'. This would be something entirely new, and therefore without a tradition of involvement such as the drama topic had

126

had. It would also give a chance to those students whose talents were not normally exploited in the academic part of the education course : students clever with gadgets and devices, nimble with their fingers, quick with invention. With a good deal of reluctance I determined to think no more about the matter until the time arrived for a new topic group, for fear that I should myself become too committed to any particular approach.

Preliminary discussions

When, some months later, I faced a new second-year group, I gave no more details than the ideas that had already occurred to me : that we should mount an exhibition on the subject of puberty and adolescence; that it should involve participation on the part of the viewers; and that it might possibly be based on a psychedelic approach. I explained how the idea had come to me, and emphasized that I had got no further with it, and that it would therefore be up to the topic group to develop it.

For various administrative reasons we had less time to allocate to topic work that year : five Thursday afternoon sessions of one and a half hours in place of the eight sessions the year before. This seemed an absolute minimum, if anything of value was to be done. Thirty-eight students elected to join the puberty topic group; slightly more than a quarter of the year group. Topics offered by other tutors were : an environmental historical study of the city in which the college was situated, with the nineteenth century as the period under review; an investigation into the local schools' response to the Certificate of Secondary Education, with a particular interest in any Mode III schemes that were being developed; and an improvized drama topic on etiquette and manners entitled 'The Polite World'.

As before, we held a preliminary meeting a few days before the end of the Summer term, to enable the students to make a provisional choice of topics. As soon as this first choice had been made, I held a brief meeting of the newly-formed puberty topic group. I repeated that I had thought no further about the exhibition than the outline I had already given, and I asked for ideas as to how we might proceed.

Suggestions were immediately forthcoming, a veritable flow of ideas. We might put our visitors in the middle of a huge, dark hall and suddenly turn on a hundred lights and loudspeakers; we might expose them to obscene pictures, and photograph their reactions; we might process them, like commodities, through a series of treatments. Lights, buzzers, bells, *musique concrète,* smells, physical shocks – we could give them the lot. It became necessary to take some decisions, even at this early stage, in order for our ideas to develop constructively. One important matter to be solved was whether the exhibition should be sequential or not; that is, should it consist of a number of displays, to be either presented or visited in sequence, or should it be a single, though no doubt complex, display? It was agreed that it should consist of a series of separate displays, to be visited in sequence. It was pointed out by the students that, in some lecture or other, they had been told that it was an important principle of child development that the stages of development were always in the same sequence, though not necessarily at the same chronological age.

A second question which had to be answered was whether the series of displays should be visited by the participants singly, or *en masse.* If they were to be visited singly, then some procedure would have to be devised to ensure their steady progress through the exhibition. Someone said that adolescence was essentially a lonely experience and that the exhibition should therefore be something experienced alone. This was generally agreed, and it led to the suggestion that the topic group could be divided into subgroups, each responsible for one of the displays.

The physical structure of the exhibition was beginning to take shape in our minds. It was to be a series of displays in separate rooms or cubicles, visited in sequence, alone. What would the visitor find? Would the displays be examples of adolescent behaviour or activities? Or would they somehow remind him or her of adolescence? I suggested that we might try to contrive a display that would somehow evoke, in the participant, the feelings of becoming adolescent. This idea was accepted enthusiastically. But should we try to evoke, in our visitors, the feelings of early adolescence in terms of the contexts of that stage of development, or should we try to evoke emotions comparable with the emotions of adolescence, but in relation to situations that had meaning to the students themselves, the majority of whom had at least reached puberty some five years or so before? Simply to try to recreate the conditions which aroused the anxieties and embarrassments of early adolescence might fail altogether. What we wanted was full participation – emotional as well as physical. We agreed that we would try to evoke in our visitors a series of emotions that would be reminiscent of adolescence in their feeling-tone, though not necessarily in the content of the stimuli which evoked them. In other words, we might have to use as stimuli, situations which would not be typical of adolescence.

The next step was, clearly, to decide what emotions were in fact characteristic of early adolescence. It was agreed that the students' own adolescence was not far behind, and that they would be able to have recourse to their reminiscences. At the same time, someone pointed out that each individual's own case might well not be typical, and in any case, they might have repressed some of their own more significant emotional experiences. It so happened that the college library had recently produced a long, annotated list of novels and autobiographies concerned with childhood and adolescence, and I suggested that we might use these as comparative source material. We worked our way quickly through the list, and various volunteers undertook to read and report on those that seemed likely to be relevant. Before breaking up, we agreed that the first meeting of the group the following term should be spent in trying to isolate and identify the separate major emotional areas which together constitute the main subjective experience of adolescence.

The question of where we were going to mount the exhibition was a difficult one. It would obviously take us more than one weekly meeting to set it up, and that meant that we had to find some place where we could safely leave it. A further requirement, if the exhibition was to be effective, was that it should not be seen during its preliminary stages. The college had among its buildings a rambling old house which had been used as a private school, and was now awaiting demolition and rebuilding as a hostel. Some of the rooms were in use as temporary lecture rooms, but there remained a large, low-ceilinged hall which was used as a store for furniture. This had the merit of being out of the way, and it was also kept locked. I arranged with the college bursar that the room could be used for an exhibition, and that the furniture could be moved, provided it was returned to its original condition.

The characteristics of puberty and adolescence

We held the first meeting of the puberty topic group proper in this room the following term. It was middle September, and the room was cold, damp and filthy dirty. We sat around on dusty tables and argued about the characteristics of early adolescence. We had in front of us only five weekly sessions of one and a half hours each, and I had already announced to my colleagues – perhaps rather rashly – that we expected the members of their topic groups to visit the exhibition in the fifth week.

We began simply by listing as many characteristics as occurred to us, as a result of experience or reading or both. At the end of twenty minutes' discussion we had agreed that adolescents were characterized by :

Irresponsibility
Insecurity
Frustration
Confusion
Growing self-consciousness
Idealism
Moodiness
Brash self-confidence
A growing awareness of the outside world
Inhibitedness
Non-conformity
Rebelliousness
Indecisiveness
Preoccupation with sex
Physical awkwardness
Social awkwardness

We felt by this time that, though we could have gone on, we had enough to work on. The question now became one of trying to reduce this to more manageable proportions, and we reconsidered our list to see of we could reduce it to a few general areas, within which all our agreed characteristics would find a place. After a good deal of argument about the meaning of terms, we emerged with the following five headings :

(i) *Insecurity*, which included indecisiveness and moodiness, and which derived from :

(ii) *Self-Consciousness*, based on physical and social awkwardness and a growing awareness of the outside world, as well as on a

(iii) *Preoccupation with Sex*, and the frustration consequent upon it.
These, we thought, led to both

(iv) *Escapism*, through idealism and a brash self-confidence as well as to

(v) *Rebelliousness*, non-conformity and irresponsibility.

We agreed that we would concentrate on these five main areas, and that the exhibition should consist of a series of five participatory displays, each one representing one area.

The next step was to try to define these emotions more precisely, and to consider ways in which they might be evoked in the visitors to our exhibition. For this purpose we agreed to divide into five working parties for the rest of the session, each to be prepared to report back to the whole group next time with a clear statement of the emotional response that was to be sought, together with some suggestions as to how it might be evoked.

I did not at this stage think it necessary to formalise these groups, nor to suggest that they should go through the procedure of electing chairmen, keeping records, and so forth. Moreover, I suggested that we should not feel it necessary to keep the same groups eventually for mounting the various displays, so that people would have a chance to change if they wished. This enabled me to go on to say that, for the purposes of these initial discussions it would be a good idea to have approximately the same number in each group. As there were thirty-eight members of the topic group altogether, this would mean about eight to each sub-group. I then went through the headings we had suggested, asking for volunteers, and in fact this worked out fairly well, with people offering to join each group until the right number had been reached.

I think, incidentally, that this procedure of beginning with temporary working parties with the possibility of changing later has a number of important advantages. It means that members of the whole group can make choices between topics which might still be too vaguely defined for longer term preferences to be declared. It is reasonable that, before you decide which of a number of alternatives you are going to spend the next month or so working on, you want to be clear what they entail. But this may be a vicious circle for until some work has been done on them, it may not be possible to make the alternatives any clearer. The procedure of temporary working parties allows work to be done in clarifying alternatives without members of the whole group having to choose finally.

A second important advantage of this procedure is that it enables people to have a trial run at working in certain groups. You might think that you would like to work with A, B and C, but after a short spell with them in a working party, you realise that you would be better off in another group. Of course, if everyone decides to change for the final groupings, you might be worse off than before, but this rarely happens, and usually only a few changes are made. Thus, unsuspected incompatibilities can be resolved.

Another advantage is that it enables those who find it difficult to make up their minds even when the choices are clear, to express a preference without feeling that they are committing themselves to something they may not subsequently enjoy. No doubt as a result of the kind of schooling and upbringing endured by a large majority of our students, in which virtually everything is decided for them and any attempt at initiative usually earns reproof or punishment, a large number of schoolchildren reach maturity with little or no experience of decision-making. Hence, when faced with a real choice, and in the absence of parental or teacher guidance, they find it difficult to choose at all. Moreover, their previous experiences on the few occasions when they have acted on their own initiative make them fearful of making the wrong choice. Such students are in a pitiable condition. While accepting that the choices offered are for their own enjoyment, and that there are no penalties for making a wrong choice, they confess themselves still unable to choose, and hover wretchedly between one alternative and another. For such as these, the possibility of reconsidering their decision enables them to plump, arbitrarily, for one at random. It is my experience that they then rarely change their minds. Having once acted on their own, and finding no dire results to follow, this experience itself is so exhilarating that the actual content of their choice is of secondary importance.

Thus, working parties having been made up, the rest of the session was devoted to discussion in these new sub-groups. It is worth making two further points about the organization of the topic group at this stage. One concerns the question of a co-ordinating group. Unlike the drama topic, in which there was a good deal of administration and technical organization to be undertaken outside the various sub-groups, with the exhibition it seemed to me that there would be very little to be done outside the various displays. For this reason, instead of having a separate co-ordinating group with representatives from the sub-groups, it seemed to me more satisfactory to co-ordinate the whole exhibition with a small group of representatives from the display groups, who could meet when the occasion arose.

The second point concerns the overall direction of the enterprise. Unlike the drama topic, in which the appointment of a director was an essential, the exhibition did not seem to need a single directing intelligence. A number of general decisions had already been taken by the whole group in discussion, and such other general questions as arose could be decided, I thought, either by the group of representatives, or again through a general meeting. Moreover, the limited time available argued the need for minimizing organizational procedures and getting on with the displays themselves.

We had arranged for the display groups to report back the following session, and a number of them made informal arrangements to continue their discussions in their own time in the intervening period. Thus again was demonstrated the readiness of students to devote their own time and energies to work for which they had been given prime responsibility.

The first part of the second session was devoted to hearing these reports, which were mainly concerned with definition of the emotional areas we had agreed upon, though initial suggestions for the displays were also looked for. Further reading had been undertaken, and this was used to justify the definitions proposed. After each report, the whole group offered comments. The final definitions that were agreed to were :

Insecurity : that state of anxiety which arises from not knowing what is going to happen, and from not being sure of one's own responses, physical and emotional, to what does happen.

Self-consciousness : a state of embarrassment from feeling that one is somehow making a fool of oneself in front of people, perhaps from doing or saying the wrong thing, or from the apprehension that one's private fantasies and pre-occupations (with power, honour, glory, sex, etc.) will be made public and ridiculed.

Preoccupation with Sex : a combination of a guilty and shameful but obsessional curiosity about the actual facts of sexual behaviour, including the facts of menstruation, masturbation, animal sexuality, perversions, etc., and the sense of lyrical rapture which accompanies first love, holding hands, shy kissing, etc.

Escapism : a feeling of being persecuted by parental and other adult authority, which does not recognise one's true worth but keeps up a kind of persistent nagging about all manner of unimportant matters (dress, manners, personal appearance, social behaviour, tidiness, lateness of hours, etc. which prevents one from giving one's attention to the vital problem of realizing one's own potential, coupled with a desire to escape from this nagging.

Rebelliousness : a combination of hostility towards adult authority, and a pride in everything which enables one to demonstrate one's independence and rejection of it.

It was agreed that these characteristics did not constitute the total emotional picture of adolescence, and that to attempt to isolate certain aspects was itself a somewhat falsifying procedure. Nevertheless, in so far as adolescence was a process which took some time, during which at any particular moment one aspect might become more important than another, it was felt more suitable that the visitor should receive these experiences in sequence, instead of all together. Moreover, the very fact that the visitor would experience rapid changes of emotion (as we hoped) would itself be demonstrative of the moodiness of adolescence – one of its more important characteristics.[1]

As to the nature of the displays, some suggestions had been made. For insecurity it was thought that we should put the visitor into some dark and ill-defined situation, in which sounds, colours and tactile experiences could be given without warning and without explanation. This might, perhaps, be the most 'psychedelic' part of the exhibition, though the aim of the display would be to arouse apprehension rather than aesthetic pleasure. The working party on self-consciousness thought that it might be possible to arouse some feeling of embarrassment in the visitor by requiring him to talk about himself, by putting personal questions. This group thought that their display would best follow the sex display, and it might be that the visitor could be asked to talk about his or her reactions to the previous display. The sex group had thought that the visitor might be exposed to fairly lurid photographs from erotic magazines, and that a typical lavatory wall with suitable graffiti might arouse some of the curiosity and embarrassment which they had agreed were mingled in the adolescent's experience. This group, incidentally, asked me : 'How far may we go?' I replied that it was up to them, but that we did not wish to be prosecuted for pornography, and I should be sorry to lose my job! The escapist group suggested that the visitor might be subjected

---

[1] The group had been impressed with Anna Freud's well-known and vivid description of adolescence as a continuing alternation of contradictory moods; see her book *The Ego and the Mechanisms of Defence*, Hogarth, 1937, pp. 149 et seq.

to some kind of unpleasant experience – such as bright, flickering lights, or unpleasantly loud music – from which he would wish to escape. The rebellious group envisaged subjecting the visitor to a number of humiliating demands, towards which he would feel hostile.

The preparation of the displays

It seemed that the exhibition was taking some kind of shape, and certainly the members of the topic group were anxious to get on with the practicalities of their displays. I suggested that when the groups to set up the displays were formed, they should each elect a co-ordinator who should be responsible for organizing the work of the group as a whole, and should also be a member of a small co-ordinating group to meet from time to time to settle general problems. This was agreed, and we forthwith set about forming the display groups. As I had suspected, these consisted, for the most part, of the working parties, though in fact about half a dozen students changed their interests at this stage. Self-consciousness was the largest group, with nine members; escapism had eight, and insecurity, sex and rebelliousness had seven each. The rest of the second session was devoted to further discussions on the practical problems in hand. I called a meeting of the co-ordinators for half an hour before the session was due to begin the following week, and asked them to be ready to discuss the sequence of displays, and what materials each would require.

From the lively discussions that were going on, and from the purposeful way in which each group began to allocate responsibilities among its members for materials, design, further research, etc., it was evident that the topic had the interest and support of the students. I was particularly pleased about this, for although I had not met the members of this year before except as part of an audience for large-scale lectures, I knew that this topic group included a number of students who were reported to be lazy, un-co-operative or generally tiresome. It struck me once again that laziness is very rarely a natural disinclination to work, but is usually a declaration of antagonism to the kind of work expected. Given something that appeals to their interest and offers them responsibility, the laziest students are capable of self-discipline, enthusiasm and sustained hard work.

The co-ordinating committee met promptly at the hour fixed the following week. I was interested to see that several of those students whose names had been mentioned to me by other tutors as lazy had been elected. In accepting these roles, they had presumably not been motivated by a desire to evade work.

The committee worked quickly and efficiently. We agreed that each display group should rely upon its own membership for manning the exhibits, but that it could ask for guinea-pigs from other groups to try out different ideas at any stage during the construction stage. The sequence of the displays was settled. Insecurity seemed to be naturally the first, since this would set the emotional tone for the remainder of the exhibition. We had already agreed that self-consciousness should follow sex, and there seemed to be an argument for having this at the end of the exhibition, so that all preceding experiences could be drawn upon. Since escapism was a kind of rebelliousness, we agreed that it should follow the latter, and the final order was thus : insecurity, rebelliousness, escapism, sex, self-consciousness.

We confirmed that, as had been previously agreed, visitors should go through the exhibition singly, which meant that there would have to be some kind of signal to ensure that the visitor in each display moved on at the same time as the next. We agreed to work on the provisional allocation of two minutes in each display. The whole exhibition would thus take ten minutes to work through.

We then considered the layout of the rooms we had at our disposal. In fact the large hall had, at the end, a storeroom – at present filled with tables and bureaux. There was also a small store out of the corridor leading to the hall, and that corridor itself led out of a fairly large classroom which we could use as a waiting room. (See Fig. 2). It was clear that we should have to divide the hall physically into a number of cubicles, and I had previously asked the college bursar if we might use the stored furniture as a basis for the divisions. One important problem was that of ensuring that visitors who left the exhibition at the end did not meet those waiting to come in, or pass those already in the displays. We solved this problem by arranging the interior of the hall into three cubicles, bypassed by a long corridor. The store in the passage leading to the hall we allocated to the insecurity group, while the final display, on self-consciousness, we placed in the storeroom at the end of the hall, with instructions to this group that each visitor should be dismissed from this final display before the next one was admitted. Fortunately, there were some stairs leading out of the passageway, down to the old kitchens of the house, with a second set of stairs which reappeared in the entrance hall. Thus it would be possible to take each visitor round the whole exhibition, and with a certain amount

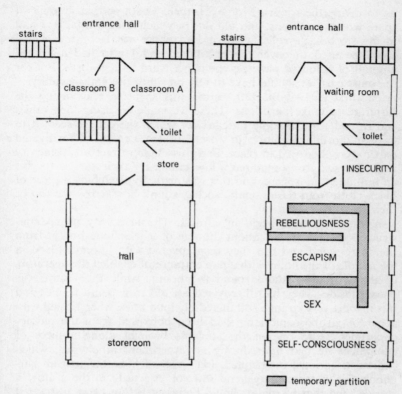

Figure 2: Available rooms before adaption for the exhibition

Figure 3: Allocation of rooms to the five sections of the exhibition

of judicious timing, ensure that no one person was seen by any other once they had entered from the waiting room. Moreover, if we were to allow all those wishing to enter the exhibition to first wait in the waiting-room, then they would not be seen by those who had left through the basement kitchen. (See Fig. 3).

There was a good deal of anxiety felt by members of the co-ordinating group lest visitors should somehow communicate their experiences to each other or to those waiting, but in fact this proved to be no problem at all when it came to staging the exhibition, as we shall see.

Finally, we discussed the problem of materials. We had been given permission to use the stored furniture, and this would enable us to divide the rooms. Moreover, there was a certain amount of spare wood, partitions, and old doors, which were available. I had in my store some rolls of corrugated paper, six feet wide, which could be used to cover the partitions, and I also had a limited amount of coloured paper, crêpe paper, card and so forth. But for the most part we should have to rely on simplicity and ingenuity.

The first part of the full session was spent in rearranging the furniture to make partitions. These we made by using long tables end to end, and standing bureaux (of which the college seemed to have an inordinate number in store) on them. Lengths of corrugated paper were then tied in place, and this made in fact a satisfactory wall. The sex group required a low ceiling for their cubicle to give an intimate atmosphere, and this was made by stretching a piece of black cloth from the dramatic society's junk box across the top of their section.

Work could now begin in earnest. The insecurity group constructed a small frame, about the size of a telephone booth, from the spare wood and this they then covered with hessian. Fixed in the middle of the floor, with a flap entrance, it enabled the operators of the scheme to stand round the booth, while the visitor was placed inside. They had discovered an old iron piano frame, and this made a very strange and incredibly loud noise when rasped with a bar. A stroboscopic lamp had been borrowed from the physics department, and one of the students brought along a piece of equipment he had built during an experiment in physics, which emitted a curious, interrupted, high-pitched buzz through an earphone. To increase the general state of insecurity in the visitor, it was decided that his pulse should be taken before being instructed to get inside the booth. As this operation took place in the dark, and the flap through which he had to scramble was thick and difficult to manage, the whole experience was likely to arouse some degree of apprehension.

Meanwhile the rebelliousness group had hit upon the ingenious idea of subjecting the visitor to a number of arbitrary orders from an authoritarian person whose outline could be made out by the visitor through a screen. A low stool was to be provided for the visitor, and the authoritarian figure was to be ensconced behind the screen, on a table, looking down on him. While the visitor was responding to these instructions, two or three members of the group would appear from round the corner, and urge him to ignore them. They would themselves reply to the figure behind the screen, questioning its right to give orders and generally answering back.

In this way, they would 'wean' the visitor away from the authority, encourage his sense of defiance, and send him on to the next display.

Here, in the escapism section, he would be met with a barrage of arbitrary orders, questions, demands and personal criticisms from two members of the group, who would ignore his attempts to answer. There was also to be a revolving flashing light, and a tape-recorder, playing a hotchpotch of jazz, classical music, pop music and *musique concrète*.

In the sex cubicle the visitor would be required to participate in three ways, directed by three arrows hanging from the low ceiling. The first would direct his attention to an exhibition on one wall, arranged in three parts: the first a montage of photographs of large-breasted nudes in provocative postures, the second a display of romantic scenes of young lovers, the third a collection of sanitary towels and contraceptives. The second arrow would point to a screen with a small gap, through which he would be asked to put his hand. On doing so, he was to be given a rubber sheath to hold. The third arrow would lead his attention to the wall on which a number of obscenities had already been chalked. A piece of chalk was hanging from the ceiling on a string and he would be instructed to write something. Meanwhile, in the corner of the cubicle a young couple would sit opposite each other at a small table, lit by a candle, and gazing into each other's eyes, totally ignoring the visitor.

Finally, on leaving the sex cubicle, the visitor was to be ushered into the dark storeroom, given a cup of water full to the brim on a saucer, and ordered to walk along a raised platform, made of old bedsprings, covered with sheets of paper. Rounding the corner he would find a cushion on the floor, on which he would be instructed to sit by one of a row of seated persons, high on a table above him, whose faces he would not be able to see in the dark. Having sat down, with a bright light in his eyes, he would find in front of him, fixed to the dais, more nude erotica. He was to be asked questions about what he had written on the wall in the sex display, his reasons for writing what he did, his views on the pictures in front of him, and so forth.

Work in progress

During the third session, the displays began to take shape. The insecurity booth was constructed and trials begun on the effects of various noises and lights. The rebelliousness group made a wooden frame which they covered with a large sheet of tracing paper. This was mounted on the end of a table, and the sides built up with crêpe paper. The 'authority' sat, cross-legged, on the table, with a table light throwing his silhouette on to the screen. The fact that the visitor, crouched on a low stool on front of this screen, could see under the table, made the figure behind more effective, since it appeared to consist solely of head and shoulders. The escapism group experimented with various lights and tapes, though their attempts to construct a flickering device proved abortive in view of the fact that the light outlets were limited, and we had agreed not to put more than a hundred-watt load on each socket, having regard to the antiquity of the wiring.

The sex group succeeded in making their cubicle dark and inviting. The low ceiling with the candle-lit couple at the table provided a most effective setting. A portable screen was arranged in one corner, behind which a member of the group could sit, putting sheaths into the hands that would, we hoped, be obediently thrust round according to the directions. The graffiti wall was already covered with a good collection of obscene words and drawings. I noticed that when I first inspected the wall, the members of the group, though busy elsewhere, were covertly watching to see my reactions and they seemed quite relieved when I added my own contribution for good measure. The self-consciousness group had used the remaining pieces of furniture to subdivide their room again. This enabled each visitor who had finished to be led out while the next was busy negotiating the catwalk made of bedsprings.

At a meeting of the co-ordinating committee towards the end of the third session, the suggestion was made that the reactions of the visitors should be recorded, and it was agreed that a new sub-group should be set up, with a representative from each of the display groups, to work this out. Accordingly, during the fourth session (which was the last before the exhibition itself), this new sub-group got together to consider ways to try to judge the success of the exhibition. A number of alternatives suggested themselves. One might be to call a meeting, subsequently, of all the visitors, to ask for their opinions. But it was felt that they might not all bother to come. On the other hand, it was pointed out that if we were to attempt to get their views immediately after the exhibition, they might not be prepared to give honest answers, particularly if they had in fact been emotionally moved by the experience, whereas if we were to wait until they had been able to achieve a more detached, objective view of their experience, their answers might be more accurate. The possibility of a questionnaire, issued at the time but to be completed later, was discussed, but again it was felt that we might not get a 100 per cent return. The only sure way of getting a response from every visitor would be to interview them immediately after they had finished. It was suggested that an objective check on whether or not they had experienced any emotional reaction at all might be provided by a comparison of pulse rates before and after.

After agreeing on an interview as soon as the visitors emerged from the exhibition (which would have the added advantage of delaying longer their 'contamination' of any people who might be waiting to enter), the group drew up a simple pro-forma for use by the interviewers.

The exhibition

On the day of the exhibition we had agreed to assemble early, so that the display groups could have a last chance at testing their displays. In accordance with our agreement, 'guinea-pigs' from other displays were asked to try out the different arrangements, and a number of the members of the group (including myself) went through the whole exhibition. What was particularly interesting about this last was that, although we knew more or less exactly what was going to happen in each section, we were all nevertheless apprehensive about going through, and certainly ourselves experienced a number of emotions (most of them appropriate!) as we did so. This augured well for the success of the exhibition itself.

A few last-minute alterations were made. The sex group decided to change the couple who had been sitting at a small table, gazing into one another's eyes, and instead they lay down on a mattress, locked in each other's arms. This new arrangement seemed to gratify the two who had been cast for this role (who were already known not to be averse to each other!) but I felt this change a pity, as when they were simply sitting at a table, their continued ignoring of the visitors seemed more effective and emphasized the idea that being in love somehow removes one from the ordinary world of communication. Moreover, it seemed to me that there was already too much emphasis in the sex cubicle on what might be called the flesh, and not enough on the romantic, idealised spirit. However, this seemed to be the wish of the group and I did not want to interfere at the last minute.

We had advertized the exhibition on the students' notice board, inviting not only the other second-year students who were busy with alternative topics, but also first years whose response was thought more likely to be authentic. We had no idea how many would in fact attend and at the last minute we began to wonder whether anyone would come at all. However, as the time drew near it became apparent that we should be reasonably well attended, and five minutes before the exhibition was due to be opened, a respectable queue of twenty or so, including one or two of my own colleagues, were found waiting outside the door of the waiting room in the hall.

We admitted them to the waiting room singly. We had hung the walls of this room with notices: 'Do not talk', 'No smoking', 'No spitting', 'Silence', 'No radios' and even 'No breathing'! The incoming visitor had first to sit in front of the receptionist who took his pulse and made a record of its rate, giving him a numbered token to hold. (Position (1) in Fig. 4). He was then told to wait on the benches, which had been drawn up in lines. (2) Visitors were admitted to the waiting room until the benches were full; the remainder queued outside the door. Those waiting were admitted to the exhibition itself at timed intervals of one and a half minutes; as each visitor went in, so all those waiting moved up one position, and a new one was allowed in from the queue outside the door.

The atmosphere in the waiting room was tense. Despite the somewhat facetious tone of our notices, everyone appeared to take the matter very seriously, and there were only a few attempts at talking; these were quickly silenced by the members of the group on duty in the room. By the time the waiting room was full, it took over half an hour for a visitor to move from the back of the queue to the front, yet these normally impatient students all sat quietly and obediently waiting their turn. Nor was this the full extent of their patience, for a number were prepared to wait in the queue outside the door before ever gaining admission. I spent a part of the afternoon interviewing visitors both before and after admission. Those I spoke to in the queue mostly said that it was curiosity that led them to wait, though one or two found it difficult to explain just why they were there at all. Most admitted to some kind of apprehension about what they would find inside. None, it appeared, had much idea of what in fact the exhibition consisted of, and it seemed that the group had managed to keep the details secret from their friends. It was also clear that the exhibition was looked upon as some kind of ordeal, and several of the waiting visitors seemed to regard it as a challenge and had assumed a nonchalant they-can't-scare-me attitude. I pointed out to those waiting that there was absolutely no obligation on them to go. They laughed somewhat uneasily, but remained in the queue.

Meanwhile, in the waiting room there was silence. We had arranged that the signal for visitors to move forward to the next

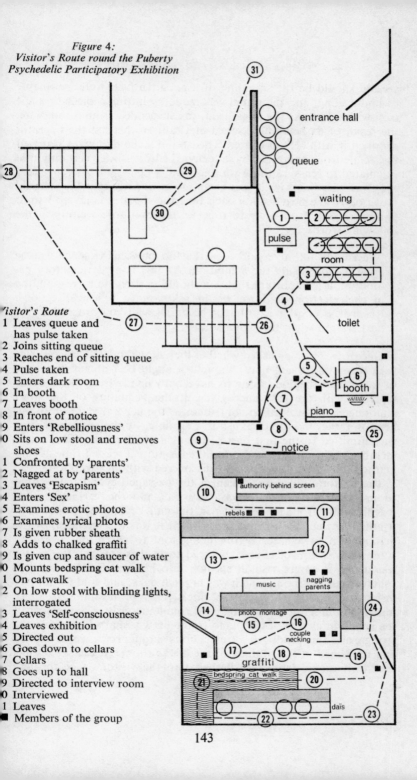

Figure 4:
Visitor's Route round the Puberty
Psychedelic Participatory Exhibition

entrance hall

queue

waiting

pulse

room

toilet

booth

piano

notice

authority behind screen

rebels

music

nagging
parents

photo montage

couple necking

graffiti

bedspring cat walk

daïs

Visitor's Route
1 Leaves queue and
  has pulse taken
2 Joins sitting queue
3 Reaches end of sitting queue
4 Pulse taken
5 Enters dark room
6 In booth
7 Leaves booth
8 In front of notice
9 Enters 'Rebelliousness'
10 Sits on low stool and removes
   shoes
11 Confronted by 'parents'
12 Nagged at by 'parents'
13 Leaves 'Escapism'
14 Enters 'Sex'
15 Examines erotic photos
16 Examines lyrical photos
17 Is given rubber sheath
18 Adds to chalked graffiti
19 Is given cup and saucer of water
20 Mounts bedspring cat walk
21 On catwalk
22 On low stool with blinding lights,
   interrogated
23 Leaves 'Self-consciousness'
24 Leaves exhibition
25 Directed out
26 Goes down to cellars
27 Cellars
28 Goes up to hall
29 Directed to interview room
30 Interviewed
31 Leaves
■ Members of the group

143

section should be the sounding of a gong. In fact, were we unable to find a gong, and the signal was made by hitting a piece of angle iron with a bar. As the angle iron was suspended from a thin wire, the result of its being hit seemed inevitably to be that the operator dropped it with a loud clatter. This sound – the dissonant clang of the angle-iron, followed by a heavy clatter – was certainly not calculated to reassure those waiting.

Before they went in, it was necessary to explain that they should move on to the next section each time the signal was given. I took it upon myself from time to time to address those waiting in the following words:

'We should like to assure you that no physical violence will be done to you inside the exhibition. As this is a participatory exhibition, it is important that you should participate by responding in each section, and we would ask you to follow directions. Regardless of what you might be doing, will you proceed to the next section when the signal sounds?'

One or two women asked whether they should take their handbags with them, and I said that I thought it might be better if they were to leave them behind, so as to have both hands free. This advice, together with the assurance given at the beginning of the short announcement, seemed to contribute to the general state of apprehension rather than to diminish it. Certainly, by the time the visitor was admitted to the first part of the exhibition, where there was a member of the group waiting to take his pulse a second time, a very marked increase in the rate was discovered without exception.

The visitor's pulse was taken in the passage beyond the waiting room (4). The light here was very dim and the various sounds reaching him from the displays in the hall beyond no doubt contributed to the state of insecurity which it was the intention of the first section to arouse. Before being told to enter the Insecurity room (it was not, of course, referred to in these terms), the visitor was asked to insert a small speaker into his ear (5). He was then ushered into the room, which was in pitch dark, and told to clamber inside the booth, through the thick folds of hessian (6). Once inside, a number of things happened simultaneously. The member of the group in charge of the piano frame drew a sharp bar across the strings, and this produced a tremendous surging roar, which echoed and re-echoed in the confined space of the room. At the same time, the stroboscopic lamp was flashed into the visitor's face through

144

the hessian, and another member of the group doused the material liberally with a pungent-smelling chemical, which smelt curiously of a mixture of rubber and almonds. The amplifier wired to the earphone began to emit an intermittent high-pitched buzzing.

There is no doubt that the experience of all this, particularly in the blackness of the booth, was disturbing. Even those of us who knew what caused the several stimuli found it disquieting, and the effect on those unprepared for it must have been considerable. The piano frame in particular produced an immense sound which gave one the feeling of being almost physically assaulted in some vast cavern. Moreover, this charivari was succeeded by a period of silence and darkness, which, although it lasted for only a few seconds, was in fact more alarming than what had preceded it.

The visitor was then extricated from the booth and instructed to proceed down the passage and turn right (7). At the same time, the member of the group who sent him on sounded the signal, in the manner already described, and at this, a new visitor was admitted from the waiting room.

Facing the first visitor at the end of the passage was a wall constructed of furniture and corrugated card, on which was pinned a small notice which read: 'Remove your shoes'. In fact, however, the passage was so dimly lit (the windows having all been covered with black or red paper), and in any case the visitors tended to be in such a state of confusion that this notice was generally unobserved (8). Hence, when the visitor rounded the corner and found himself in front of the illuminated screen, behind which could be seen the outline of an apparently detached head and shoulders, he was still in his shoes (9). This gave the authority the opportunity to say sharply:

'Why haven't you removed your shoes?'

Most visitors replied that they had not realised that they were required to.

'There was a notice telling you plainly to remove your shoes. Do you usually ignore instructions?'

The visitor was afraid that he had not seen the notice.

'It was perfectly clear. Sit down and take off your shoes.'

Upon receiving this instruction, most visitors began to comply with it. As they were sitting on the low stool, struggling to remove their shoes, two or three members of the rebelliousness group would appear and ask them what they were doing.

'Well, he told me to take my shoes off' might be the reply.

'Why take any notice of him?' the newcomers would demand. 'You haven't got to do what he says.'

At this point the authority behind the screen would repeat his instructions peremptorily.

'Get on and take your shoes off! Why don't you do what you're told?'

The newcomers would side with the visitor and begin to answer the authority back.

'Why should he take any notice of you! Why don't you shut up!'

And to the confused, irresolute visitor:

'Don't you do what he says. He's got no power over you.'

This section of the exhibition was, in fact, extremely effective. On going round myself, prior to its opening, despite the fact that I knew exactly what was going to happen, I nevertheless found myself caught in that strange state of irresolution, and there was no doubt that the appearance of the 'rebels' and their 'cheeking' the authority produced a definite state of defiance and a feeling of temporary but strong loyalty to the rebellious group.

The irresolution was exacerbated by the fact that, at the outset of the exhibition, visitors had been asked to co-operate by following instructions, and so, whatever they might have felt about the order to remove their shoes, they felt an obligation to comply. No doubt this willingness was heightened by the half hour or more spent in the waiting room, in which, as I have mentioned, visitors obediently did as they were told. And we may suppose that the brief spell in the Insecurity booth was not without some contributory effect to the irresolution.

Moreover, although the authority figure was anonymous, there was a circumstance which added to its power and this was a small hole, not much larger than that made by a compass point, in the middle of the opaque screen. This was originally intended for the purpose of allowing the authority to be able to observe the reactions of the visitor to his directions. But it also was found to contribute to the sense of power he was able to exercise. The visitor, squatting on the low stool, was able to make out, through the hole, the movement of an eye behind it, and this gave greater immediacy to the figure, without detracting from its anonymity.

My own feeling was that this display was most ingenious and the students responsible were to be congratulated for contriving an extremely successful situation with such simple materials. It certainly was effective in arousing, in the majority of visitors, exactly the emotions prescribed at the outset.

When the signal was sounded, the rebels ushered the visitor, who by this time had replaced his shoes, on to the next section, where he was met by a couple of parent-figures who immediately began to abuse and criticise him, asking sharp questions without waiting for his answers and generally subjecting him to a barrage of personal criticisms (12). This barrage was complemented, if that is the word, by a tape-recorded programme of electronic music, played extremely loud, and it had been intended to add the effect of flickering and revolving coloured lights, though the mechanics of these broke down.

Again, most visitors tried to participate in the exhibition by answering at least some of the questions. As many of the visitors were well known to the 'parents', a good deal of the criticism could be well-informed, and in some cases a dialogue arose. But on the whole I think this was the weakest section of the exhibition; it was too like the previous display, and did not grow logically out of it, as it should have done. It was interesting that the student who had been elected convenor of this group was not exactly famous for his industry, and I had the impression that the whole display group lacked the degree of enthusiastic enterprize that was common among the others. On the other hand, it could certainly be argued that the convenor gave more to this than to any other part of the education course, so the topic-work approach was at least justified in this respect.

From the escapism section the visitor passed, at the sound of the gong, to the Sex cubicle (14). The low ceiling produced a sensation of a cave, which was somehow enhanced by the fact that the only illumination came from a number of flickering candles. Three large white cardboard arrows hung from this ceiling, directing the visitor's attention, first to the montage of photographs of alternate erotically-posed nude women, romantic pictures, and menstrual and contraceptive apparatus; then (17) to the screen, behind which he was instructed to reach his hand; and lastly (18) to the wall partly covered with graffiti, to which he was invited to add his contribution. In the corner, the necking couple lay on a mattress.

The reactions of visitors to this section were mixed. Some were genuinely interested, others were embarrassed, a few were unmoved. Most of the men students added to the graffiti the four-lettered words that the situation seemed to demand, while the women for the most part contented themselves either with mere inspection or ambiguous remarks. Perhaps this section was less effective than it might have been because the students visiting it were determined not to be embarrassed or surprised. Moreover, even though the details of the exhibition did not seem to have become widely known outside the topic group itself, nevertheless the possibility of there being displays connected with sexuality was a reasonable guess, and no doubt most visitors came prepared to find something of the kind.

Finally, at the sound of the signal, the visitor moved to the door of the last room, where a member of the group gave him a cup and saucer to hold, the cup filled to the brim with water (19), and instructed him to mount and walk along the cat walk leading round to the self-consciousness interviewers (20). In the mean time, the last visitor was ushered out.

The catwalk itself was a successful device. Sheets of cardboard had been laid across old bedsprings, which were raised a foot or so above the ground. These were treacherously insecure to walk upon, particularly in the semi-dark, and trying at the same time not to spill the cup of water. As the visitor rounded the corner, he was ordered to sit down on a cushion placed below the interviewing bench, and in front of a strong light (22). Before him, pinned to the foot of the dais, were more erotic photographs. (The members of the topic group seemed to have access to an unlimited supply of these, incidentally!)

Most visitors asked what they should do with the cup and saucer of water, but they were given no answer. Certainly the majority seemed to feel the need to explain what they were about, as for example by saying: 'Well, I'll put it down here' or 'I was asked to bring it round'.

The interviewers varied their techniques with each visitor; most were asked to describe the photographs in front of them and to say what they had written on the wall. A typical reply to the first question was the answer:

'Well, they're photographs of nude women.'

'How do you know they're women?' they would be asked.

'Well, it's obvious, isn't it?'

'Is it? Why is it obvious?'

One or two of the bolder spirits were seemingly well-prepared to detail and name the anatomical clues which identified the sex of the photographed subjects, while others were most reluctant to do so, and skated round the subject in a variety of ways.

On the whole, I thought this section quite effective. Certainly when I went through the exhibition myself, I found it difficult to talk naturally about the photographs or to give good reasons for what I had written on the wall. The insecure walk in the dark on the bedsprings, the low cushion, and particularly the cup of water, all served to accentuate the oddness of the circumstances. Moreover, though I knew perfectly well who was on the platform, yet I could not make out their faces in the dark, and the disembodied questions were disturbing and certainly succeeded in arousing a sense of self-consciousness. This experience was confirmed by the other members of the topic group who went through the exhibition as guinea-pigs, and though a number of our visitors denied that they found the interrogation at all unnerving, their speech was noticeably unrelaxed. Some spoke too quickly, even breathlessly; others gave clipped, brusque answers. One of my colleagues, a tutor from another topic group, kept up a running commentary during the whole of the interrogation, scarcely allowing the hidden figures time to put their questions!

This section concluded the exhibition proper. The gong was the signal for the member at the door to give the next visitor, arriving from the sex cubicle, a cup and saucer of water, and to set him off on the catwalk. This took long enough for the previous visitor to be relieved of his cup, and ushered out. He passed down the long corridor formed by the backs of the bureaux, and was directed down the stairs to the old kitchens. Here further members of the group led him to the servants stairs, back up into the hall, and into the interview room, where he was asked for his views on the exhibition.

It is difficult to know what significance to attach to the answers given at the interviews. A number of our visitors, in particular our male visitors, avowed that they had not been in the least moved by the exhibition which they had found, so they said, rather boring. Yet our pulse-rate test showed that there was not a single visitor whose pulse did not increase significantly, and for many, the increase was considerable. It seems likely that the emotions experienced were, in fact, sufficiently disturbing for the students to wish to disavow them – certainly to us, possibly to themselves.

Some of the visitors agreed that the exhibition had been successful, or partially successful, in arousing various emotions, but not all agreed that the emotions were those they had experienced in adolescence. Again, we experienced difficulty in interpreting these results. It was possible that they spoke the truth. On the other hand, it was also possible that they did not remember their own emotional experiences, especially those at a time in their lives which had been not only disturbing, but also only very recently put behind them.

After the interviews, our visitors were free to go. Very few stayed to say anything to those waiting in the queue, so we could be fairly confident that there was little 'contamination' of those waiting to go in by those who had already gone through.

In all, we managed to get fifty-nine visitors through the exhibition. A fair number were still anxious to attend, and were prepared to queue and wait to do so, but by half-past four the members of the topic group themselves were exhausted. We had a quick cup of tea, and then dismantled the entire exhibition in three-quarters of an hour.

Post-mortem on the exhibition

I called a meeting of the members of the topic group for the following week, in order to enable us to draw what conclusions we could from the exercise. Topic work was now officially over, and the students were making preliminary visits connected with their group work in schools. I was therefore anxious to use the experience of the exhibition as a learning situation while it was still fresh in our minds, and then to round the matter off. However, I had not reckoned with the interest which the topic had aroused in the members of the group.

Although, I think it would be fair to say, from the amount of discussion that the exhibition had given rise to in the rest of the college, and from the enthusiastic attendance of our visitors, that the puberty participatory exhibition had been fairly successful, yet the tone of the post-mortem was far from self-congratulatory. The members of the small sub-group that had undertaken the interviews began by pointing out the various reasons why the answers they had received could not altogether be relied upon – reasons which have already been mentioned, such as the reluctance of students to admit to emotions which they might be ashamed or embarrassed about, or the possibility that those visitors who claimed to have experienced different emotions during their own adolescence might in fact be genuinely deceiving themselves in their recollections. But, having pointed out these possible sources of error, they went on to say that it seemed to them that the exhibition had failed, in most cases, to achieve what had been intended: that is, the re-evocation of the emotions of early adolescence. They reported to the group a number of criticisms that had been made by the visitors: in particular, that the exhibition exaggerated the unpleasant aspects of adolescence, and laid far too great an emphasis on sexuality, particularly on what might be called its sensational aspects.

While there was a certain amount of defensiveness in the reactions of the topic group to these reported criticisms, nevertheless their general attitude was serious and self-critical. A lively discussion followed which led the members of the group increasingly towards the view that they had made a basic initial over-simplification in assuming that there was such a thing as a typical emotional pattern to adolescence. Despite the caveats about accepting our visitors' evidence, we eventually came round to accepting that the criticisms made were sufficiently general as to be convincing.

I was immensely impressed by the readiness of the group to accept these strictures on something into which, after all, they had put a good deal of energy and thought. They did not – as well they might have – use the perfectly valid objections to their visitors' criticisms as a reason for ignoring them. They became conscious, not only of the shortcomings of the exhibition, but also of the limitations of their own understanding of the topic itself, and this led to their request that more time should be found in their programme for further discussions on the subject.

I was, of course, delighted at this spontaneous suggestion from the students. If the topic had had the result of leading them to want to know more, then it had certainly justified itself. We agreed on a further meeting the following week, and also on a suggestion that we should put up a notice, inviting any first- or second-year student who had actually visited the exhibition, to join us and contribute to our discussions.

In the event, only two visitors turned up for our discussion. Both admitted that the exhibition had been effective in arousing various emotions in them, though both went on to say that these emotions were only a part of the whole emotional complex that they had themselves experienced during adolescence. The members of the topic group were willing to accept this criticism and to admit that the exhibition as a whole had suffered from a number of short-comings, of which this particular oversimplification was but one. In passing, I think it is important to notice that readiness to accept informed, objective criticism is itself a sound criterion of intellectual maturity, and there is no doubt in my mind that part of that maturity derived from the fact that these students had been given full responsibility for the exhibition.

This admission led in turn to a recognition of the fact that the members of the group themselves had only just come to accept the truth of the generalization that any generalizations about the characteristics of adolescence are almost certain to be dangerous oversimplifications. I reminded them of the fact that, during my own first-year lectures on the subject, I had emphasized this very point. No doubt many of them had made a note of it at the time. They agreed that no doubt they had, but that learning something from lectures and reading was one thing; coming to see the truth of the matter for themselves was another – a splendid justification of the topic approach, and further confirmation of my own view of the limited value of lectures.[1]

This led me to ask the group whether they thought that it was in any way possible to communicate these important truths more effectively than had evidently been the case in my own lectures. As it happened, I had to give a similar lecture to the present first-year students in two months' time. Could they suggest a means by which the new generation of students could be persuaded that what was said during lectures was not simply something to be written down and then forgotten, but was intended as something which would illuminate their own understanding of the children they had to teach. The generalization under discussion, which the topic group had finally arrived at by themselves, was a case in point. Too often teachers prepared and gave their lessons as if all children were the same, intellectually as well as emotionally, despite the fact that the teachers had, without doubt, made notes during their student days of the fact that individual children develop at different rates and in different ways. Would it be possible for the topic group to persuade their fellow students of this central truth in such a way that it would be meaningful information for them, instead of simply another lecture note?

[1] It may be reasonably asked, then, why did I give lectures at all, particularly in view of my brave resolution, made during my study leave, not to do so? In fact, the whole question of large-scale lectures is one that has occupied the members of the education department at my college a great deal. If the expertise of one person is to be made available to two hundred and fifty students, and given that he does not have time to meet them in separate groups, small enough for question and answer, there must clearly be some kind of formal confrontation. Education tutors devote a good deal of time and thought to the problems of making these confrontations effective, by the use, among other things, of transparencies on the overhead projector, of films and slides, of recordings, of dramatic interludes, of worksheets and working situations, and of the importation of children and adults. It is extremely unusual for a year lecture in education to consist of a formal lecture on the traditional model. There is, of course, the danger that the use of our teaching aids will become more important than the content of the lecture itself. One way by which we hope to overcome the limitations of lecturing is by holding discussion groups immediately following lectures in which education tutors, who have themselves attended the lecture, act as chairmen. Sometimes the lecturer is freed from this role in order to circulate among the discussion groups to answer technical questions outside his colleagues' own competence.

This question was one that the students naturally found challenging and interesting, and they agreed that they might try. How might this be done? Presumably not by lecturing themselves since, as they generously pointed out, it might be supposed that I had some little skill in the art of lecturing which they lacked. No, it was the form of the lecture, rather than the content, which was at fault, they decided. If the content could be presented more vividly, more dramatically, then it might make an impact on the student audience. It had already occurred to me that the topic group might agree to a dramatic performance of some kind, but I preferred to wait until the suggestion came from them, which it did, soon enough.

In fact, two alternative proposals were put forward: the group might mount a straightforward dramatic presentation of emotional and social development at adolescence, with emphasis on individual variations; or, alternatively, the group could dramatise the problems which had attended the mounting of the psychedelic exhibition, including this very discussion. It was argued that this latter might have a particular impact, in so far as the audience would be expected to identify with the student players. Both proposals had a group of supporters and after some discussion of the merits and demerits of each, it was agreed that the two groups should discuss among themselves further details, and that we might then have a further meeting together, at which we could decide between them.

In the event, at this next meeting, only one group turned up – that supporting a straightforward dramatic presentation of puberty. It included one or two students who were already particularly interested in drama, and who wanted to experiment with a performance in the round. As the supporters of the alternative scheme had not appeared, we went forward with preparations on the lines suggested. But what was particularly interesting was that as the plans progressed, so the group found itself committed to precisely the same heresy that they were supposed to be combating. In order to give the performance dramatic impact, it had been decided to centre the events round the life of a particular adolescent. He was to be played by Willis, one of our more unconventional students, with a reputation for that quiet effrontery which, as E. M. Forster reminds us,[1] is the proper attitude of any good democrat towards the establishment. In the event, Willis turned out to have a natural talent for acting. But in the working out of the scenes, the group found itself forced to make precisely the kind of generalizations about adolescence which it had

[1] In *Two Cheers for Democracy*.

already decided to discountenance. Attempts were made to over-come this by introducing other characters – the precocious, rebel-lious leader of the gang; the shy, and somewhat conformist girl-friend; but there was no doubt that the dramatic interest of the performance centred on the adolescent himself, who Willis depicted as a shambling, confused and indecisive youth, whose fantasies of himself were at sad variance with the facts. This was undoubtedly an effective portrayal of one kind of adolescent, and it also high-lighted characteristics to be found in most adolescents, but it was again being presented as the *typical* adolescent, and after two meet-ings at which the running script had begun to take shape, this fact was admitted by the members of the group.

However, at about this time, two members of the rival group turned up, demanding to know why their own approach had been neglected. After agreeing that they had, in fact, been given the opportunity to present their suggestions (with which, as it turned out, they had made little progress), they agreed to join the present group. The latter had just reached this point of recognition that they were well on the way to repeating the error of the exhibition. The newcomers then suggested that one way of overcoming the problem would be to adopt at least one of their suggestions – to re-enact this very discussion, and invite the participation of the audience.

This proposal struck us as a good one, and we made rapid progress. The form the presentation was to take was to be that of a straight-forward lecture by myself, interrupted by explanatory scenes played in the round in the centre of the audience. These scenes, depicting incidents from a day in the life of our 'typical' adolescent, would be designed to illustrate points made in the lecture. The lecture would end with some statement about its having been an attempt to depict the characteristic traits of adolescence, At this point, members of the cast would interrupt from the body of the hall, and we would then settle down to a discussion of whether we had not, in fact, made the same mistake again. This discussion would end with an invitation to the members of the audience to continue the argument in their own discussion groups.

We drafted out a rough script, in which cues were agreed for the alternate sections of lecture and drama to come in. Lighting was tried out with a student with experience of stage lighting, co-opted for the purpose. It was agreed that it would be a mistake to learn parts – the presentation would be partly spontaneous – but we went through the whole lecture twice, to get a sense of continuity and rhythm, and agreed upon most of the incidents. The 'adolescent'

154

recorded some fantasies, which could then be played over loud-speakers to represent his thoughts at different stages. One or two props were found, and the layout of the hall was worked out, but there was in fact very little rehearsal in the normal sense of the term, and I was very impressed with the mixture of ready co-operation and relaxed insouciance with which these young people, the majority of whom had never acted before, faced the prospect of acting without a script before an audience of 250 of their fellow-students.

The main preparations took place an hour before the lecture was due to begin. We set up a small stage in the centre of the auditorium with some moveable rostra, arranged the lighting and tested the speakers. The chairs were arranged in rows on all sides of the stage, facing inwards. A table doubled as the breakfast table at home, desks at school, dining tables and an air-raid shelter (in which the adolescent gave his girl-friend a characteristically unsuccessful kiss!) A rug was the only prop – it was used to cover our adolescent who was asleep in bed when the audience trooped in .

In fact, the dramatic lecture went off extremely well, and without a hitch. The players ad-libbed convincingly, but without over-doing it; no cues were missed for the changes from lecture to drama (there were seven dramatic interludes in all); the recorded thoughts came over well on the speakers; and the final discussion seemed to go well. The audience dispersed to their discussion groups stimulated in a way that I could never have hoped to have done by my own efforts.

It would be wrong, I think, to say that this was the end of the puberty topic. Several of the members of the group showed a continued interest in the whole problem of adolescence, and there is no doubt in my mind that this will lead in turn to further reading, discussions and activities. During their third year, these students will be offered a choice of study groups, several of which include some aspect of adolescence, and I shall be very surprised not to see several members of the topic group opting to attend those groups. Part of the legacy of formal education, which affects college curricula as much as it does those in secondary schools, is the assumption that all studies are neatly defined, with a clearly recognisable beginning and end, so that one's 'knowledge' of the subject can be pinned down, by notes or essays. This assumption goes with the sadly prevalent practice of regarding school or college learning as something which is divorced from everyday life, having relevance only to that remote and frightening world of examinations.

PART THREE

Participation in Planning

8

Student Participation in Course-Planning

The examples of group and topic work described in the previous chapters allowed the students to take a more active role in organizing their courses than is customarily the case in higher education and, as we have seen, provision was made for students to propose topics, as well as to organise their approach to them. All this, however, took place within a framework which had been planned by the college tutors. Indeed, there was a feeling that topic work was something set aside from the main course: a kind of educational treat within a more orthodox administrative structure of lectures, demonstrations and other classes. If I was really to test my belief in student acceptance of responsibility, I should have to go further than this. In this chapter I propose to outline some of the ways in which we have tried to give students a more direct part in planning and evaluating education courses.

The Education Consultative Committee

At a fairly early stage after my return from study leave, I set up an Education Consultative Committee. This consisted of an equal number of student representatives and education tutors. It was emphasized that the student members of the committee should be representative of the whole student body, and to this end we agreed that there should be two representatives for each of the three years of the certificate course, and that, preferably, one of each two

159

should represent students preparing for primary schools, and one those going into secondary teaching. We asked for these representatives to be elected by and from all the students of their year. In the same way, the six tutors were elected by the whole Department of Education, and an attempt was made to ensure that there were representatives of the various age-range and other specialist interests.

This committee normally meets once a term, though there is provision for an emergency meeting. The agenda is circulated beforehand, and consists of items put forward by both students and tutors. The committee has no executive function, but its recommendations are tabled for discussion by the Education Department's Executive Committee (which consists entirely of tutors), and they are often adopted.

During its early meetings, the Education Consultative Committee tended to concern itself with somewhat unimportant details, as if both students and staff were wary of discussing more basic issues in an atmosphere which was deliberately non-authoritarian. Too, the discussion was stilted; both sides were over-anxious to see the other's point of view, and there was little argument. If one of the tutors put forward a reason for some decision, then it was accepted without question by the students. However, as the members of the committee became more accustomed to meeting each other in this neutral context, they relaxed and began to deal with some of the central problems of the education course. (The committee was necessarily limited to discussing only education matters.) Arguments were made more forcibly, and students began to question the tutors' assumptions. Moreover, the students' confidence in the value of the committee grew once some of its earlier recommendations were seen to be adopted.

While the majority of items tabled by the student members tend to begin from complaints about the course, their contributions are by no means limited to criticism. Suggestions for improvement are put forward, both of the administrative arrangements and of the content of the course. Tutors use the committee to sound out student opinions on various proposals, and sometimes the student representatives are asked in advance of a meeting to conduct a survey of student opinion on a proposed major change.

There is no doubt that the Education Consultative Committee has made for improved student-staff relations, and has enabled the Education Department to adjust its course more nearly to student needs and problems. Critics of the committee sometimes argue that if the relationships between staff and students were satisfactory, there would be no need for the formality of a standing committee of this kind; students could mention problems to their tutors, and tutors could ask their students for their views. I think this criticism is based on a self-deceptive belief that everyone is reasonable and tolerant of criticism. The committee has the advantage that it constitutes a formally-recognized channel through which complaints, criticisms and suggestions may be put and will be discussed. Moreover, it enables students who are reluctant to approach tutors with personal criticisms to ask their representatives to put them forward in general terms. And the student representatives need not and do not hesitate to mention views which they know will be unpopular with tutors, since they are not necessarily their own views. A further advantage is that since there are several tutors present, no one tutor can dismiss a complaint as irrelevant unless it can genuinely be shown to be so. And the fact that the committee exists and meets regularly, means that problems are often brought forward before they have developed, whereas without a recognised channel of communication, students might well wait until a situation has developed to a major irritation before taking action, by which time it may be difficult to do anything about it.

At the same time, there are several shortcomings to the Education Consultative Committee. One is that the student representatives do not necessarily represent majority student opinion. As with any system of elections, it is often the more active, more outgoing students, or those with strong views, who are nominated. The latter often feel so strongly about the various matters discussed that they do not see the need to consult other students, and it is possible to get the impression that a particular course of action would be supported by the whole student body, whereas in fact enthusiasm for it is limited to a small but vocal minority which includes the representatives. However, an interesting development took place at the last meeting of the Education Consultative Committee which almost entirely meets this objection. I had given the student members notice of the tutors' intention of raising for discussion a proposal which involved a major change in the Education course over the three years. The editor of the student weekly news-sheet asked me for details of the proposed changes, which he then published in the news-sheet. Simultaneously, the student representative members of the Committee distributed a questionnaire, based on these details and inviting student opinion. A large number of replies were received, several of them containing extremely useful comments and suggestions, and having done an analysis of the replies, the student members of the Committee were in a very strong position to claim to be able to represent general opinion on this issue. All this took place spontaneously, without any suggestion from the tutorial staff, and it is a development which I very much welcome.

The main criticism that I would make of this committee, however, is of its purely advisory function. While it is true that several of the suggestions made by the students have in fact been adopted, there is no guarantee that they will be so, nor will the reasons for their rejection necessarily be brought back to the committee (though they normally are). The committee works at a stage removed from effective participation and consequently there is a certain air of remoteness about the discussions. Too, there is a temptation for tutors to withhold their most telling objections to a particular suggestion, knowing that they can advance them at a subsequent meeting of the Executive Committee. If students suspect that the real objections to a scheme are not being put forward, they may well come to feel that the committee is simply a palliative device.

On the other hand, it is worth reporting that the students have petitioned other departments in the college to set up similar consultative committees in other subjects, so it would appear that they attach some importance to the work that has already been done in education.

Staff-student working parties
A more direct participation in course-planning by students has been achieved by staff-student working parties. These are usually *ad hoc* groups, convened for a specific purpose. They may meet no more than once or twice, to plan a particular activity, or they may be constituted rather more formally, and meet regularly over a long period. The present basic structure of the junior-secondary course in education was worked out by such a working-party, consisting of three tutors and three students, which met throughout one academic year.

It has been the tutors' experience that, once they have accepted the idea of having students on course-planning committees – and this acceptance is not as effortless as it might sound, since it involves the voluntary abandonment of often deeply-held views of the proper relationship between tutor and student – the rewards are considerable. Not only do the students bring to the discussions new ideas and a relative freedom from the trammels of tradition, but also the very fact of joint planning leads to a sense of commitment from both sides that gives the course the vitality that comes from shared

162

purpose. Of course, it is only fair to say that not all students are full of new ideas; there are always a few who are more reactionary than the most conservative of tutors. Another problem is that the student members of working parties often see the aims of the course in terms of more practical and short-term objectives than do the tutors. For this reason, it is of the greatest importance that any joint planning committee begin its work with a discussion of course objectives.

The provision for the creation of such *ad hoc* working parties has now been built into the three-year course in education, and it may be of some interest to explain how this works in detail.

The general framework of the first-year course is planned the previous year by a team of tutors, and in so far as there are not yet in college any of the students who will be taking the course, there is obviously no opportunity for them to participate in the planning at this stage. However, comments on its outline are invited from the Education Consultative Committee and indeed, the distribution of questionnaires described above was in relation to proposed changes in the first-year course.

Within that framework, provision is made for first-year students to make some choices: for example, in their topic work, which is now done in the first term of the course. Group work has been moved back into the first year, and this also provides opportunities for choice and for a certain amount of autonomy in planning schemes, forming groups, and so forth, though all within the overall structure provided. In this way, the students learn to accept responsibility for their own learning by stages. To expect them to be able to take part in major decisions regarding their course before they are fully aware of the implications would be unreasonable. Perhaps even more important is the fact that many of them have had very little prior experience of making decisions at all, and they must first learn to do so within a relatively secure framework, which enables them to accept without too much personal hardship the consequences of wrong decisions.

It was decided to put group work into the first year of the course for a number of reasons. One was the very success of the group work itself, which has been accepted by an increasing number of local schools as a normal part of the curriculum, particularly in those comprehensive and secondary modern schools which have adopted team-teaching approaches.[1] Indeed, group work can no

[1] Participation in group work is not limited to such schools, incidentally; several independent schools are taking part in the scheme.

longer be regarded as experimental in secondary schools, but as a normal approach in the teacher's repertoire. And in primary schools, in which it had always found a place in the progressive class teacher's curriculum, the development of co-operative teaching has provided added opportunities for group work. Hence, it was felt that, instead of introducing group work to students in their second year of training as an 'experimental' approach, it should be included in their first year as part of (but not, of course, the whole of) their normal preparation for teaching practice.

The pattern of the first year's work in education for the three-year course thus includes the following elements:

TERM 1 (Year I)

1.1 A week's introductory course, followed by:

1.2 Two weeks' observation practice in primary schools (for all).

1.3 Topic work in the area of child development, undertaken by groups of students in small groups under the guidance of their education tutor.

1.4 Professional studies in, e.g. the teaching of reading.

1.5 Teaching aids workshops in the use of simple aids.

1.6 Towards the end of the term, a course in the organization of group work.

1.7 The formation of groups and provisional preparation and discussion of schemes for group work.

1.8 Preliminary visits to schools in which group work is to be done.

TERM 2 (Year I)

2.1 Group work a morning a week throughout the term, under the joint supervision of tutors and teachers.

2.2 A parallel course of lectures in the social psychology of groups.

2.3 Occasional lectures and demonstrations on aspects of group work; for example, planning visits, organizing displays, etc.

2.4 Discussions in college on the progress of group work in schools.

2.5 Further opportunities for work with teaching aids.

TERM 3 (Year I)

3.1 Teaching practice preparation groups.

3.2 Block teaching practice.

3.3 After teaching practice, the formulation of questions in discussion groups arising out of teaching and observation, the answers to which would enable the students to teach more effectively next time; for example, Why do some children learn to read at an earlier age than others? Why are some children rude or disobedient? etc.

The above outline relates only to their course in education. In addition, students pursue main and second subject studies, and follow curriculum courses in English, mathematics, art and craft, physical education and so forth. Nor does it include all the studies in education; parallel courses in, for example, health education are taken, but need not concern us here.

This framework provides students with opportunities to participate in the planning of their own courses at a number of points: for example, in the determination of the topic which they study in 1.3; in forming groups and deciding upon schemes for group work in 1.7; and in the formulation of questions in 3.3. This last activity enables the students to take part in planning ahead, for the content of Term 4 is based upon the questions which are formulated by the students during 3.3.

It will have been noticed that virtually no provision is made during the first year for the formal introduction of what might be called the contributory disciplines of psychology (except for child development), sociology, philosophy and the history of education. It has been our experience that if formal disciplines are introduced to students too early in the course, there is a considerable danger of their learning them as discrete bodies of 'pure' knowledge, unrelated to their teaching needs. This is particularly so with students who have developed the skills required to absorb and regurgitate factual data for presentation at written examinations. It is, of course, perfectly understandable that they should continue to apply these skills, especially as they owe their places in higher education to their mastery, and it is therefore necessary to wean them away from their indiscriminate application. This is a further reason for the placing of group work in the first year, which, as may be seen, contains a good deal of practical work with children.[1] From their practical experience, students begin to identify problems which they seek to be able to deal with. These problems in turn can lead to specific

[1] Visits and work in schools also form part of the first-year course; details o these have been omitted from the outline given above.

questions, and it is through the formulation of these questions that the students come to see the need for and the relevance of theoretical inquiry.

The first term of the second year is given over to an introductory presentation of the various contributory disciplines, organized in such a way as to lead towards (and to be seen to lead towards) answers to the questions the students have formulated. The content of the course is thus in a very real way the outcome of student participation, though the manner in which that content is organized and presented is, of course, decided by the tutors responsible.

During the second term, the students are given a second block teaching practice, this time unsupervised by college tutors (except in the case of weak students). In their preparation for this practice, the students are required to formulate their objectives, and to use the conceptual apparatus they have developed from the previous term's theory in doing so. Particular importance is attached to the comments written in their teaching practice files after every lesson given, and to ensure that time is available for this, they are expected to undertake not more than a half a full teaching load. It is intended that these comments should be analytical in approach; that is, they should be used to analyze the problems (and successes) of the lessons. At the end of the practice, students are required to use their experience to evaluate the theoretical conclusions they had previously arrived at. On their return to college, they use these notes to formulate further questions: this time attempting to place the problems they see in the broader context of modern society.

At this stage, a full-scale *ad hoc* team is formed of tutors and students to plan the course for the last term of the second year, which is designed to provide a theoretical approach to the answers to some of these problems. Seminar groups are formed, and reading lists drawn up. The names of those students who are to introduce the various topics to the seminars are decided upon, and the related lecture topics allocated to tutors on the basis of their expertise. A pattern which has so far proved extremely successful is for a lecture to be sandwiched between two discussion periods. The first discussion period, lasting for an hour, is given over to a seminar, introduced by one or two students, on preselected topics. All the members of the seminar group are required to have done a certain minimum amount of specified reading, while the seminar introducers have done further reading to enable them to elaborate on the topics. The whole year of students then attends the lecture, in which the tutor attempts to identify the main arguments of the topic, to explain any points likely to cause particular difficulty, and to summarize the general findings from research. He will also have suggested a number of questions for further discussion, arising out of the material so far. During the following and second discussion period, another member of each group will suggest answers to these questions, again based on suggested reading, and the discussion will become rather more speculative.

In planning the work of this term, based on problems raised in the first instance by the students themselves, the *ad hoc* team ensures that provision is made for continuity of study, and for each problem to be examined from different points of view. An example of such a problem, identified by students after their second teaching practice, was 'Streaming'. Four days (one in each of four successive weeks) were allocated to the study of this topic, which was approached from the point of view of (i) historical developments and administrative arrangements; (ii) psychological considerations; (iii) sociological considerations; and (iv) philosophical implications.

It will be appreciated that, if lists are to be published before the end of the second term, giving synopses of lectures, details of topics and questions before and after the lectures for seminar introducers, with annotated reading lists for (a) all members of discussion groups, (b) seminar introducers, and (c) those who wish to follow up the topics, a great deal of hard work has to be done by the *ad hoc* team responsible, and particularly by the tutors who are members of it. It would seem that there is an objection to this procedure in that insufficient time might be thought to be available for tutors themselves to undertake necessary reading, and to plan their work carefully. And yet it is surprising how much can be done under pressure, and in the conviction that the students' participating both in the planning and in the discussions themselves will be doing so because they feel that the studies they will be embarking upon are relevant to their own felt needs. Moreover, and this is the same point that was made above in the first chapter of this book, it need not be supposed that the tutors themselves will be entirely unprepared for the kind of problems which students will identify as relevant to their needs, just as it need not be supposed that primary teachers will be unprepared for the kind of topics likely to be selected by junior children for investigation at their level. Nevertheless, and this point cannot be stressed too strongly, it is through the identification of the problem by the students themselves that is aroused the kind of commitment to its detailed and rigorous study which is both the aim and reward of this approach to learning.

167

I have used the word *rigorous* in the last sentence deliberately. In a sense, the fulcrum of the argument of opponents to student participation in course-planning is the conviction that, given the chance, students and schoolchildren will choose easy and superficial studies to disciplined and systematic ones. This has not been our experience. Given the initial requirement that the students see the problems as relevant to their own needs (and this requirement is met by the provision that they identify the problems for themselves), then there has been an appetite for hard work and a willingness to embrace academic rigour that has not only been extremely heartening, but has also given us the necessary encouragement to extend the principle of participation further.

The outline of the second year of the three-year course in education, therefore, is as follows:

TERM 4 (Year II)

4.1 Theoretical introductory courses of lectures and discussions on the contributory disciplines, organized towards the answering of the questions formulated by the students in 3.3 above.

4.2 The above courses include both required elements for all students, and elective elements for student to specialize in further study in one of the disciplines.

TERM 5 (Year II)

5.1 Preliminary visits to schools in which students are to undertake their second teaching practice.

5.2 Professional studies, including opportunities for more advanced work with teaching aids.

5.3 Discussion and formulation of teaching-practice objectives.

5.4 Second block teaching practice.

5.5 Formulation of problems arising from teaching practice.

5.6 Formation of *ad hoc* working party of tutors and student representatives to plan course for Term 6.

TERM 6 (Year II)

6.1 Course of seminars, lectures and discussions the content of which was determined by the activities of 5.6.

6.2 School visits and conference.

6.3 Loobiad (see page 177).

Again, in the above outline, a number of details of parallel courses in education are omitted, and no reference is made to the work in main subjects, and in curriculum studies.

The final teaching practice is taken in the first term of the last year of the three-year course; that is, in Term 7. This arrangement has a number of disadvantages, and was originally made as a result of the problem of finding places for teaching practice during a period of rapid expansion in colleges of education in an area in which the schools were already heavily used by a large variety of training institutions. However, it does have one important compensatory advantage. It enables the student to put behind him or her the immediate anxieties and problems of the teaching situation, and to spend some time standing back from classroom in order to examine the wider implications of the role of the teacher. Again, as with classroom approaches, it is stressed that there is no one 'correct' interpretation of this role, but that every student must work out for himself or herself a personal synthesis; one that is, let us hope, consistent and logical, but one which rests ultimately upon personal values.

It is towards providing the opportunity for the student to arrive at this personal synthesis that the major part of the third year of education is directed. During the few weeks at the beginning of the first term (that is, Term 7), when a good deal of energy is necessarily given to preparing for teaching practice, time is also found for meetings of discussion groups to formulate the programme for the last two terms of the course. Again, an *ad hoc* working party is formed of tutors and student representatives, the latter of whom act as intermediaries between the working party and the student discussion groups. An outline of the course is worked out, and for this purpose no prior assumptions are made by the tutors, so that the working party is free to start from scratch. We have thus arrived at full participation of the kind that we could not feel able to make provision for earlier in the students' course. The working party is free, not only to determine the content of the course, but also its framework and organization.

It would be dishonest to pretend that the third-year courses, arrived at in this way, have been 100 per cent satisfactory. We have made many mistakes. One of our particular problems is that of ensuring that any given year is able to learn profitably from the mistakes of the previous year. One important procedural rule we have learnt as tutors, however, is that our misgivings should never be kept to ourselves, but should be spelled out at meetings of the working party. It often proves to be the case that these misgivings are echoed by the students themselves, and having once agreed upon their particular nature, it has generally proved possible to agree

PARTICIPATION IN PLANNING

upon necessary safeguards. As with all planning discussions, it usually proves most profitable to begin by examining objectives. And just as in schools, when a teacher who is embarking upon a child-directed project finds it necessary to remind the children at the outset of any requirements which may have to be met, so as to avoid disappointment and frustration when suggestions from the children prove to be impracticable, so tutors need to outline their requirements and objectives.

This is, after all, participation and not full democracy. The tutors are ultimately responsible for the course, and they cannot abrogate that responsibility. Nor should they seem to be doing so. A not unimportant aspect of outlining requirements at the beginning of a planning session is that it makes manifest that the tutors accept fully their own teaching responsibilities.

The third year of the course in education, then, cannot be spelled out, even in outline, beyond the following:

TERM 7 (Year III)
7.1 Teaching practice preparation.
7.2 Discussion groups to make suggestions for the course in Terms 8 and 9.
7.3 The formation of an *ad hoc* working party to consider these suggestions and to formulate and plan the course for Terms 8 and 9.
7.4 A final block teaching practice.

TERMS 8 and 9 (Year III)
The course as formulated in 7.3

Student-set assignments

An area in which student consultation has been particularly successful is that of the setting of assignments. The college course is assessed, not by a final examination, but by what is termed 'continuous assessment'. This is a misnomer, since the assessment is not continuous but intermittent, being based on a number of assignments set and marked at intervals throughout the three years of the course. These assignments are not done under examination conditions, but they are usually framed in such a way that students are required not only to give evidence of relevant reading, but also to quote and evaluate their own experience in schools or working with children. That part of the assignment which is given most credit in marking is usually the section in which the student is asked to give a critical evaluation of relevant reading and experience, and to advance suggestions for the solution of problems. Hence there is little opportunity for simply copying out sections of textbooks in answer to set questions. Moreover, the assignments themselves are not necessarily written essay-type answers to questions; they may and often do consist of practical work; for example, the staging of an exhibition to illustrate a particular topic, or the mounting of a dramatic interpretation of some educational question, or the construction of a filmstrip, or recorded programme or set of other visual aids.

Students participate in the setting of these assignments in two ways. One is by joining the team responsible for drafting the assignments. A successful example of this approach took place during the academic session in which I am writing this. One of the major education assignments is that which is set towards the end of the first year's work, to be done during the summer vacation and handed in the first day of the second year; this is referred to as the summer assignment. Last year's summer assignment for the junior-secondary students was drawn up by a team of tutors on the basis of a critical examination of various current changes taking place in school curricula and organization. A certain amount of choice was provided for, but within the framework of this general topic. During discussions with the second-year students, a number of criticisms were voiced of this assignment, and particularly of the fact that no opportunity was provided for them to use their summer vacation experiences in a meaningful way. Most students are obliged to find employment for at least a part of the summer vacation in order to supplement their grants and indeed, many tutors feel that this work experience, occasional and superficial though it may be, is of value to students who may have come to college straight from school. It was pointed out that the work experience could be made more valuable if an assignment required them to examine it critically from an educational point of view.

The tutors felt the justice of this criticism and at a meeting of the year group of students, asked for volunteers to join the team drafting the assignment for next year's first years. A small number came forward or were nominated, and they proposed several alternative questions. These were redrafted by the joint team of tutors and students, and ultimately three questions were accepted: one consisting of a modified form of the one set last year by the tutors, and two new questions, based on suggestions proposed by the students: one asking for a critical examination of the relevance of school curricula to school-leavers' employment, to be based on work experience; the other asking for the construction of a piece of learning apparatus to be based upon the observation of children (for example, at an adventure centre or playground). There is no doubt that the new assignment is a great improvement on the old.

The second way in which students take part in the setting of assignments is by the simple expedient of requiring them as individuals to propose their own titles. At least one of the assignments in the third year of the education course consists of what is termed 'a chosen topic'. This is any title of the student's own proposing within the whole field of education. The draft title has to be submitted to a tutor, together with a proposed bibliography. The tutor then normally discusses the range of the assignment with the student, and may make further suggestions about reading. The title may then be approved, or the tutor may require a synopsis before approving it. In marking such an assignment, credit is given for the fact that the title is of the student's own proposing, particularly if it demonstrates ingenuity or careful thought on his part.

Group assignments

Provision is made for students to offer the joint work of a small group as an assignment. Two or three students may propose a title which involves a co-operative piece of work. This is discussed by the supervising tutor with the members of the group and is subject to his approval, as with a chosen topic.

The education tutors have had several discussions among themselves, and with external examiners, on the problem of marking such an assignment. To require the members of the group to state which part of the assignment is the work of which student is to place an artificial limitation on the study as a whole. As a student once remarked to me: 'You often urge the need for a co-operative approach to education. To ask us to divide the work in such a way that we can identify individual contributions is not only to defeat a good deal of the aim of a joint enterprise, it is also to sacrifice ideals to expediency.' I felt this was fair comment. In the end we agreed to accept group assignments without any indication of individual contributions and to mark them as such, though naturally we require evidence of more work than with an individual assignment, in proportion to the number of students in the group. This is rarely more than three, though one of the best assignments I have ever had was from a group of six students on the postgraduate course. For this course, students are required to do a special study, which is a fairly substantial piece of work on a chosen topic, the equivalent of two or more normal assignments. Fairly early on in their course, the six students came to me with a proposal for a joint special study on the problems of immigrant children. I told them that we had never before accepted a group assignment from more than three, and that in any case the whole system of immigrant children was a highly sensitive area, in which even experience and skilled social researchers moved with extreme caution. Moreover, all research projects involving the use of schools (which this undoubtedly would) required the approval of the local education authority, and it was extremely unlikely that such approval would be given. I suggested that they go away and think again. As a final discouragement, I gave them a list of some twenty or so titles in the field of sociology of immigration, and said that they would in any case have to acquaint themselves with the literature before deciding on a title.

Ten days later they were back again. They had not only between them read all the books on my list but also had compiled a much more comprehensive bibliography of well over fifty relevant references which they were about to embark upon. They had decided upon a topic, which was the attitudes of schoolchildren of different ages towards non-white children. They had drawn up an outline scheme of research. And they came with renewed determination.

After a discussion lasting over two hours, I began to see a remote possibility of their accomplishing what they had evidently set their hearts on doing. They had clearly put a very great deal of time and thought into their proposals. They had mastered the reading, and were able to refer to it critically. And they showed an impressive understanding of the immense methodological problems which were involved. I said that I would be prepared to act as their supervisor under certain conditions. Firstly, that if, at any stage of development of the project, I felt myself unable to support it any longer, they would abandon it, and undertake alternative individual special studies. Secondly, that they would have to persuade the Chief Psychologist of the local education authority of the validity of the scheme. Thirdly, that they would have to approach an independent sociologist of repute, and obtain his approval of the research from the methodological point of view. And finally, and by no means least important, that they would have to secure the willing co-operation of any heads of schools they might want to use. I pointed out that the schools in the area which had a proportion of immigrant children were over-visited by inquirers, welfare officers, research workers and other visitors, and that several heads felt that their task of giving these children an education was made more difficult by this constant stream of investigators, however worthy their aims might be.

The group accepted my terms without cavil. I made an appointment with the Chief Psychologist, and went down with them to see him, though I left all the talking to the group. They were immensely impressive in their approach, not merely in their appreciation of the difficulties, but also in their tactics in dealing with him. They had realized that they would need to overcome an initial opposition to the project, and they had also realized that they would do so only by showing their own competence. Hence they had prepared a detailed outline of their proposed research scheme, including samples of the various tests and questionnaires that they proposed to construct and use. They anticipated his technical questions, and they showed themselves not only sensitive to the possibilities of interfering with the work of the schools, but also ready with suggestions as to how to overcome this difficulty. They were courteous without being unduly deferential. When they were sure of their facts, they said so; when they were uncertain, they admitted it, and explained how they proposed to remove their doubts.

As I have implied, when they entered his office, the Chief Psychologist was ready to turn their scheme down, after the hearing he had agreed to give them. When they left his office, he had been completely won round and was offering them wholehearted support.

They asked for further meetings with me to discuss their proposed solutions to some of the technical difficulties the Chief Psychologist had raised. I was again impressed by their methodical approach, and by their determination to undertake what even they were coming to see was a very much more difficult scheme than they had first realized.

In the event, the meeting with the Chief Psychologist was the first of a series of meetings with various officials, all of which they conducted with success. They secured not merely the approval, but the enthusiastic support of an extremely eminent sociologist, himself an authority in the field of race relations. They met a number of heads of schools with varying proportions of immigrant children, and they managed to win them all round to willing co-operation. They sought frequent sessions not only with myself, but also with several of my colleagues, to ask for and obtain their critical advice on different aspects of the project. They worked out a research plan, devised and validated tests, checklists and questionnaires, carried out a pilot investigation, revised their tests, carried out the research on a carefully selected sample, and finally wrote the research up into a considerable volume of several hundred pages, supported by a large number of tables of data, statistically treated and presented, and they did all this, moreover, while fulfilling the demands of what was, in any case, an intensive course of study.

Copies of the study, the last chapters of which were typed during the small hours by members of the group, were delivered to me (after an epic car drive!) a half an hour before the date and time by which special studies were to be handed in. It was an outstanding piece of work, which constituted a genuine contribution to our understanding of the subject, and the external examiner agreed with the high mark that I awarded it, and which was given to each member of the group.

I do not wish to give the impression that all group assignments are as successful as this one. But there is no doubt that part of the success of this piece of work derived from the sense of shared purpose and co-operative effort that it involved. Moreover, I feel pretty sure that it would have not been nearly so successful if the members of the group had been required to organize the work in such a way that their individual contributions could be identified. Having attended a good many of their planning meetings, I was satisfied that this was a genuinely co-operative project, and while the routine chores were shared out amongst the members, the creative aspect of the work was the result of an interplay of their ideas.

Nonetheless, provision for group assignments does raise the legitimate question of how one can guard against the possibility of a group 'carrying' a member whose contribution to the project does not justify the mark awarded to the work as a whole. There is also the similar problem of making allowances for the fact that the participation of one outstanding member of the team may raise the level of achievement far above what the other members might have been able to achieve either individually, or without his help. And this might easily happen, especially where the more able member of the team takes on the role of team leader. One cannot count on the supervising tutor being necessarily aware of the calibre and contribution of each member of the group. I think I had a reasonable awareness of the role played by each of the six postgraduate students, but then this team was unusual in the demands they made upon me. There was no need for me to call for regular progress reports, for example, since their own requests for discussion meetings far surpassed the number of meetings I would have normally thought necessary. And in any case, the amount of time available to tutors for such discussion is sadly limited.

I think myself that the educational value of a successful group assignment far outweighs these assessment problems. So much of our educational system is already crippled by the attempt to fit the curriculum to the Procrustean bed of examinations that it seems criminal to extend this policy to the field of teacher training where one would hope a more balanced view of the function of assessment would prevail. In our department we have accepted the principle of group assignments, with the following limitations: it is the responsibility of any group of students who wish to offer a joint assignment to obtain the approval of a supervising tutor of their proposed title, bibliography and scheme of work; the group should meet their supervisor at regular intervals to report on progress; no student may offer participation in group assignments for more than a third of his or her total assignment requirements over the three years of the course. In fact, it has been our experience that no one has yet approached a third; most students who take part in group assignments only do so once. And it is still only a small minority of students who offer joint work. These two last considerations are, perhaps, a reflection of the sad fact that the vast majority of students arrive at college with little if any criticism of the existing educational system, and seeing their task as being simply that of preparing to carry on the good work as before. As I have said above, the students themselves have, on the whole, coped successfully with the demands of the examination system, and are usually already committed to the notion of individual achievement and the competitive society. I would myself think that one indication that we are making some inroads into this complacency would be if all the students offered at least one group assignment as part of their course, and if a substantial number of them offered the maximum number of such assignments allowed, and even petitioned for that maximum to be increased.

Evaluation meetings and 'loobiads'

An important part of the education course is the provision for evaluation meetings. All students are urged to offer comments, criticisms and suggestions at any time, and tutors normally invite such comments as part of their tutorial meetings with individual students. The Education Consultative Committee, as explained above, also provides a vehicle for views and suggestions by students to be put forward. In addition to these provisions, it is now common practice for large-scale evaluation meetings to be time-tabled as part of the course. These are customarily held at the end of, for example, a course of lectures, or a series of practical classes. Sometimes, however, evaluation meetings are held while a given course is in progress, particularly if it is an experimental course, or if there are indications that there is general unrest about some aspect of the work.

One regular evaluation meeting, involving 150 or so students, is the second-year 'Loobiad', or Look-Back-in-Anger Day. This tradition arose in the first year in which experimental group work was adopted as a general requirement for all students preparing to teach in secondary schools. It so happened that this was only one of a large number of far-reaching experiments that were set on foot in that year; in fact, it was the year after I returned from study leave, and it bore the brunt of my experimental zeal. In this year, the age-old tradition by which education tutors were individually responsible for virtually the whole of the education course for small groups of students was abandoned as departmental policy, and we began, at least as far as those students on the junior-secondary course was concerned, to work in tutor teams.

It had seemed to me when I first came into training college work that there was a considerable weakness in what is often referred to as the 'mother hen' system. This is the arrangement whereby a group of twenty to thirty (or more) students, preparing for a particular age-range of teaching, are allocated to one education tutor, who is then responsible for their course in education throughout the three years. When I first joined a training college staff, there was virtually no contact with the other tutors in the education department beyond an occasional year lecture (i.e. one to the whole year of students), and an opportunity in the third year to join a special study group concerned with some topic in depth, and even in this latter case it was still possible for students to elect to go to the study group run by 'their' education tutor.

There is no doubt that this system allowed tutors and students to get to know one another very well indeed, which was presumably a good thing from the point of view of the development of *rapport* between them. On the other hand, the system has a number of what seemed to me obvious disadvantages. The field of education is a large one, and it would be ridiculous for any single tutor to claim competence in more than a few of its areas, let alone in the various contributory disciplines. It follows that students are limited in the intellectual stimulation they are offered not merely to the field covered

M   177

by the members of the department as a whole, but to the particular range of interests and knowledge of that single tutor to whom they happen to be allocated. Moreover, while it is no doubt true that over three years a tutor can form a very thorough picture of a given student's abilities, he can also develop and persist in a very prejudiced and one-sided view, as there is no opportunity for his judgments to be tested against those of anyone else. It is true that provision was made for the transfer of students from one tutor's group to another in cases of personal incompatibility, but such transfers were unusual.[1] And of course, misjudgment need not be based on an underestimation of a student's abilities; indeed, experience suggests that tutors are more likely to exaggerate the qualities of 'their' students than to underestimate them. Nor is this surprising, since their students' achievement may be supposed to reflect, in some degree, their own tutorial competence.

There are other obvious drawbacks to the 'mother hen' approach; for example, that discussions in a group whose membership does not change over three years must necessarily become somewhat stale, with its members fulfilling predictable roles which there is little need or opportunity for them to change. However, there is no doubt that many tutors and students find this arrangement comfortable, some perhaps, sadly, precisely because it does not make intellectual or personal demands upon them. I have always taken the view that changes cannot be forced successfully upon people, but that they must come about as a result of a conviction, on the part of the people concerned, that they are desirable. Hence, I did not feel able to require the tutors of the department to abandon the 'mother hen' principle on my say-so. Instead, I instituted a series of discussions centring upon the education syllabus and the objectives of the course, with the suggestion that we re-examine our overall approach.

[1] The fact that transfers on the grounds of personal incompatibility were rare is itself suspicious, particularly in the light of the increasing importance which is coming to be attached to the differences in working modes between teachers and taught. The research of H. A. Thelen is of the greatest significance in this respect. In his book, *Classroom Grouping for Teachability* (New York, Wiley, 1967), Thelen demonstrates the relevance of 'teachability' to teachers' assessments of their children's work. By 'teachability' is meant a subjectively-determined group of personality characteristics and attitudes which any given teacher considers will enable his pupils to benefit most from his teaching. What is of vital significance is the fact that these characteristics and attitudes vary considerably from one teacher to the next. It is my view that Thelen's work constitutes a major advance on our understanding of the psychology of learning bearing, as it does, upon the whole question of the allocation of children to earning groups or classes.

178

Ultimately, a number of proposals arose out of these discussions, several of which included a team-teaching approach. After further discussions, members of the department were invited to vote for the adoption of these alternatives. In the event, about two-thirds of the tutors voted for a modified team-teaching approach, with education groups for the first year of the course only, while the remainder preferred to retain the traditional responsibility for groups of students throughout the three years of the course. As it happened, the division of tutors was not random, but reflected their different interests and experience as far as the age-ranges of teaching were concerned. Those prepared to experiment with a team-teaching approach were also the tutors who specialized in preparing students for the middle school (8–13 years) and secondary school (11–18 years) age-ranges, while those tutors who preferred the 'mother hen' approach were specialists in infant (5–7 years) and junior schools (7–11 years). And it may well be that the kind of close personal relationship between teacher and children which is necessary to effective teaching in a primary school is more successfully fostered in this way.[1]

For the junior-secondary (i.e. middle school) and secondary students, however, a team-teaching approach was planned, in which the students were divided into education groups as usual for their first year and allocated to various tutors, but were then reallocated at the beginning of their second year to a team of tutors. While there was an attachment to individual tutors for the purpose of tutorials, the second-year course was presented by the whole team to the whole group of students (about 150 in number). The course did not necessarily consist of large-scale lectures; a good deal of it was done in much smaller groups, but here again students found themselves working with different tutors at different times, according to what they had elected to do.

There is no doubt that this abrupt change in tradition upset the first year of students who were confronted with the changes when they became second-year students. No longer did they have the security of 'belonging' to a small group of students, nor were they the sole responsibility of 'their' education tutor. Moreover, they were not merely cast adrift in this way, they were also required to adjust to a whole number of new and different groups: they had to join a group for the purpose of topic work (as outlined in Chapter 5 above), and they also had to form among themselves smaller groups for the

[1] Since writing this, all the tutors have elected to join the year teams.

purpose of group work in schools (see Chapter 6). Then there were various workshop activities in college for the purpose of which they were again divided into groups. And on top of this, they had a tutorial attachment to one of the team of tutors, who would occasionally call together all the members of this tutorial group for administrative purposes.

It was altogether too much for many students. 'Group' became a dirty word, and their restlessness showed in absenteeism from classes and lectures, in complaints, and in their written work, which revealed not merely an initial opposition to some of the new ideas that were being put to them, but a substantial reluctance even to consider them. Perhaps the low point was reached about two-thirds of the way through the first term, just before the actual group work in schools began, when late at night, a group was heard chanting in the junior common-room: 'Down with Education! Down with Education!'

I called a meeting the following day of the whole junior-secondary year.[1] I explained that we sympathized with their uneasiness, part of which no doubt lay in the unfamiliarity of the work in schools we were asking them to undertake. I said that I thought that they would very quickly get the feel of the new approach, but that in any case, we were appealing to them to suspend judgment on the year's course until they had seen it through, when a great deal of what must appear obscure or even irrelevant would fall into place. I also promised that an opportunity for full and frank criticism of the year's work would be made available at the end of the year, as part of the time-tabled programme.

In the event, my guess that a good deal of the undercurrent of disquiet was simple apprehension about the group work itself proved correct, and once they had begun to work with children, most of the complaints died away. Too, we had undoubtedly ourselves made mistakes of timing and presentation; some of our lectures on the theory of group work were virtually meaningless to the students because they had had no experience of children working in this way, and could not imagine the conditions. Moreover, we had planned a series of demonstrations of the 'creative use of audio-visual aids' and invited a number of outside speakers, some of whom we knew only by repute. Several of these proved to be unused to communicating their expertise to large audiences, and although their demonstra-

---

[1] We use this term as a convenient shorthand reference for all students who are preparing to teach children of secondary school age, whether or not that is their main or indeed their only aim. Most of them prepare to teach in *both* junior and secondary schools.

tions were interesting enough, the students were unable to see parts of them, or to follow all the technicalities. Nor were the faults confined to outside speakers. We ourselves misjudged our students' level of understanding in a number of ways, and we made elementary faults of presentation.

The atmosphere eased quickly as the term progressed. The topic work was highly successful, and most of the students found the children's response to group work exciting and challenging. We were able to offer courses on lectures and demonstrations that were immediately relevant to the problems they found themselves facing in schools, and some of the less successful courses ended. The year passed all too quickly, and as agreed, we set aside the last day on the programme for a large-scale evaluation meeting.

I had by this time a good deal of confidence in the students' ability to handle their own affairs, and I decided to invite them to join me in planning the day. A planning committee was formed of six students and myself, and we worked out a programme whereby provision was made for detailed criticism of each constituent of the year's work, for comments and suggestions about the course as a whole, and for a general discussion of the policy behind it. Having regard to the strong feelings at the beginning of the year, I proposed that we call it: 'Look-Back-in-Anger Day', and one of the other members of the committee suggested that it be conducted somewhat in the manner of a Victorian palace of varieties. One of the students, Mike, an outgoing character with a ready turn of wit, undertook to be master of ceremonies, and others were primed to introduce discussion on various points with burlesque speeches and dramatic sketches. We mimeographed the programme on bright red paper and awaited events.

Look-Back-in-Anger Day proved tremendously successful. One of the things that had upset the students at the beginning of the year had been the plethora of duplicated sheets which the team had issued, dealing with the various administrative problems of the new course, the group work, membership of the various groups, and so forth. These sheets had been printed on various coloured papers, as we had adopted in the department a colour code for our various documents. Again, these documents were part of the change from the informality of the small groups, in which administration could be arranged verbally by general agreement, to the necessary large-scale organization of 150 students. Moreover, I have always felt that a document, in which arrangements are clearly and definitely stated, is to be preferred to a verbal arrangement, not only because it is possible to check it, but also because it is less time-wasting than going through things during time which could be devoted to teaching.

Anyway, these variously coloured sheets had become something of a symbol to the students of the frustration and irritation they had felt at the time, so it had been agreed by the Loobiad planning committee that the day should begin as if it were yet another of those administrative meetings which began with the hand-out of documents. Accordingly, when the students were assembled, I mounted the rostrum armed with a large sheaf of sheets of all colours, and began to explain that I was about to distribute several new documents pertaining to the course next year. There was hardly time for the familiar chorus of groans before one of the planning committee jumped up from the front row, snatched the documents out of my hand, and began to tear them up and scatter the pieces frenziedly about the hall, shouting as he did so:

'Oh no you don't! We've had just about enough of all these bloody documents!'

The effect was quite electric. The audience, not realizing that this was a rehearsed scene, sat stunned at this display. One girl, I recall, even called out in her alarm:

'No, no!'

At this point, Mike stood up and announced:

'As it seems that the teacher is unable to control this class, I shall have to step in and take over.'

And as I crept, cowering, to the back of the hall, he called upon the first speaker.

This set the pace of the discussion, which was lively, witty but good-humoured throughout. One turn which earned a great deal of applause was a satirical demonstration of how not to give a demonstration of the use of a projector. The criticisms were sharp, but relevant and deserved. Moreover, comment was not confined to the students. The tutors, who were distributed among the audience, at one stage began an interminable list of reasons why a certain suggestion would not work because it presumed that students were rational and responsible beings. We felt able to say what we wanted to say, without pulling any punches, because the atmosphere of the Loobiad encouraged the free exchange of opinions.

The morning was given over for the most part to criticism of the course that had just finished. For this purpose, the audience was first divided into small discussion groups, and this gave Mike an opportunity to make a good point.

'We have heard a great deal during the year about the problems of forming groups, and we have ourselves been formed into groups in more ways than I care to remember,' he said. 'We have been formed into groups by numbers, alphabetically, by subject, by age-range of training, sociometrically, according to interest, and geographically, to mention only a few. The tutors have expended a great deal of time explaining to us the immense problems in forming groups; they have demonstrated, with elaborate charts, matrices, sociograms and so forth, the subtleties of forming into groups; we have even had a dramatic interpretation of group formation.' (Which indeed they had.) 'What the members of the Education Department do not seem to realize is, that there is really no problem to it. All you need do is simply say: Right, now form yourselves into groups.'

And the audience, laughing, forthwith did just this. They turned their chairs round, and arranged themselves into suitably-sized discussion groups.

But what was most impressive about the Loobiad was the calibre of the discussions themselves, and the thoughtful and practicable suggestions that came out of them. We took a record of the suggestions, and were able to incorporate many of them into the course for the following year.

At the end of the day, after a plenary session at which the recommendations of the various discussion groups were reported, the students themselves proposed a vote of thanks to the Education Department for a stimulating and successful year, and the tutors in turn expressed their appreciation of the students' magnaminity and co-operativeness. We had come a long way since the chanting of 'Down with Education!'

I suppose all innovations soon become part of the tradition. We still hold Loobiads at the end of the second year, but now the complaints are about details, and the suggestions are for relatively minor improvements. I dare say that we ought to congratulate ourselves on the fact that the students now accept topic work, group work, team-teaching and their reorganization into different groups as part of the education course, but I fear that complacency into which it is all too easy to slip, and which is the enemy of true education. As I walk past the junior common room these days, I sometimes catch myself listening almost hopefully for the sound of 'Down with Education!' again!

9

Participation as a Learning Process

I have outlined in the previous chapters of this book a number of experiments in teacher training that have in common a provision for the participation of students in the determination of their own courses. The degree of such participation varies from that of merely deciding upon a topic for group investigation within a highly-structured framework to that of planning both structure and content of an entire course. The assumption that lies behind these experiments is that participation of this kind leads to more effective or more worth-while learning, or both. It is the purpose of the present chapter to examine the nature of participation and to suggest some principles by which it might be administered.

Participation and democracy
We may begin by considering an assertion made in the previous chapter, that participation is not democracy.[1] What is, in fact, the nature of the distinction between these two processes?

The critical difference lies in the fact that in democracy, an assumption is made that all effective members have equal rights and equal responsibilities in terms of self-government, whereas participation is based on the assumption that responsibility is not equally shared. In a democratic organization – whether it be a nation of several million people or a small community of only a few – every member has an equal right to take part in decision-making, and that right is

[1] See p. 170 above.

184

normally exercised through the procedural principle of 'one man, one vote'. Of course, it may be the case that in a democracy, representatives are elected to exercise their electorates' rights of voting for them, but technically it is still true to say that every vote cast is of equal value. Participation, however – in the sense in which the word is used in this book – assumes that at least one member of the group in question has a greater responsibility for the success of the outcome of the group's activities than do the other members. Full democracy in such a situation is not possible unless those members with particular responsibility are prepared to abrogate that responsibility.

In a teaching situation, the responsibility of the teacher for the pupils' learning is one that cannot be abrogated; it is built into the job itself.[1] This does not mean, of course, that every teacher guarantees that his pupils will in fact learn effectively, but it does mean that he undertakes to ensure that, as far as he is able and with good will, his pupils are presented with such circumstances and opportunities to learn as, in his knowledge and experience, are most likely to lead them to learn effectively. He may be willing to experiment with various approaches in the belief that out of these experiments will come effective learning, but he must necessarily reserve the right to terminate them if he comes to feel that they are not meeting this requirement.

Thus the teacher, if he is to continue to discharge his responsibility as a teacher, cannot join with his pupils in a learning situation that is completely democratic. Even if provision is made for what are normally regarded as democratic processes within the group of which he

---

[1] That is, so long as present social expectations hold. Of course, a situation in which teachers and students share the pursuit of learning without either having ultimate responsibility for its attainment, and in particular, without the teacher's being required to assess the student's progress, would entirely alter the circumstances. In such a situation, full democracy would be entirely acceptable, and the Argentine students' plea for *cogobierno* in the *Cordoba Manifesto* of 1918 could be realized. The current student argument for the complete democratization of higher education is in accord with the current view of psychologists that a very much larger proportion of the population could benefit from university or college study than are at present admitted. Indeed, the logical next step is that of 'higher education for all', in which a degree becomes within the reach of all as no more than a certificate of attendance. The problem of selecting the most able administrators, technologists, executives, etc., will, of course, remain, and it is noticeable that those students who argue that assessment should have significance only as a means to further learning (an altogether admirable argument, in my view) do not concern themselves with the problems of selection; see, for example, Tom Fawthrop: 'Education or Examination?' in Cockburn and Blackburn, op. cit., pp. 100 et seq.

is a member, he must reserve the right to interrupt those processes if it seems to him necessary to do so. Of course, he may well be prepared to allow a good deal of freedom for the group to decide on activities which are not obviously of educational value, on the grounds that it is not always possible to determine beforehand what the outcome of any particular activity may be and his experience may have led him to be cautious in rejecting proposals which at first appear fruitless; or he may be prepared to allow his pupils to embark on plans which he alone knows are foredoomed to failure, on the grounds that they will learn something of value from their mistakes. But in the long run he must be prepared to exercise an ultimate right of veto, even if in fact he never uses it.

By participation in learning, then, I mean a situation in which a teacher allows his pupils some measure of freedom in deciding upon the content of and the approaches to their course of study. Such participation has two short-term objectives: firstly, that it will lead in some circumstances to more effective learning than teacher-directed methods; and secondly, that it fosters a sense of responsibility in those pupils for their own learning. I would argue that there is justification, in the various experiments outlined in the previous chapters, for a belief that both of these objectives have been met therein. Moreover, I think there is a further, long-term objective in adopting this approach to learning, which is that it encourages a belief in the value of the application of democratic processes to everyday problems in our society. For while, as I have said above, participation is not itself the same thing as democracy, yet it should entail – if it is to be successful – many of the detailed procedures of an effective democracy.

Now it is in my view essential that the teacher who seeks to teach through participation does not allow his pupils or students to confuse this process with democracy proper. It is the case in our society that, at least in some circles, the word 'democracy' carries with it overtones of approval. Hence there is an understandable temptation for teachers to seek to exploit this fund of emotional goodwill by using the words 'democracy' and 'democratic' whenever they can. But in doing so I think they are in fact undermining the success of participation, for they are liable to create expectations in the minds of their pupils which they cannot then subsequently meet. In embarking upon any programme which involves participation in learning, therefore, I think it is imperative that the teacher should make clear that it is *not* democracy, in the full sense. And he should then go on to explain the nature of the difference.

But there is a more important reason for spelling out the limitations of participation than the possibility of frustration on the part of pupils who have been misled into thinking they are being offered more freedom than the situation allows. This reason derives from the fact that most of us become uneasy in any situation, the nature of which is not clear to us. A good deal of the disorder that is sometimes to be found in the classrooms of poor or inexperienced teachers stems, not so much from the fact that they are using wrong methods, as from the fact that they have not made clear just what methods they *are* using, and the children's response is symptomatic of their unease and consequent feelings of insecurity. Effective teachers nearly always explain carefully beforehand what they propose their pupils should do. This is even more important when dealing with situations that entail some measure of freedom of choice on the part of their pupils. As someone has wisely said, freedom is meaningless unless we know when we are free, where we are free, how we are free and what we are free from. It is even better if we can also know why we are free. As the teacher moves from highly structured, teacher-directed lessons towards learning situations in which a good deal of informality and self-direction is possible for his pupils, it becomes of even greater importance that the circumstances and limitations of those situations are carefully spelled out, this providing a framework within which the pupil can act meaningfully and confidently.

There is yet a further reason why it is desirable that the teacher should spell out the limitations of participation, which is that, in doing so, he also commits himself to allowing freedom of choice in those areas in which such freedom is in fact provided for. Nothing is worse than the situation in which the teacher appears to be liberal-minded in his views, and to be offering his pupils a good deal of opportunity for choice, but subsequently disallows the choices which the pupils have made. This is a tyranny the worse for being concealed. It follows, then, that in making clear the conditions of choice, the teacher must also be clear in his own mind that he is prepared to accept the outcomes of that choice. This is often more easily said than done. For it is one of the inseparable conditions of allowing choice that one is prepared to accept the consequences of such choice, even if it is not the choice which one might have wished had been made. And if, in fact, there are certain alternatives which the teacher is *not* prepared to allow, then this fact must be stated clearly before choice is made.

187

Participation and open-ended inquiry

So far I have been speaking as if the kind of freedom which participation allows is that of choosing between clearly defined alternatives,
and this indeed may be the circumstances in which teachers first
experiment with participation. But experience suggests that, before
very long, they will find themselves contemplating circumstances in
which it is not possible to specify alternatives beforehand. Such
a situation is involved when students or pupils undertake inquiries
which are 'open-ended'; that is, studies or investigations in which,
while their starting-points may be clearly specified, and even the
directions in which they might go may be known beforehand, their
final outcomes are not predictable.

Now it is an interesting fact that while such inquiries are commonplace in the primary school, and encouraged in postgraduate studies,
in the intermediate stages of education their proposal is greeted by
teachers with alarm and protest. We encourage our young children
to be adventurous in their thinking. We praise their initiative and
imagination, and proudly display the fruits of their enterprise on
the walls of our junior classrooms. Then we are surprised when
those same children, encapsulated by the rigid specifications of their
secondary schooling, become either rebellious or apathetic. And
when a few have managed to learn to inhibit their natural curiosity,
and to develop instead that capacity for the absorption and periodic
regurgitation of facts to which I have already referred, we are again
surprised when they seem unable to come up with imaginative
suggestions for an investigation for a thesis or special study, but
prefer instead to travel along wellworn paths, or to rely on their
supervisors' proposals.

We must be prepared, I suggest, not only to allow more room for
enterprise in our secondary schools and colleges, but actively to encourage it by the provision of opportunities for open-ended inquiries.

Two objections to this proposal will immediately spring to the
minds of those in whom it arouses foreboding—both eminently
reasonable.[1] The first objection is that open-ended inquiry, being

---

[1] Less reasonable objections, which may well not be made explicit, are
suggested by Frank Musgrove and Philip H. Taylor in their provocative and
stimulating book: *Society and the Teacher's Role*, Routledge & Kegan Paul,
1969, pp. 70–1, where they point out that academic subjects 'have become highly
organized social systems with heavily defended boundaries' which 'resist curriculum change – particularly when this involves the amalgamation of subjects.
"Subjects" provide their members not only with a livelihood, but with a sense
of identity. While curriculum change may not often threaten a member's livelihood, it frequently threatens his sense of identity. An academic subject may
afford safe anchorage for a teacher's self concept.'

188

necessarily undirected to some extent by the teacher, does not guarantee the learning and application of those standards of academic rigour which are among the main objectives of secondary education, and may instead lead to woolly and superficial results. Now of course woolly and superficial results are not altogether unknown under a system of teacher-directed lessons. But putting that consideration on one side, I think this objection arises from the mistaken belief that a regard for rigorous standards will not be voluntarily accepted, but can only be inculcated through a process of conditioning. I have already suggested in the first chapter of this book that a readiness to apply systematic methods of study is to be found even in young children, given that they are interested in the outcome,[1] and I think this is no less true of older pupils or students. What, I suggest, we must rid our minds of is the false conviction that academic rigour is somehow inseparable from the study of traditional academic topics. A regard for accuracy, for precision, for system, for logical deduction – and it is of these desiderata that we are speaking – can, I suggest, be fostered other than in the study of isobars, or of Marlborough's campaigns.

This leads us to the question of 'integrated' studies – an unfortunate term, since presumably all studies aim at some kind of integration. In a well-known article, Hirst defines a liberal education as one which includes experience of all the different forms and fields of knowledge that go to make up the heritage of Western culture.[2] The implication might seem to be that it is possible to have experience of the various forms of knowledge only through the study of those topics which, traditionally, have been associated with them. But in fact, of course, there is no intrinsic reason why the methods of history (for instance) should not be mastered with equal facility in the study of birth-control propaganda in the nineteenth century as in the study of Anglo-French relations during the same period. And if the student happens to find birth-control propaganda a fascinating topic,[3] and Anglo-French relations deadly dull, then he is more likely to profit from the former than from the latter.

[1] See above, p. 27 et seq.

[2] P. H. Hirst: 'Liberal education and the nature of knowledge', in R. D. Archambault, ed., *Philosophical Analysis and Education*, Routledge & Kegan Paul, 1965.

[3] I give this example simply because I myself first came to find the fascination and reward of historical study in the pursuit of this topic, on which I wrote an essay during my first year at university, after finding political history utterly boring and unrewarding throughout my secondary schooling.

By an integrated study, then, I understand a study in which the approaches from the various disciplines are brought to bear upon a particular topic or group of related topics, upon the pursuit of which no limitation is laid by virtue of the argument that it would lead outside the traditional boundaries of any particular field of knowledge. And education is an area (or field or whatever) of knowledge that lends itself to such integrated studies. Indeed, I would argue that unless the student teacher has had the opportunity of undertaking such an integrated study, the point of much of what he may have learned in psychology, sociology and the rest will have been lost.

A second objection to open-ended inquiries that will be made is that they exclude or, at any rate, make more difficult the precise formulation of the objectives of a course of study before it is embarked upon. With the development of curriculum studies in education, the whole notion of defining educational objectives has become a fashionable preoccupation in the world of academic theory of education.[1] Like many other preoccupations in the history of education, while perfectly valid as one consideration among many, it has tended to so dominate current educational discourse and activity as seriously to endanger it. Twenty years ago it was not generally thought necessary to go beyond a few grandiose and empty phrases in seeking to justify educational enterprise. While it was right and proper that educationists should be made aware of the need to be more precise in the formulation of their aims, there now seems to me to be a very real danger that all worth-while experiments will grind to a halt in an effort to spell out precise behavioural objectives which can then be evaluated according to measurable criteria. We are in risk once again of allowing a laudable concern for precision to prevent us from recognizing that some of the most valuable educa-

[1] I say the 'notion' rather than the actual activity of defining educational objectives, for though there has been a great deal of discussion over the last decade or so about the advantages of defining objectives, there has been very little evidence of such definition in fact, and I do not know of any rival to the much-referred to *Taxonomy of Educational Objectives*, edited by Bloom and Kratwohl. (B. S. Bloom, ed.: *Taxonomy of Educational Objectives. Handbook I: Cognitive Domain*, New York, McKay, 1956' D. R. Krathwohl, et al.: *Taxonomy of Educational Objectives. Handbook II: Affective Domain*, New York, McKay, 1956.) While admirable as a first attempt, the *Taxonomy* seems to me to lean far too heavily on behaviouristic principles, and I hope that alternative formulations which make more provision for imaginative, inventive and creative factors (among others) will become available before too many curricula have been reorganized to fit in with the Bloom-Kratwohl categories.

tional objectives of all are not, as yet, susceptible to precise definition and measurement.

Moreover, and this brings me back to my present concern, it is by no means certain that the most desirable sequence of events in every educational enterprise is necessarily that in which objectives are defined before the course itself is embarked upon. It may well be that the formulation of objectives is itself an activity that ought to arise out of the process of the course itself. Or, to put it another way, among the educational objectives of a course for student teachers ought to be the formulation of the educational objectives of that course. And this is what is entailed in participation.

I see the insistence upon the formulation of precise objectives at the outset of every course of study as likely to lead to a further narrowing of education into only those activities which can be precisely measured. One has merely to examine some of the contortions into which objective-test constructors have been led who have tried to formulate multiple-response items for tests of aesthetic sensibility or literary criticism to see the sorry state to which this might bring us. On the other hand, I would at the same time support a move towards the more precise definition of objectives in areas where they can, without distortion, be precisely defined, provided that this does not lead to a neglect of those areas where comparable precision is not yet attainable. And among these latter areas I would include, as an important contributory study in a course of education for student teachers, some provision for open-ended inquiry, particularly in the field of integrated studies in which approaches developed in the traditional disciplines are learned through being brought to bear upon a topic which has aroused the students' interest. And as we have seen, the approach to such studies can be successfully made through participation in course-planning.

Some principles of participation in course-planning
It may be helpful at this stage to suggest some of the principles which, in one college of education, we have sought to follow in applying participation as an approach to learning. In doing so, I should like to emphasize that they are suggested merely as pragmatic solutions which have been found useful in an approach which is still very much in the stage of intial try-out, and I would not wish it to be thought that they have yet attained the status of experimentally validated procedures.

The first consideration we have found it vital to have regard to, is the time available, both in terms of the time in hand between the beginning of planning and the actual presentation of the course being planned, and the time available for planning meetings. As a working principle we have taken the view that course-planning must be set in motion at the very least half a term before the term in which it is due to begin, and preferably earlier. Moreover, it is essential that sufficient working time is set aside for the necessary meetings and one can be fairly confident that about twice the amount of time will be needed as for the more conventional situation of tutor-planned courses, not only to allow for students and tutors to master a mutually comprehensible language of planning, but also because – with students present – tutors find themselves looking rather more methodically at arrangements that were apt to be dealt with in a perfunctory way under the old system. This last is not intended disparagingly; it is often not until one has students present at planning meetings that the complications and implications for them of what might appear to be simple administrative matters become apparent to all.

To have sufficient time, then, is vital and without both time and the willingness to take it, one would be best advised not to embark upon participation at all. Otherwise the temptation for tutors to use their expertise to anticipate difficulties and to propose solutions before their need has become apparent, will be too great to be resisted, and the student members of the working parties will cease to have a part to play. Such a situation can easily lead to frustration and resentment.

However, it must not be supposed from the preceding paragraph that the presence of student members in a course-planning team is seen simply as a device to give students the impression that they are contributing. The fact that tutors can, from their experience, anticipate problems and propose solutions to them does not mean that alternative and preferable solutions might not have been arrived at, had the problems been allowed to arise in the normal course of events. For while tutors may bring to working discussions their experience and their knowledge, students bring their inexperience and their relative ignorance (which I prefer to call innocence), and it is a guiding principle of participation that both experience and inexperience are equally necessary to a fruitful discussion, as are both knowledge and ignorance. Innocence properly heeded by wisdom will lead to a synthesis at which neither could arrive without the other.

It goes without saying, I hope, that it is not enough to secure the intention of tutors to attend all planning meetings; it is necessary also to secure their actual attendance. For meetings to be attended by all the student members but by only a few of the tutor members will lead not only to justifiable ill-feeling on the part of the students, but also to procedural difficulties when important issues are voted upon. Similarly, the absence of student members without adequate excuse should not be accepted by the tutors without a reminder that they are responsible for their fellow students as well as for themselves.

Having decided to embark upon a measure of participation in course-planning, having secured the willing (and preferably the enthusiastic!) co-operation of one's colleagues, having done both of these sufficiently in advance to allow sufficient time for reasoned discussion, and having provisionally set aside time for such discussion, it then becomes necessary to explain what is intended to the students concerned. Again, sufficient time to do this fully to all should be allowed, and provision should be made for questions and further explanations so that – as far as possible – the procedures intended are clearly understood by the students well in advance. An important principle to be followed here, and one that has already been mentioned, is that the nature of participation and the way in which it differs from democracy should be carefully explained, not only so that the students know where they stand, but also so that they appreciate that it does not mean that the tutors are repudiating their responsibilities.

The election of student representatives should also be discussed at this first general meeting, and this brings us to a further important principle, which is that the responsibility for decisions and actions should be clearly seen to rest with the student-tutor team, and not to be subject to ratification by the whole student body concerned. This does not mean, of course, that opportunity should not be provided for comments, suggestion and criticism by the student body; indeed, it is strongly advised that such provision in fact be made. But in electing representatives, the student body should be clear that they are electing colleagues who will then have the power not only to speak for the rest, but also to act for them. This is a principle which experience has shown to be very necessary to establish clearly at the outset, otherwise there is a considerable danger of initiative passing from the student-tutor team to the student body itself.

It is suggested that the actual methods of election of representatives be left to the students themselves, though it may be thought desirable to suggest certain categories. For example, on the college teams that we have from time to time set up, we have generally asked for representation to include the various age-ranges for which the students are preparing (for example, infant, junior, junior-secondary or middle, and secondary), to include a minimum number of representatives of each sex, and to include at least one representative of mature students. As to numbers, it is our own experience that equal numbers of tutors and students work best, with the chairman (so far always a tutor, though not necessarily so) having the casting vote if necessary.[1] Requirements as to number and representation should, of course, be made beforehand.

A further suggestion that we have thought worthwhile making is that representation on student-tutor working parties should be as widely shared as possible among the students, and that, as a general principle, students who had once served should not be eligible for re-election. Again, the reason for this suggestion – that serving as a representative is itself a valuable learning experience which should therefore be available to as many students as possible – should be explained beforehand. Indeed, an important general principle which we have always tried to follow (and have regretted not following on the odd occasions when, for some reason or other, we have not done so) is that of always giving the reasons for any proposed action or requirement.

An anxiety which I have heard voiced is that the students may choose to represent them fellow-students who have views which are in fact not representative, perhaps because they are articulate in discussion, or energetic, or simply because they put themselves forward. Now of course this danger is one inherent in any democratic system, and there is no certain way of ensuring that it is avoided. It is one of the reasons why it is important to emphasize to the whole student body that representatives are elected to act for all. Moreover, the presence of one or two articulate minority opinions, while sometimes irritating, can also be a valuable insurance against complacency on a team, in that matters on which there is general agreement, the advantages of which might therefore be taken for granted, may have to be explicitly justified.

A variant of this last anxiety is the apprehension that 'trouble-makers' might be elected by their fellow-students. Now the term 'trouble-maker' is one that means different things to different people, and one might well argue that the whole purpose of having student members of working parties is that they *should* make trouble, in the sense that unless they have some suggestions to make, there is no

[1] Any expectations there might have been that members of working parties would vote in two blocks – as tutors and as students – have not been borne out in fact.

point in their being there at all. Too often lecturers are ready to interpret any suggestion of change as due to 'trouble-makers' and of course, if new ideas are suggested, or new implications of old ideas pointed out, this is bound to make trouble for those who are then obliged to take cognisance of them. Certainly participation is not for those who seek to avoid change, and those who feel that their courses are already as good as human endeavour can reasonably make them, are strongly urged not to try it.

The merit of the working party is something to which the tutors ultimately responsible for the course are advised to give a good deal of preliminary thought. The formula which should be kept in mind is that of 'flexibility within a framework' and the tutors should be satisfied that the framework is sufficiently explicit for them to feel perfectly happy about allowing the fullest measure of flexibility within it. Curricular requirements should be spelled out carefully, as should any limitations of approach, materials, time, place, etc. As has been said above, it is essential that all limitations are known beforehand, to prevent the necessity of vetoing a proposal after prior thought has gone into its formulation. Though at the same time, the tutors responsible should genuinely seek to provide flexibility; there is no point in participation which is merely a rubber-stamping exercise.

Thus, while the framework should be clearly defined beforehand, the tutors should resist the urge to go further and formulate proposals for the course itself until the working party has had an initial meeting to discuss objectives. And indeed, experience suggests that the most fruitful way of spending the first meeting of the working party is in a discussion of course objectives.

The procedures used to reach agreement at planning meetings should be known and followed. Often, of course, these meetings are quite small, and there is a temptation not to take formal votes on policy suggestions but instead to rely upon 'the feeling of the meeting'. Experience suggests that if the chairman is a tutor, he is likely to interpret the feeling of the meeting in line with his own views, or with what might appear to be tutorial views. I think myself that there is much to be said for taking a quick count of hands on policy and administrative decisions, though one clearly wants to avoid the whole panoply of formal committee procedure.

Similarly, it saves a good deal of misunderstanding and subsequent resentment if such decisions are recorded and circulated afterwards. Indeed, being able to judge the degree of formality and the amount of documentation that is appropriate in participation is an important skill for the chairman of student-tutor teams to develop.

Having once reached a decision, it is of vital importance for the future success of participation that it is in fact implemented. Tutors are bound to discover improvements that might be made after a decision has been taken. They would be well advised not to make any alterations to agreed plans, however, for if they do so, they may secure minor improvements only at the cost of jeopardizing the whole relationship. Of course, this is not to say that, in arriving at a decision, it may not be appropriate for a good deal of detail and interpretation to be left to whoever is responsible for its implementation. Indeed, there must come a time when, plans and outlines having been agreed upon, tutorial expertise is sought to give some body to the skeleton, and at this stage tutors must naturally be given full autonomy in carrying out what has been agreed. What is important again is that the point at which this happens should be known beforehand.

From all that has been said in the last few paragraphs it must be evident that the role of chairman of the working party is a crucial one to the success of a scheme of participation in course-planning. The chairman must ensure that full weight is given to tutorial expertise without thereby effectively inhibiting all student comment. On the other hand, he must encourage suggestions and criticisms from the student members without thereby appearing to condone personal attack on tutors, whether past or present. He must be a stickler for such procedures as are necessary to ensure full participation, without being pedantic in the application of the kind of procedural minutiae which prevent ready discussion and agreement. He must ensure that all members of the working party are clear about decisions which they have to take without at the same time preventing the kind of free-ranging discussion out of which fruitful proposals often develop. And he must, above all, foster the kind of working atmosphere in which all members of the team feel able to express freely, not only their constructive proposals, but also their anxieties and reservations, and this itself may be said to be an important principle of successful participation – that both tutors and students should spell out any apprehensions which are felt. There is a temptation not to make anxieties explicit. Tutors may be reluctant to explain that they are afraid that certain important parts of the syllabus may be left out, or that students may take advantage of greater freedom of action not to act at all. Students may be equally reluctant to reveal their suspicion that they may not be permitted to investigate certain areas. If these

PARTICIPATION AS A LEARNING PROCESS

anxieties are made manifest, it then becomes possible to discuss ways and means of overcoming them. Moreover, it very often proves to be the case that the viewpoints of tutors and students are not nearly so different as either might suppose. Discovery that they share a common concern for certain values enables planning to proceed in a much more relaxed atmosphere.

Finally, as has been mentioned above, provision should be made to enable the student members of the working party to get the views and suggestions of their fellow students before decisions are finally taken. Our experience has been that two large-scale meetings of representatives with the student body are necessary: one right at the beginning of the course-planning, when the remit alone is known, to enable suggestions to be made at the outset; and a second when the working-party has arrived at a provisional plan, but not decided upon detail, again to permit comment and suggestion. The first meeting may also be that at which the representatives are elected. However, it is suggested that to attempt to get into a single general meeting all the preliminaries – that is, the tutorial outline of the whole course, the election of representatives, and suggestions from the student body, is too much. Thus, the following general programme suggests itself:

An initial meeting of the whole student body at which the tutors outline the intention to embark upon a scheme of participation; explain the nature of participation and the procedures; detail the actual remit of the course, including the limitations; and finally make suggestions for the election of representatives.

A second meeting of the whole student body at which representatives are elected, and proposals made from the floor for them to take to the working-party meetings.

A series of meetings of the working party to arrive at a provisional plan.

A third meeting of the whole student body to hear the plan, and to make comments and suggestions.

Further meetings of the working party to finalize the plan and agree upon details.

The tutors concerned then work out such details as may be necessary to implement those parts of the plan which call upon their expertise (lectures, reading lists, etc.).

A final meeting of the working party to go through the various details.

197

A meeting of the whole student body to hear the detailed plans. This meeting also enables the tutors responsible for the course to thank the student representatives for their help and to announce the disbandment of the working party. (It is assumed that comments and suggestions from students during the course will be provided for by some alternative channel; for example, through a consultative committee.[1]).

[1] See above, p. 159 et seq.

PART FOUR

Conclusions and
Suggestions

10

Some Shortcomings of Colleges of Education

The qualities desirable in a teacher

If I were asked what qualities the student teachers of today most noticeably lack, I would say: originality of thought and the capacity for the critical analysis of ideas. These also happen to be the two qualities most urgently needed in a changing society. To achieve improvement in any sphere of activity, it is necessary to have a fund of new ideas, and the ability to subject them, together with existing forms, to a disinterested critical examination. Moreover, one must have *both* these essentials. Originality of itself may lead simply to fads and gimickry. Just because something is new, it is not necessarily better. On the other hand, a critical attitude by itself may lead simply to sterile cynicism.

There is a third component which a society needs in good measure if change is to be for the better, and that is agreement on basic values, for these constitute the criteria by which both existing institutions and proposed improvements must be judged. In this respect it is my opinion that we are fortunate in our young people, for they frequently display a fundamental moral code which puts their elders to shame. One of the most heartening signs for the future welfare of mankind is the moral purpose and integrity of the students of today. Moreover, they have the capacity for seeing through the often outworn forms and trappings of existing social codes and of judging them by which I can only call the great copybook maxims governing

201

personal relationships upon which, in the last resort, all social organizations must depend: I mean the primary virtues of honesty, generosity, tolerance, friendliness and love without which any contractual relationship must ultimately founder.

It is my experience that student teachers share with the other students of today the conviction that it is upon these primary values that the social structure of tomorrow must be built, though – sadly – they are perhaps less ready than their fellow students in universities and colleges of art to come forward in defence of their principles. For this is what contemporary student protest really is about. Behind the complaints about restrictive syllabuses, old-fashioned regulations and unsympathetic teachers is a more fundamental concern with the nature of social relationships in the world of today. Students are rightly concerned, for instance, not only with the relevance of the history of Renaissance art to the design of automatic ovens, but also with the relevance of the present marriage contract to the sexual and social needs of members of an automated society.

Basically, there are two ways in which a social institution such as marriage can be examined with a view to change. One is by starting from the assumption that the present form of the institution represents also its best possible form, and that therefore the fewer changes in it that are made, the better. Acting on this principle, one then attempts to make adjustments in detail where there is evidence of its failure to meet particular needs; for example, by making divorce easier. The alternative approach is to start from the human needs which the institution is supposed to provide for (provision for the upbringing of children, emotional security, sexual fulfilment, companionship) and then to ask what alternative forms of the institution, or indeed, what alternative institutions, might provide for them more satisfactorily.

If one adopts the first procedure, then there is little need of a criterion other than that of expediency. The institution as it stands constitutes an end in itself, and the question simply becomes: what is the least change we can make in order for it to work? If one attempts to follow the second course, however, one is obliged to recognise criteria against which the success or otherwise of the institution can be judged. This is naturally an infinitely more difficult approach, but it is also more likely to lead to success in the long run. As I have said above, its adoption depends upon agreement about basic values. And it is to the credit of the younger generation of today that such agreement appears to be widespread amongst them.

I am speaking as if social change is inevitable and that, certainly,

is my belief. It is also my belief that one of the teacher's most important functions is that of preparing his pupils to adapt to, and to participate in, a changed society. It follows that, if teachers are to fulfil
this function, they must themselves be adequately prepared for the
task, which brings me back to the opening sentence of this chapter:
the relative lack of originality of thought, and of the capacity for the
critical analysis of ideas, among student teachers. It is, I hope, clear
that the various experiments outlined in the preceding chapters had,
as their main purpose, the engendering of these qualities. But it must
be remembered that they took place within the limitations of a traditional training-college environment, with its often obsessional preoccupation with the minutiae of personal appearance, its overt
emphasis on conformity, its preference for assessment based upon
impressions and guesses rather than upon objectively-demonstrated
criteria.

The pressure towards conformity

Those who are unfamiliar with colleges of education (as training
colleges now prefer to be called) and who suppose them to be somewhat like academically inferior universities, often do not realise what
a world of difference in fact there is between these two institutions of
higher education. In a university a student is judged, in the main, by
his intellectual calibre. It is true that he may have to give evidence of
conformity to a certain academic tradition, and that originality of
thought may not be acceptable to his teachers if he departs too far
from traditional ideas. Of course, he may be sent down if he contra-
venes university or hall regulations, and these regulations may well be
petty and unreasonable. But the judgment that is made of him, at
his final examinations, is essentially a judgment of his intellectual
capacity.

In a college of education, however, the emphasis is upon his
personality. His academic achievement is of some importance, but it
is not sufficient of itself, without evidence of what is often referred to
in the regulations as 'suitability for entrance to the teaching profession'. A splendidly meaningless phrase, which can bear any interpretation whatever that the examiners choose to put upon it! The interpretation that is normally put upon it is in terms of conformity to a
certain stereotype in the minds of the college tutors. Indeed, it is far
easier to say what qualities are not suitable for entrance to the teaching profession than what are. Any eccentricity of behaviour, for
instance, is not. In a woman student, any form of dress or personal
adornment which might be regarded as sexually provocative, or even

sexually attractive, is not. All but the least obstrusive forms of make-up are not. (I know of a student who was reprimanded by a tutor for turning up to a lecture wearing 'too much make-up', as if the quantity of cosmetics somehow affected her capacity for taking notes!) Indeed, probably the best way of defining the ideal student teacher, according to prevailing college standards, would be to paint his opposite: a man whose speech is somewhat ungrammatical and idiomatic and often interpolated with swear words; whose personal appearance is either flamboyant or else untidy and perhaps a little grubby; whose preoccupations are those of sex, food, politics and pleasure; whose manner is hearty, affable and familiar; who has a good stock of dirty jokes and a fondness for telling them; who is ready with his opinions, argumentative, curious about his fellow creatures, tolerant of their shortcomings, and fond of their company. In short, the average man. For it is the curious and perhaps arrogant assumption of the vast majority of those responsible for training teachers to deal with society's children that those teachers should be as unlike what the children themselves are going to become as possible.

So it is not, perhaps, surprising that our student teachers lack originality of thought if, by manifesting it, they are likely to be regarded with suspicion. Nor is it surprising that they are not remarkable for displaying a critical attitude if it is likely to earn them the label: 'unsuitable for entry to the teaching profession'. And to be fair to the college tutors, it is not only from them that the pressure to conform derives. All too often the students themselves contribute to it. Teaching is a profession which is unlikely to attract the adventurous in the first place. The vast majority of college applicants have already had a career which argues their orthodoxy and ability to please those in authority over them: they have nearly all been school prefects, form captains and vice-captains, chairmen of the school debating society. Many have also been Sunday-school teachers. They turn up for interview at the college either in their school uniform, or in sensible clothes. The girls have a freshly scrubbed look, and wear no make-up; the boys are usually keen on some healthy outdoor activity, such as canoeing.

I am not wishing to imply that canoeing is not an excellent thing, nor that the use of make-up argues a lively intellectual scepticism; only that there is something depressingly predictable about the kind of young person who is likely to apply to a college of education, and even more likely to be accepted. Having been accepted, they in their turn contribute to the general pressure towards conformity. Those few students with unorthodox ideas or unorthodox ways of behaving who have somehow got through the selective net tend to disappear during the first year of the course – they find the atmosphere too limiting, they fall foul of the heads in the schools in which they do their teaching practice, or they are deemed by the tutors to be 'not suitable for entrance to the teaching profession'.

So that not only is there pressure to conform from the tutors and the heads of schools in which students do their teaching practice, there is also pressure from among the students themselves who, by the process of selection and perhaps from the nature of the appeal of teaching itself, tend to be conservative in outlook before they ever arrive at the colleges of training. Moreover, the prospect of teaching practice itself is a severe discouragement to enterprise. However irresponsible and light-hearted students might feel towards their academic and theoretical studies, they rarely regard the periods of teaching practice with anything but serious concern. An important element in this concern is, of course, the anxiety that they will not be able to deal adequately with a class of forty or so children. The prospect of chaos in the classroom is not one which many can contemplate with indifference. But, to be fair to the students, there is also a genuine concern for the children they will be teaching, and a desire to give them an educational experience that will be of value. Some form or other of teaching practice normally occurs at least once every year, so that its prospect is never far from sight, and thoughts about it rarely altogether are out of the student's mind.

When faced with a task, the failure to deal with which is likely to bring acute mental and even possible physical discomfort, most people are anxious to master the skills needed to deal with it, and they are often prepared to put up with inconveniences and minor difficulties in the process. Teaching practice acts as a kind of recurring discipline to student teachers. And, sad to relate, too often its prospect is used as a kind of threat by their tutors. So that even if there were not already that predisposition to conform which, as I have suggested, is endemic to the recruitment of student teachers, the circumstances of their training and, in particular, the always imminent demands of the classroom tend to create a situation highly unfavourable to the development of originality. And it has been my experience that even when students are encouraged to try out new ideas, and are persuaded that no blame or penalty will be attached to their failure, they are most reluctant to abandon methods which, whatever their shortcomings, are nevertheless known to work.

The lack of objective criticism in colleges

But if the students themselves are partly to blame for their con-
formism and generally conservative attitudes, I think it is the college
staff who are responsible for the other major lack in the students'
education: the relative lack of a capacity for objective, analytical
criticism. It is in this respect that colleges differ most from universities. In a university, whatever may be the prejudices and personal
bias of any individual professor or student, the test of the validity of
an idea or assertion accepted by both is whether it stands up to
objective analysis and critical investigation. In a college of education, however, this is not always the case. There are whole areas of
experience, central to the life and work of the college, where not only
are impressions, guesses and 'intuitive' judgments accepted as valid
evidence, but where also there is strong resistance to any attempt to
replace them by more objective tests. This is particularly true, for
example, of the assessment of a student's skill in teaching itself.
Tutors will see no logical inconsistency in asserting on the one hand
their ability to make fine discriminations, often expressed mathe-
matically (or pseudo-mathematically), between the classroom
achievements of two or more students, and in steadfastly refusing on
the other, to subject these judgments to analysis. Phrases such as
'good *rapport* with the class' and 'a sympathetic understanding of
children's needs' come naturally to the college tutor, but he would
argue strongly that any attempt to define these undoubtedly desirable
qualities in objective terms would be a waste of time, since there
would always be some quality which would evade definition, but
which he himself takes into account in his judgments.

This kind of woolly thinking, while most evident in the assessment
of students' practical teaching ability, nevertheless tends to spread
into other areas of college life. One factor encouraging its spread is
the already-mentioned responsibility often laid upon college tutors,
and certainly always claimed by them, of judging the suitability of
students for entrance to the teaching profession. This no doubt in-
tentionally vague phrase is usually taken to mean not only that
teachers must be competent at providing an environment for their
pupils in which effective learning takes place, but also that their
personal lives should be free from the kind of vice which would be a
bad example or influence on their charges. And most people, and
certainly most parents, would agree with the need for preventing,
say, uncontrollable paederasts from having responsibility over their
children. But again, it is rarely if ever the case that college tutors spell
out the qualities that are necessary to a student's suitability, or the

particular shortcomings which militate against it. They prefer to rely upon their own judgments, for which the criteria are never made overt, even if they are known to themselves. This has the result that those students who are in fact judged unsuitable can never prove otherwise, since they have no way of knowing precisely their faults. They are like K in Kafka's *The Trial*, judged for an offence which is never defined, and which can therefore never be disproved.

One would like to think that college tutors' judgments are infallible, but both experience and commonsense suggest otherwise. What rapidly becomes evident to anyone who works in a college of education is the readiness with which personal prejudices enter into these assessments. And what is worse, are concealed in the process. Too often the damning entry on a progress report form, 'I wonder if this student is really suited to teaching?' proves to be based, upon investigation, on the fact that his hairstyle was not to the tutor's liking, or on some similar matter. Indeed, the importance attached to the student's personal appearance, and the alacrity with which judgments of his personality are based upon it, would scarcely be credited by those outside the teaching profession.

It can be readily appreciated that an atmosphere in which subjective judgments are allowed but the criteria of which are never discussed, is hardly conducive to the development of a capacity for objective criticism. Nor is the reluctance to analyze arguments confined to discussion between staff and students. In the internal affairs of the college, tutors are often equally suspicious of a logical and systematic approach to problems, preferring to rely upon tradition or 'intuition'. One important reason for this, in my opinion, is the hierarchical system of college organization.

Traditionally, the position and function of a college principal is very much like that of the head of a school.[1] He was, and in most cases still is, responsible to a board of governors for the whole running of the college, and it is very unusual for any member of the college staff other than the principal to attend meetings of the board. This means that, unless the governors are very active in their interest in college affairs, and provided he does not do anything outrageous or scandalous, the principal has a free hand in the organization and

---

[1] Taylor suggests that the increase in the size of colleges consequent upon expansion will lead to a shift in the principal's role away from expressive tasks, such as those concerned with student-staff relations, tutorial work, etc., towards instrumental tasks of organization and administration, and that this shift may be away from what many principals see as their 'real' work; see Taylor, op. cit., pp. 238–41.

administration of the academic and domestic affairs of the college, without even the restraints which the need to please parents normally place upon a school head. The tradition, dear to the hearts of the English establishment, of appointing one man to run an institution, and then giving him full powers and freedom to do so, may well be more successful than the Continental pattern when that one man is of outstanding imagination, competence and integrity. But, alas, for every one principal or head with a combination of such talents, there are ninety-nine with an ordinary or even less than ordinary run of abilities, who then use their power either to conceal their ordinariness behind a panoply of minor rules and regulations, or to give rein to some private fantasy or other.

This is, in my view, unfortunate enough in a school, where the imagination and creativity of both pupils and staff may be stifled by a dull, unimaginative head. It is even more unfortunate in a college of education, which should be a powerhouse of ideas for the continual reinvigoration of the teaching profession, but which all too often proves to be a factory for churning out conformists, whose main interest in life is a secure job and a desire not to upset the powers that be.

One might suppose that the opportunities offered for a modification of the hierarchical principle in college government, and greater participation by the staff in its affairs, by the Robbins Report,[1] and still more by the Weaver Report,[2] whose main recommendations have been adopted by the government, would be enthusiastically grasped by college tutors. But alas, the habits of intellectual subservience die hard, and in many instances the tutors themselves are unwilling to accept the responsibility of democracy. For example, even in those colleges who have managed to achieve academic boards as responsible policy-makers (as opposed to the principal himself, with or without the advice of his staff), it is not uncommon for any matter of importance to be referred to the principal (usually chairman of the board) for decision. An example came to my notice recently in which, as a result of the expansion of numbers of students, additional mem-

[1] *Higher Education: Report of the Committee appointed by the Prime Minister under the Chairmanship of Lord Robbins* 1961–63, H.M.S.O., 1963. The Robbins Report recommended that training colleges, to be renamed 'Colleges of Education', should be integrated into university schools of education, and no longer controlled by local education authorities or voluntary bodies. The change of nomenclature is, so far, the only part of the recommendation that has been adopted by the government.

[2] Department of Education and Science: *Report of the Study Group on the Government of Colleges of Education*, H.M.S.O., 1966.

bers of college staff could be appointed, and the question of which departments within the college were entitled to them came up. This had, in the past, been a matter of the principal's discretion and this fact was no doubt one of the reasons why heads of departments might have hesitated to do anything which might have led to his disfavour. It is obvious that the number of tutors in each college department ought to bear some direct relationship to the responsibilities of that department, and yet the matter is not at all the simple one that might at first appear, since the teaching of some subjects legitimately require a much higher tutor-student ratio than does that of others. It would be untrue to say that all members of this college's staff were satisfied that in the past the principal's decisions in this matter were equitable. There were strong feelings on the part of some tutors that their departments had been unfairly discriminated against, though such was the atmosphere of the college that these feelings were rarely expressed openly. It is interesting to notice that the question of the allocation of staff between departments is obviously of such fundamental importance to the well-being of a college, that it was one of the functions which the Weaver Committee spelled out as proper to an academic board.[1] Nevertheless, when this particular academic board was faced with this particular decision, that is, given the opportunity to exercise a basic responsibility, instead it chose, with not more than one or two dissentient voices, to hand the decision back to the principal. A sad example of the corrupting influence of subservience, perhaps outmatched only by the reported case, less well substantiated but, alas, certainly not incredible, of the college staff who, when faced with a request from the Ministry to form an academic board, asked whether the principal and deputy principal together might not form the board! Here is total renunciation of responsibility and one can well imagine the kind of intellectual atmosphere that must flourish in such a community which not only tolerates despotism but begs pitifully not to be released from it.

It might seem to some – perhaps to many – that my criticisms are over-severe, my language intemperate. 'Despotism', 'subservience' – can he really be talking about our colleges, in which students are so carefully looked after, and in which there is rarely if ever disagreement? I dare say several college tutors will claim that they know of no opposition to the principal's wishes or ideas in *their* colleges, either from the students, or still less from the staff. Indeed, they will claim that there is almost universal agreement about everything. And

[1] Ibid., para. 110, page 21.

it is, of course, precisely this atmosphere of universal agreement about everything that I am condemning. Progress can only be made where there is opportunity for disagreement; where criticisms of existing institutions, and equally important, of proposed alternatives, are not merely tolerated, but are actively encouraged. And the more reluctant we might be to expose our convictions to the cold winds of dispassionate analysis, the more important it is that we should do so.

The influence of the B.Ed. degree

So far I have confined my remarks in the present chapter to the conditions prevailing in colleges of education, rather than to those in university departments of education. This is not because it is my opinion that the latter are beyond criticism, but rather because the vast majority of teachers in England are trained in colleges, and with the coming of the B.Ed. degree it seems likely that this majority will increase.

All universities in England and Wales now admit college of education students to take a new internal degree, that of Bachelor of Education. As a result, partly of the fiercely-guarded academic autonomy of universities and partly of the sheer lack of any co-ordinative machinery, the regulations and provisions for this degree and the course leading to it are as diverse as may be imagined. Some universities accept the normal three-year Certificate course as Part I of the degree course, others require B.Ed. students to take a different course from that followed by non-degree certificate students after the first year. In some universities, the B.Ed. is a classified honours degree, in others it is only a general degree, without honours. The proportion of education theory to other subjects varies from one course to another. In some universities, the teaching for the degree course is carried on by lecturers in the university; in others, it is undertaken at the colleges, by college tutors who are either themselves recognised as university teachers, or are members of departments so recognized.

Despite the tremendous variation, however, there are some trends which are common to all areas. One is the pressure for higher academic standards. This is bound to be felt most strongly in those colleges in which little or no distinction is made between B.Ed. and non B.Ed. students before the fourth year, but even in colleges in which students are 'streamed', or those in which students attend lectures and classes for the degree work at the university itself, it seems highly likely that the whole level of academic work through-out the college will be affected.

This, in my view, is no bad thing. While there are no doubt lec-tures and seminars in some colleges of education which are on a par, academically, with their university equivalents, the general level of academic work in colleges is undoubtedly below the general level in universities, and anything which works towards a raising of stan-dards is to be welcomed, always provided that it is not accompanied by any increase in that sterile pedantry which represents the academic tradition at its worst. It is my view that while colleges have a lot to learn from universities, there is room for some traffic of ideas and attitudes in the reverse direction. As I have implied above, I would have colleges more intellectually rigorous, less inclined to allow judgments of students' personalities, attitudes and behaviour to affect their assessments of their work, more tolerant of unorthodox ideas, than they tend to be. But on the other hand, I would have universities more aware of the need for and value of tutorial guid-ance, especially with first-year students, more concerned with the opportunities, at both staff and student levels, for the relation and integration of subject areas, less intolerant of modes of thought other than those traditionally recognized by their syllabuses, and more ready to experiment with new approaches in both content and method.

The limited working experience of the teaching profession

Even supposing that it is possible for colleges of education to improve their academic standards without at the same time exchanging the tyranny of conformity to an undefined ideal of personality for the tyranny of conformity to an all-too-rigorously defined and narrow set of academic traditions; that it is possible for them to encourage and foster originality of thought in their students without sacrificing their sense of concern for the children they are going to teach; that it is possible to develop a capacity for critical rigour without losing sight of the importance of those basic virtues which I referred to above as the great copybook maxims – even supposing all these things, there remains one major drawback, in my view, to the trend towards a course in a college of education as the predominant form of teacher training in this country. And this has nothing to do with any preference for university departments of education, but derives from the fact that students who take a postgraduate course of pro-fessional training have, at least, already spent three or more years in the company of students other than those preparing to teach, whereas college students often meet none but their own kind. Teachers already tend, by virtue of their profession, to be shielded from the realities of life in the competitive society of industry or commerce. The majority of them, especially in primary schools, have had little experience of working conditions outside school beyond the occasional vacation job while they were students. Anything which reduces the already tenuous contact between the teaching profession and other occupations and professions in society must be deplored, and whatever disadvantages there may be in the pattern of degree plus postgraduate professional training as a preparation for teaching, it does have the merit that at least some teachers have mixed with non-teachers, even though this was in their student days. Colleges of education are, by definition, exclusive; their only concern is with teaching. This may make for high professional standards, but it also makes for professional isolation. The majority of college-trained teachers have done little to break away from the myopic circle of school-college-school, yet the children they are responsible for will themselves have to enter a working life of which their teachers know little or nothing.

This is a serious limitation. We often hear nowadays of the need for curriculum reform, and one of the directions in which it is generally agreed that reform is most needed is in making the curriculum more relevant to the needs of the school-leaver. One cannot help suspecting that the main reason why this desirable change is not implemented more rapidly is not any special attachment on the part of teachers to the subjects which they teach (indeed, if the truth be known, I dare say that the majority are heartily sick of them) but a total and appalling ignorance of any alternative. What is the use of asking a teacher to make his syllabus more relevant to working conditions in a factory if he has never in his life been inside one? I would ask the reader to read once again my description of the average man on page 204 above, and then to ask himself whether or not he knows many teachers who bear any resemblance to that picture? Is it not a fact that, as a social group, teachers both are regarded and regard themselves as something of a class apart from and – dare I say – above the common touch?

I am not recommending the general adoption of the degree-plus-postgraduate-year pattern of training as a cure for this limitation. Apart from the unsatisfactory nature of this pattern from the point of view of time spent in schools, I do not think it goes nearly far enough to ensure some functional experience of common humanity as an essential element in a teacher's training. What I *would* support,

212

as a requirement for both college and university-department student teachers, is a minimum of a year spent in industry or commerce. For graduates, this year might well come after their degree finals and before the professional course. For college students, my own view is that it would come better during their course than before it, and I would suggest that the penultimate year would be the best time.

This requirement would not cost anything to implement. Once the system was adopted, students could easily be interviewed and accepted for entrance to university departments a year ahead of their course, while college students' grants could be suspended for a year. Moreover, the fact that the present critical shortage of teachers seems likely to be coming to an end means that there is more room to manoeuvre and a diminished college output, to allow a proportion of accepted students to spend a year at work, might be acceptable nationally.

The advantages of experience of a year or more in the kind of working situation that the majority of school-leavers must expect would not be limited to giving student teachers a frame of reference for curriculum reform, desirable though this is. The very fact that the whole of the senior student body had been obliged to support themselves, and to establish a working relationship with other forms of authority than that of college tutors, would both give the students a sense of their own dignity and responsibility, and would also make them less tolerant of precisely that kind of petty restriction that is such an unattractive aspect of college life. Indeed, one cannot help thinking that a highly desirable preliminary to requiring a year in industry of all students would be to require the same of all college tutors.

11

Some Suggested Changes

The function of this book is not that of presenting an exhaustive analysis of the shortcomings of the present system of teacher training, and I have discussed the points raised in the last chapter only to offer some kind of background against which the various experiments described in the second part of the book might be judged. I have concerned myself with colleges of education rather than with university departments, as it would seem—particularly with the advent of the B.Ed.—that the trend towards a wholly college-trained profession is likely to increase.

I have suggested that the prevailing intellectual atmosphere of the average college of education is one in which conformity in both behaviour and opinion is seen to earn approval, while non-conformity is regarded with suspicion or even outright condemnation; one in which judgments are based on impressions and intuition, often coloured by personal prejudices, while there is considerable resistance to the application of analytical and critical thinking to many of the areas central to the college's function. On the more positive side, however, there is a sense of professional commitment to the welfare of the children whom the students are preparing to teach, and there is also evidence among the students of that understanding of basic human values which is, for me, the most encouraging characteristic of the younger generation of today.

I have claimed that the various experiments outlined in previous chapters must be judged against this background. At the same time, it would be feeble of me not to indicate, at least in outline, some of the ways by which I think that the main shortcomings of the present system could be overcome without at the same time losing its merits, and this last chapter is therefore devoted to such an outline. Again, I have preferred to take as a frame of reference a hypothetical college of education rather than a university department. Whatever their faults, it is my opinion that the colleges of education have the potential for development, whereas the mere lack of time available for professional studies and, more important, for practical experience in a one-year postgraduate course (which is, effectively, a nine-month course) is such an overriding disability that I have not felt it worth while discussing its other limitations. It is as centres for advanced educational studies and research that I myself see the present departments of education which, in any case, will presumably merge into the schools of education which are already developing in several universities.

Given the present three- or four-year course in a college of education, what remedy can be offered for the shortcomings suggested in the previous chapter? Is it possible for teachers to be prepared for their responsibilities in such a way that originality, inventiveness and creativity are not discouraged but instead are fostered and allowed to develop, though subject to a critical intelligence, which in turn is used in the service of a commitment to basic human virtues? I think it *is* possible, but only if we are ourselves prepared to re-examine the aims and methods of training teachers.

To begin with, I think we must abandon the idea of a college of education as a place where the ignorant and brash come to learn from the wise and experienced. Instead, we must think of it as a kind of community workshop in which both staff and students learn together from experimentation and the critical examination of results.[1] To such a workshop, the college tutors will certainly contribute their knowledge and experience, but the students will not be without knowledge and experience of their own—no doubt very different from that of the tutors, but potentially just as relevant. Instead of a planned programme of lectures, classes and assignments, based on a syllabus drawn up beforehand by the tutors, the course should begin with a discussion of objectives. These should include psychological and social as well as academic objectives; that is to say, it should be concerned with the kind of future citizens the schools

[1] I hasten to admit that in the various activities described in the previous chapters, there may have been a certain amount of experimentation, but there is very little examination of results that justifies the term *critical*. That is, I hope, to come.

should aim at producing, as well as the kind of society in which they might live and the ways in which they might contribute to it.

This discussion would not be limited to an exchange between staff and students. It would include visits not only to schools and other institutions, but also to housing estates and villages. Opinions would be collected from parents, shopkeepers, teachers, bus conductors, educationists, factory workers and politicians, and as many as could be prevailed upon would be invited to join the discussion groups.

A term would not, in my view, be too long to devote to these preliminary discussions. They would include the defining of the course objectives and some first agreement on the methods by which they might be achieved. Some built-in procedure for the interim assessment of the degree of success in such achievement would have to be adopted, as well as overall methods of evaluation.

Part of this first term would be devoted to the problem of presenting and recording the agreed objectives in such a way that they would be available for reference. There would also be need for each intake of students to compare their objectives with those of previous years, and the opportunity might be welcomed by previous intakes of making some kind of assessment of their general progress. But it must not be supposed that each intake's programme would be the same, or even broadly similar. It it were so, then indeed there might be little to commend this approach compared with that of having a prearranged course organized by the tutors. For it is an assumption upon which I am working that not only do individuals' needs differ, and hence their modes of self-expression and optimum working conditions, but also that the same is true of the needs—social, emotional, aesthetic, spiritual – of groups.

Now it will be seen that such an approach requires a totally different relationship between tutor and student from that to be found at present. For whereas in the traditional training set up, the tutor's knowledge and experience gives him authority and perhaps entitles him to respect, in the kind of ongoing exploratory community I am envisaging, one might well say that the tutor's knowledge and experience are almost disqualifications. At any rate, one can say that the student's inexperience is as valuable and necessary as the tutor's experience. And – as with the kind of group work in schools outlined earlier in this book – the tutor's problem will often be that of freeing himself from his experience, rather than of relying upon it.

One of the contacts that the students would make during their first term is that with the children for whom they were going to be responsible on teaching practice, and hence among the discussions they took part in would be those with the teachers and the children themselves about the work they were going to do. This would, of course, give an impetus to the students' own studies, which would be directed to some extent by the children's work plans. Moreover, the responsibility would be a real one, not only for the students but also for the tutors, for after a period of co-operation, with teachers, tutors and students working side by side – at first perhaps on a day-a-week basis, and then increasing – there would come a time when tutors and students took over full responsibility for the whole school, allowing the teachers a term off for study leave.

It would not be appropriate, even if it were possible, for me to give precise details of the timing of this. No doubt it would vary with the special needs and circumstances of the schools and students. Nor is it possible to be dogmatic on the question of how often such a cycle of preparatory work, co-operation and full responsibility should be repeated. It occurs to me that there might be much to be said for the students to maintain contact with the same group of children throughout the three years of their course – sometimes visiting them occasionally, sometimes co-operating with them in school or in college over a project, sometimes having full responsibility for their work. This would not preclude occasional working visits to other schools, possibly at the invitation of other groups of students.

The work preparatory to and in relation to school would, of course, represent only a part of their course in college. At least once during the year, the whole college might participate in some joint project – the mounting of a festival perhaps; the organization of some piece of social service; or the investigation of, and reporting upon some local or national problem. Thus, students would take part in three such projects during their three years at college, and it might be suggested that they should fulfil different roles in each: in one, say, an administrative or organizational role; in another an artistic or practical role; and in a third, a research or investigatory role.

Academic studies would be planned, not in accordance with some mythical notion of what constitutes a scientific or liberal education, but arising out of the needs of students in relation to their plans and commitments. Courses would be short and highly specific, with a good deal of the basic information being provided in the form of self-operated programmes and work-kits. The planning of courses in relation to group and college activities would be an important responsibility of steering committees, composed of both staff and

217

students, and their provisional plans would be discussed by all parties involved.

Among the needs which the steering committees would have to consider would be not only those in relation to planned school work, and group and college activities, but also the individual needs of students. Approximately a third of a student's time might be spent on courses of his own choice or suggestion. These might include not only courses within traditional subject areas, but also inter-disciplinary courses, and courses offering opportunities to learn and develop particular skills.

I see this college as having widely-reaching and functional relationships with the community of which it would be a part. It would be a centre for social research and social action and it would bear a continuing responsibility for a wide range of local social services: youth clubs, citizens' advice bureaux, family service units, an old people's welfare centre, a community entertainment office, a local arts, drama and music workshop, and so forth. But this would not be the only way in which its students would gain that experience of everyday working life outside school which is, in my view, an essential condition of becoming a worth-while teacher. At some stage during his course, and preferably in the latter part of it, every student would be required to leave college for a minimum of a year in order to take a job of the kind that would bring him into contact with ordinary people. As I have said above, the advantages accruing from this requirement would not only be those of a heightened sympathy with an understanding of the problems facing the majority of school-leavers, but also the greater personal dignity resulting from the fact of the students having had to provide for themselves. This experience, together with the kind of social service outlined above, would go a long way towards overcoming that sense of inferiority which is usually at the bottom of acts of irresponsibility on the part of students.

Such a college would offer its students a wide range of social and educational experiences as a preparation for the crucial responsibility of teaching our children. As much provision as possible would be made for the exercise of personal choice in the selection of courses and participation in activities. At the same time, there would have to be some system of guidance to ensure that students did not become too one-sided in their approach to their studies, and that they did not miss out altogether some vital area of educational experience. Such a system of guidance would be framed in terms of broad areas, however, and not of narrowly defined subjects.

Finally, it would be an essential part of the course as a whole, and indeed a distinguishing characteristic of the intellectual atmosphere of the college, that progress in every sphere, whether that of individuals, groups or even the college as a unit, would be continually subject to evaluation and assessment, and that all members of the community would be taking part in such evaluation would be taken for granted.

Such a college would clearly be very different from the majority of colleges functioning today. That it would produce more successful, more effective teachers than those which now enter the profession every year is at present only a matter for speculation. And perhaps the most serious criticism of all that can be made of the present system of teacher training is the consideration that it is likely to remain so. For while there are signs that teachers themselves are prepared to re-examine their traditional roles, and to experiment with new approaches to their responsibilities, there is little evidence of a parallel readiness on the part of those who train them. It is my view that in no part of the contemporary educational scene is experiment and research more desperately needed than in that of teacher training.

Index

Note: The letter 'n' after a page number denotes a footnote.

221

described, 16–17
obsessional nature of, 35–6
order in, 39, 83, 107
personal qualities in, 36
predetermined syllabus for, 16, 35
preparation for, 18, 33, 37, 41, 111
pupil-teacher relationships in, 37–8, 39, 41
responsibility of the teacher in, **35–9**
role of the teacher in, **36–9**, 40, 44
skills of teachers in, 38–9, 40
students' experience of, 55, 57, 61–2, 71, 111
students predisposed towards, 55–6, 61–2
Teacher-pupil relationships, 37–8, 39, 41
Teachers' attitudes
  conservative, 61
  towards children, 18n, 35–6, 95, 107n
  towards lecturers, 61
  towards students, 61
Teachers
  limited working experience of, **211–3**
  must act, 7
  personality of, 7, 36, 56, 178n, 203–4, 206–7
  qualified, 46
  students' attitudes towards, 61
Teaching
  aids
    audio-visual, 180
    blackboard, 15, 35–6, 37, 93
    charts, 37
    films, 37, 100, 110, 112–13, 152n
    filmstrips, 37, 171
    overhead projectors, 100–1, 152n
    teaching machines, 95–6
    television, 18n
    workshop, 164
  as a career, 49, 51, 55–6

authoritarian, 19n, 43, 78, 95, 160; *see also* Teacher-directed lessons
class, 15, 19, 31, 37–8, 39, 71
co-operative, 44, 164
infant, 15–16, 50
junior, 16–19
machines, 95–6
methods
  drama in, 110–12, 152
  formal, *see* Teacher-directed lessons
  informal, 7–8, 100, 187
  indirect, *see* Indirect teaching
  repertoire of, 8, 71, 123, 164
  revolution in, 8, 15–34, 61
  traditional, *see* Teacher-directed lessons
of basic subjects, 15, 17, 20; *see also* Basic skills
of mathematics, 15, 16, 17, 20, 30, 50, 88, 165
of reading, 17, 20, 30, 88, 164
of writing, 15, 16, 17, 20, 30, 88, 114–15, 118, 120
personal qualities in, 8, 36, 56, 178n, 203–4, 206–7
personal style of, 8, 48, 178n
practice
  amount of, 47, 48, 50–1, 164–5, 166, 168, 169, 170
  compared with group work, 118
  objectives of, 166
  pattern, 48, 50–1, 164–5, 166, 167, 168, 169, 170, 217–8
  preliminary visits for, 168
  preparation for, 164, 166, 168, 169, 170
  problems on, 56, 78
  students' attitudes towards, 48, 51, 169, 205
  supervision of, 48, 78, 166
primary, 46, 70, 167
routines, 36
suitability for, 203–5, 206–7